THOMAS JEFFERSON
AND THE CHANGING WEST

THOMAS JEFFERSON
AND THE CHANGING WEST

From Conquest to Conservation

Edited and with an Introduction
JAMES P. RONDA

University of New Mexico Press
Albuquerque

Missouri Historical Society Press
St. Louis

For Merrill D. Peterson
Keeping the past alive in the present

Library of Congress
Cataloging-in-Publication Data

Thomas Jefferson and the changing West :
from conquest to conservation / edited
and with an introduction by James P. Ronda.
—1st ed. p. cm.
Papers presented at a 1994 conference
organized by the Missouri Historical Society.
Includes index.
ISBN 0–8263–1775–8
1. Jefferson, Thomas,
     1743–1826—Views on the West
     (U.S.)—Congresses.
2. West (U.S.)—History—
     To 1848—Congresses.
3. United States—Territorial expansion
     —Congresses. I. Ronda, James P., 1943- .
F592.T47 1997
973.4'6'092—dc20   96–25330   CIP

CONTENTS

ILLUSTRATIONS

ACKNOWLEDGMENTS

Thomas Jefferson once described St. Louis as "the center of our western operations." For generations of fur traders, soldiers, Indian agents, Oregon Trail emigrants, and California gold rushers, St. Louis was the place where the West began. So it is especially fitting that a book about Jefferson and the West have its origins in the Gateway City.

More than anyone else, it was Merrill D. Peterson who brought the idea of a national conference on Jefferson and the West to the attention of the Missouri Historical Society and its director, Robert R. Archibald. The 1994 conference was fashioned in large part by a planning committee that included Robert R. Archibald, Susan Flader (University of Missouri-Columbia), Patricia N. Limerick (University of Colorado-Boulder), Gerald D. Nash (University of New Mexico), Peter Raven (Missouri Botanical Garden), James P. Ronda (University of Tulsa), Richard Etulain (University of New Mexico), and Eric Sandweiss (Missouri Historical Society). Many members of the planning committee also served as respondents and session chairs at the conference. The success of the gathering was due in no small part to generous financial support from the Liz Claiborne Foundation, the Thomas Jefferson Commemoration Commission, the Missouri Botanical Garden, and the Missouri Historical Society.

Of course, good conferences do not necessarily make good books. When collected within covers, most conference papers are too random in argument, too scattered in direction. But from the beginning it was clear that this gathering would be a memorable exception. Papers quickly became essays, and essays soon emerged as chapters in an unfolding book.

What might have been a long and arduous trek from conference to book was made shorter and easier through the creative efforts of Tim Fox, publications editor at the Missouri Historical Society. His care for words and attention to detail is evident on every page. Both Tim Fox and Jim Ronda want to express their genuine thanks to MHS intern Ben Cawthra for his tireless efforts on behalf of this project. Ben scouted footnotes and explored quotations in the best tradition of Lewis and Clark. Lee Sandweiss has from the beginning given this book the benefit of her considerable publication experience. At the University of New Mexico Press, Beth Hadas has been both astute editor and faithful promoter of the book's central premise. All involved in this book remain grateful for major financial support from Kay and Leo Drey.

Finally, Merrill Peterson opened the conference with thoughtful comments that set just the right tone, and his pioneering work informs each of the essays in this volume. The book's dedication to him is one small way to pay a debt owed by all who believe that the past still speaks to the present.

JAMES P. RONDA

INTRODUCTION

JAMES P. RONDA

More than a decade ago, the distinguished historian Joyce Appleby wrote an essay with the thought-provoking title, "What Is Still American in the Political Philosophy of Thomas Jefferson?" Like Appleby, many Americans assume that Jefferson still speaks with authority across the ages. Few scholars, and even fewer people outside the academic world, would either read or write an article suggesting the relevance of John Tyler, Millard Fillmore, or Grover Cleveland to modern America. As Merrill D. Peterson explains in *The Jefferson Image in the American Mind* (1960), we have come to expect a great deal from Jefferson. Seeing his own fascination with technology and his struggle to confront questions of race and equality, we think of him as a contemporary. Perhaps more than any other national leader, Lincoln excepted, Jefferson seems to transcend time and place to become a voice for all times and all places. We have appropriated him to be the intellectual keystone in our arch of the usable past.

Americans also expect Jefferson—a man who never ventured west of the Blue Ridge Mountains—to be engaged in all the tumultuous events beyond the wide Missouri. Half a dozen presidents (certainly Lincoln, Grant, and both Roosevelts) made decisions of greater moment for the West, but we have tagged Jefferson as our first and perhaps most influential western president. As many of the essays that follow suggest, Jefferson invented much of what we call "the American West." At the most obvious level, the Louisiana Purchase and the Lewis and Clark expedition are his western credentials. But Jefferson did more than acquire territory and launch a famed exploring party; he also invested the lands west of St. Louis with a particular character and a unique set of expectations. In his important book *Thomas Jefferson and the Stony Mountains*

(1981), Donald Jackson boldly insists that the Virginian was "the most towering westerner" of his generation. Monticello faces west, and we expect its builder to be somehow western as well.

Americans want so much from the author of the Declaration of Independence because we recognize that Jefferson posed a remarkably durable set of questions about the West and the future of the region. Jefferson loved the question-and-answer format, constructing the only book he ever wrote, *Notes on the State of Virginia*, on that scheme. He would have instantly agreed with historian David Hackett Fisher that "questions are the engines of intellect." At least once, when preparing exploration instructions for Lewis and Clark, Jefferson set down the full range of his western queries. From botany to zoology, from ethnography to vulcanology, Jefferson asked what amounted to an encyclopedia of questions. While many of the answers Jefferson advanced over the years seem less persuasive today, the questions retain their power and appeal. Jefferson's questions (and regrettably, at times, some of his answers) have shaped everything from national public policies concerning land and water to individual fantasies about Rocky Mountain vacations. The Homestead Act, hydroelectric projects on western rivers, and dude ranch adventures all spring in one way or another from Jefferson's questions about the West as it was and as it should become.

As a planter and a lawyer, Jefferson was acutely aware of landscape. Measuring the land, knowing its metes and bounds, came to Jefferson as part of his cultural inheritance. His eye quickly took in terrain features and organized them with a geographer's passion for system and structure. As John Logan Allen makes clear in his essay "Imagining the West: The View from Monticello," Jefferson was thus a geographer at heart. In *Notes on Virginia*, he describes in painstaking detail the lands and rivers that characterized his cherished place. For Jefferson, Virginia was just another name for America; to write about Virginia was to describe the boundaries and possibilities of a much larger country. And when it came to the West, Jefferson eagerly joined a large company of conjectural geographers. From Giovanni da Verrazano and Jacques Cartier to James Maury and Jonathan Carver, generations of Europeans and Americans pondered the physical nature of North America. Explorers, cartographers, and armchair adventurers all advanced theories about the continent's size and shape. Virginia itself was home to an especially lively geographic tradition. Beginning in the seventeenth century with Richard Hakluyt and Captain John Smith, Anglo-Virginians imagined trails and waterways linking Jamestown to the Pacific Ocean and the fabled Orient. Hakluyt gave classic expression to this geography of hopeful dreams when he wrote in 1606 urging

London Company adventurers to "make Choise of that [river] which bendeth most towards the Northwest for that way shall you soonest find the Other Sea." The dream of a passage to India soon entered in the intellectual life of Virginia, remaining alive and well in Jefferson's time. Like other Europeans, the Virginia geographers believed in a symmetrical world, a world of balance and uniformity. The mountains and rivers west of the Appalachians were sure to be like the familiar country of the Piedmont. This vision of the West promised navigable rivers, broad passes, and mountains easily portaged.

Thomas Jefferson thus grew up in a world of questions and conjectures about the lands of the Ohio country and beyond. As Allen explains, Jefferson's tutor James Maury most likely initiated the young scholar into Virginia's geographic tradition. Rivers, mountains, and a northwest passage were fundamentals in that deceptively simple continental scheme. To those essentials was added a final and compelling feature. Speculators, whether in geography or land, agreed that the country all the way to the great western sea was a garden of boundless fertility. The West as the Garden of the World became the centerpiece of Jefferson's western geography. The garden was not only a statement of geography but of political philosophy as well. In the Garden of the West the American republic would thrive and remain forever free. Rivers and mountains might change size, shape, direction, and even location as explorers filled in the outlines of the western map, but Jefferson and his heirs—including generations of government planners, railroad promoters, and real estate speculators—never abandoned faith in the garden. They wrote that faith into national legislation and confidently plotted the garden from Kansas to the Oregon country.

Jefferson asked about the geography of the West and was satisfied with an answer that blended unequal measures of dream, hope, and fact. His explorers found neither mountains of salt nor water passages to the Pacific, and the president was probably disappointed. But for all his fascination with the West as garden, he never pretended that the lands beyond St. Louis were an empty Eden. To ask after the character of the West was to inquire about the lives and destinies of native people. Such an inquiry forced Jefferson and the American republic to confront what they might have called "the crowded wilderness"—a West filled with indigenous societies and yet by Euro-American standards an empty, unformed place. Jefferson once insisted that he had a lifelong fascination with the native peoples of North America, and indeed he spent considerable time gathering Indian vocabularies, studying archaeological sites, and collecting objects representing various aspects of native life. Historians have usually read Jefferson's interest in native people as an expression of his commitment to Enlightenment science, and his passionate defense of indigenous cultures against European criticism had the edge of reflexive patriotism as well. Jefferson's devotion to science was genuine and best expressed in his comprehensive instructions for the Lewis and Clark expedition.

But as Anthony F. C. Wallace ably shows in his essay "'The Obtaining Lands': Thomas Jefferson and the Native Americans," the fascination with things Indian had a more ominous side. Nothing attracted Jefferson and his contemporaries more than the prospect of acquiring tribal lands. Land was the measure of status and wealth. Land ownership was the road to power and influence. As long-time British Indian Superintendent Sir William Johnson put it, there was a "pestilential thirst for land, so epidemic thro' the provinces." The same Virginia tradition that introduced Jefferson to western geography also taught him that the measure of a man was the land he could survey and call his own. The message from enterprises like the Ohio Company and the Loyal Land Company was simple and direct. Indian country belonged in white hands. The garden was meant to be tilled and tended by Anglo-American farmers.

As president, Jefferson took the passion for land and made it the central feature of federal Indian policy; all other considerations were subordinated to the drive to acquire the tribal estate. Wallace makes painfully clear that talk about philanthropy and civilization made little difference when it came to "obtaining lands." But this was no simple story of intellectual hypocrisy bent on justifying national greed. As on virtually all matters of race and non-European peoples, Jefferson moved from one isolated compartment to another. In the compartment labeled "thought," Jefferson spoke eloquently about native peoples and indigenous cultures. In his most optimistic and philosophical moments, Jefferson thought that Indians could have a place in the new republic—not as Indians but as newly-made Americans. The power of the plow, private property, and republican values would sweep away tribal identity, replacing it with a new sense of national self. But when Jefferson the empire builder moved to the compartment marked "action," such considerations were quietly left behind. Instead, what counted was "our final consolidation"—a phrase Jefferson used to describe the construction of an American continental empire. Consolidation meant the acquisition of lands east of the Mississippi and the removal of native peoples to territories in the West, and even those new native reserves would eventually become part of a larger American empire. Throughout the nineteenth century, the consolidation policy had many faces, none of them promising much good to native people.

Jefferson's questions about the future of native peoples and cultures in North America prompted answers that determined federal policy for more than a century. Whether policy makers and sometime "friends of the Indian" supported removal, reservations, or assimilation, there was a Jefferson line to bolster each view. At first glance there seems to be little of value in Jefferson's ideas for either contemporary tribal peoples or non-Native Americans seeking to better understand the future of the West. In fact, at least one principal chief of a prominent western tribe recently attacked Jefferson, putting him squarely on the side of those who campaigned for native dispossession. As legal scholar Robert A. Williams asks, "Why should Indians in the changing American West of the twenty-first century expect to find anything useful in Thomas Jefferson's writings and thoughts?"

Williams' essay "Thomas Jefferson: Indigenous American Storyteller" is a provocative reappraisal of Jefferson's meaning for contemporary native people. Following time-honored custom, Williams suggests that Indians appropriate what might be valuable in Jefferson's life and thought, leaving the rest—as Jefferson did, though for opposite reasons—quietly behind. Williams casts Jefferson as a storyteller, a role with special meaning and power in native cultures. Storytellers are not only explainers; their very words change reality and make things happen. Redefined as a storyteller, the man from Monticello offers two powerful stories about native people. One story recounts the supposed conquest and capitulation of native nations—a story Williams discovers repeated as fact in several important United States Supreme Court decisions. But Jefferson's second narrative is the one Williams finds far more interesting and valuable. Throughout the era of the American Revolution, Jefferson told stories about oppressed peoples rebelling against a distant oppressor. It was certainly the narrative theme in the story told in the Declaration of Independence. Jefferson instinctively understood what political theorist Franz Fanon much later called "the colonial mentality": the tendency of colonized peoples to accept the vocabulary and world view of the oppressor. As James Axtell reminds us in his book *The Invasion Within* (1985), the struggle for America involved not only the scramble for tribal lands but also a debate about languages and visions. Jefferson knew that in the midst of the Revolution Americans needed a new story, an alternative vision and a fresh political vocabulary. An essential part of the story Jefferson told was the tale of the Norman Yoke. In Jefferson's version of English history, invading Normans put the yoke of oppression on the necks of freedom-loving Anglo-Saxons. Jefferson easily brought the story of the Norman Yoke up to date, casting the American revolutionaries as the Anglo-Saxons and Great Britain and George III as the new Normans. In a contemporary tribal setting, Jefferson's story about anti-colonialism and the Norman Yoke becomes an act of personal and communal resistance. The words of the story have the power to change perception and reality.

Surveying the West from Monticello, Jefferson and his explorers Lewis and Clark asked about the "character of the country." That question not only included geography and the human landscape but also encompassed what the West might become. For Jefferson and his intellectual successors, the fundamental fact about the West was its open spaces and seemingly sparse population. As a modern song lyric has it, the West promised "fifty miles of elbow room." While he could on occasion be charmed by city ways, Jefferson had no doubt that rural and agricultural pursuits promised national peace and individual prosperity. Cities, so Jefferson believed, could offer only violence, vice, and tyranny. Jefferson did recognize the increasingly commercial, export nature of American agriculture, and his antiurban bias did mellow over the years, but he never doubted that the rural West was the ultimate guarantor of republican virtue. An urban West was both contradiction and curse.

Jefferson's eighteenth-century view of the necessity of a rural West is in striking contrast to Robert Gottlieb's twentieth-century view of the inevitablity of an urban West. In "Reinventing Place: Community and Conflict in a Changing West," Gottlieb describes a region and its current character that would have bewildered if not horrified Jefferson. Like a number of recent western historians, Gottlieb finds the contemporary West "a collection of powerful and expanding metropolitan areas." He carefully traces the region's often-troubled transformation from resource colony to empire, a transformation that took not much more than half a century. From the 1930s to the 1970s, by Gottlieb's calculation, the West became an urban, industrial place. Water projects, large-scale manufacturing, and massive infusions of federal funds through defense industries remade the West. Jefferson's Garden of the World became something more akin to Alexander Hamilton's vision of America as city and factory.

A hasty reading of Gottlieb's elegant essay might suggest that Jefferson is wholly irrelevant to a West dominated by Los Angeles, Denver, Seattle, and Salt Lake City. But just as Williams found a Jeffersonian voice and vocabulary that could speak to native people, so Gottlieb has uncovered a Jefferson surprisingly at home in urban places. The evocative image of the Pico Market in Santa Monica that begins Gottlieb's essay reconnects California to Jeffersonian ideals. Here is the Garden of the World in all its tastes, smells, colors, and shapes. Furthermore, Jefferson believed in, and sought to create, livable and sustainable spaces, and Gottlieb concludes his tour through the urban West with a call to consider urban western environments as home. We are reminded that "home on the range" ought to mean city neighborhoods as well as the wide open spaces imagined from Monticello.

In their essay "An 'Empire of Liberty': Thomas Jefferson and Governing

Natural Resources in the West," Helen M. Ingram and Mary G. Wallace consider one aspect of Gottlieb's twentieth-century West, natural resource management, through a more explicitly Jeffersonian lens. Offering one of the oldest and most traditionally Jeffersonian answers to questions about conflict, community, and the future of the West, Ingram and Wallace contrast Jefferson's promise of the West with the contemporary realities of wealth and power concentrated in the hands of a few. They tell a compelling story of real estate ventures and irrigation projects that delivered vast power to a bureaucratic elite. Western entrepreneurs, regional bankers, and federal officials all became part of what historian Samuel P. Hays calls "the gospel of efficiency." Land and water were, so the gospel taught, such precious commodities that only a highly trained corps of engineers and policy makers could be trusted to manage them. The common good, what the Constitution calls "the general welfare," needed definition and supervision from an elite neither elected nor accountable to ordinary citizens.

In a spirited argument, Ingram and Wallace counter the gospel of efficiency and its priesthood of experts with a call to reassert Jeffersonian fundamentals. They take those fundamentals to be self-government, political decentralization, and public education and open debate as integral parts of any decision-making process. Dismantling closed elites and returning power to the people will, so Ingram and Wallace argue, make decisions more equitable. Individual readers might disagree with the authors' analysis of the current resources debate in the West or with their understanding of Jefferson's political philosophy, but one thing is certain: Jefferson remains part of our usable past, whether as an indigenous storyteller or as an advocate for reform.

When Jefferson considered the economic future of the West, he usually talked about two different but related economies. One was the fur trade. Jefferson believed that much of the Anglo-Canadian power in the West was tied to the fur business and its links to native people. The president knew that fur and empire had been allies for centuries in the struggle to dominate North America. Jefferson's short-term economic strategy for the West called for redirecting the fur trade away from Canadian posts toward St. Louis and American trading stations on the upper Missouri River, but the fur trade never captured Jefferson's imagination in the way the West as agricultural paradise did. The western garden was not only a statement of republican faith; it was also a prescription for manageable growth and prosperity on a human scale.

Jefferson's vision of the American West was not only rural but also largely without room for social tension and political dissent. His imagined West has a sameness about it—the sameness of homogenized milk. While Jefferson was no stranger to controversy in his own life, he never relished the fray and did what he could to avoid conflict. Jefferson therefore hoped to fashion a West that did not have the sharp divisions and angry controversies he believed marked European societies. The lack of discord, so Jefferson thought, would be both the hallmark and the saving grace of the American empire, which could be both imperial in geographic reach and yet a safe place for liberty to grow and prosper. In fact, as Peter Onuf points out in "Thomas Jefferson, Missouri, and the 'Empire for Liberty,'" the Virginian was passionate in his efforts to keep the West free of "European" divisiveness. It was difference and division that Jefferson feared most, and the most visible symbol of what he feared was the geographic division imposed by the Missouri Compromise. As Onuf shows, Jefferson insisted that to threaten the geographic unity of the Union was to challenge the very existence of the republic. Having equated the union and the republic, Jefferson took the next step, linking the fate of the nation to the continued strength of his own political party.

Jefferson's anguish and fury in the Missouri crisis is more than an important chapter in the history of early American political rhetoric. In the last years of his life, Jefferson had to confront a West far more factious, far more contentious than he ever imagined. It was, in fact, a West much like the controversy-ridden region today. Both Jefferson and James Madison repeatedly argued that territorial expansion would lessen internal divisions by diluting controversy, but the Missouri crisis, with all its angry talk about slavery and a line between slaveholding and free states, seemed to prove the theory wrong. Geographic expansion, when tied to the explosive slavery issue, promised endless argument and perhaps the end of the union. Nothing disillusioned Jefferson more; the promise of the West seemed in default. Jefferson's own struggles concerning diversity and the value of controversy presaged contemporary arguments. His questions about the character of the West and the republic go to the heart of our own preoccupations with national unity and cultural pluralism.

Soon after Lewis and Clark returned from their epic journey to the Pacific, Jefferson expressed the hope that "some enterprizing mercantile Americans" would plant a settlement on the Columbia River. The words enterprizing and mercantile were not typically Jeffersonian; they might more readily have come from the political economy of Alexander Hamilton. But as Elliott West shows in his masterful essay "Great Dreams, Great Plains: Jefferson, the Bents, and the West," those words could best be applied to the Bent brothers. Born into an influential St. Louis family, Charles and William Bent were drawn into the West and Southwest by the promise of a dream far older than Jefferson's garden fantasy. What lured the Bents was the idea of a vast exchange network, an interconnected web of trails and trading places. As West explains, the Bents quickly became part of this traditional Native American economic pattern.

Having inherited old ways of life and labor, the Bents introduced changes that profoundly altered the human geography of the plains. From Bent's Fort near present-day La Junta, Colorado, the Bents and their partner, Ceran St. Vrain, brought a new kind of commercial pattern to the region. While older systems linked the plains to a distant marketplace, the Bents thought in terms of two markets with the plains in between. Reflecting Thomas Fitzpatrick's apt phrase "a disconnecting wilderness," the Bents employed an economic strategy that made the plains and native people less important. At the same time, the Bents were deeply involved in moving native people, especially the Cheyennes, away from traditional homelands to locations closer to new trading centers. As West explains, the Bents were "instrumental in encouraging and facilitating two changes of enormous significance." More people, more animals, and more commerce taxed the limits of a plains world.

Both Jefferson's view of the West as garden and the contrasting view of the West as desert are of little use, West argues, in explaining the Bents and their neighbors. Their world was far more complex, far more unpredictable than Jefferson imagined. But West does find value in the larger Jeffersonian legacy. It is the legacy of questions and "a commitment to intellectual breadth and a practical knowledge of living with the possible."

Jefferson never doubted that there was an intimate connection between the land and the character of the people who lived with it. He seemed to sense that there was more than a semantic difference between living with the land and living on it. In his vision of the West as republican garden, citizens found the fullest expression of virtue and independence by connection to the land. Western writers from Mark Twain, Bret Hart, and Zane Gray to Wallace Stegner, Ivan Doig, and Mary Clearman Blew have asked the same question. What is the relationship between landscape and lives lived in the daily routine of work and play, love and tragedy? What happens when familiar landscapes, the ones of imagination and memory, either vanish or no longer nurture the soul? In her essay "The Exhausted West: A Last Look at Landscape," Mary Clearman Blew finds that the old "western" stories are played out. The land could never sustain Jefferson's garden and the stories that sprang from that dream world. Blew proposes not abandoning stories but, along with Robert Williams, finding new and more appropriate ones. Wallace Stegner's "geography of hope" need not vanish just because some particular vision proved insupportable or too exclusive. "I continue to believe," Blew writes, "that in story lies possibility."

Stories are shared explanations, and as Patricia Nelson Limerick writes in her concluding essay, Jefferson sought explanations as eagerly as he posed questions. Limerick quotes approvingly John Adams' plea to Jefferson: "You and I ought not to die, before We have explained ourselves to each other." It is the struggle for explanation and the search for new questions that keeps Jefferson's voice alive in the modern West. As the essays in this book testify, Jefferson continues to engage the West and to challenge it. The Jeffersonian voice demands that the region acknowledge both its limits and its possibilities, its accomplishments and its confusions.

THOMAS JEFFERSON
AND THE CHANGING WEST

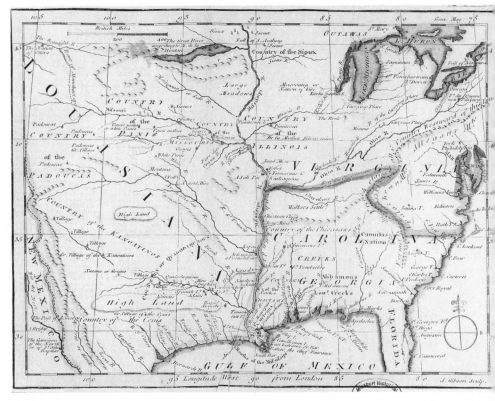

MAP I. "MAP OF LOUISIANA, VIRGINIA, AND CAROLINA, UP TO THE GREAT LAKES."
BY J. GIBSON, C. 1750. FROM *The Gentleman's Magazine*. MISSOURI HISTORICAL SOCIETY
LIBRARY MAP COLLECTION.

*While portraying the mid-eighteenth-century West that sparked Jefferson's imagination, this map
also makes plain a fundamental reality of the region: the land was already settled, already home to
native nations. Whatever European imperial aspirations, the country remained in the hands of its
first possessors. European and American territorial expansion would come at the expense of native
lives and estates. J. Gibson's map was a chart for future conquest.*

CHAPTER ONE

IMAGINING THE WEST
The View from Monticello

JOHN LOGAN ALLEN

There is something about mountains that invites us to look beyond them, to find what is on the other side. Whether these are mountains of reality, such as the Blue Ridge of Virginia, west of Monticello, or whether they are mountains of the mind, such as the Stony Mountains or Mountains of Bright Stones that appeared on only a scattering of late eighteenth-century fur trader maps, the invitation is the same. For those born, as was Thomas Jefferson, with a geographer's mentality and inclination, the invitation is so strong as to be compulsion. Looking west from Monticello, the Blue Ridge Mountains dominate the horizon and block the view of the eye but not of the mind. And in the view of the mind's eye, the farther Stony Mountains also permit penetration by the imagination. We cannot know at what point in his life Thomas Jefferson the geographer decided to pursue systematically the compulsion to look beyond the Blue Ridge, although we can (and will) make some informed guesses. What we can know is that pursue he did, and the implications were not just continental but global in scope. My purpose in this essay is to lead the reader through the development of the geographical imagination of Jefferson, the formation of his image of the West beyond the Blue Ridge and, yes, beyond the Stony Mountains.

Scholars have been prone to think and write of Jefferson as statesman, political theorist, architect, gentleman farmer, natural historian, eclectic scholar, amateur archaeologist—in short, as the quintessential Renaissance man—but few have explicitly dealt with him as geographer. Among those few who have was Donald Jackson, a man to whom I owe a great deal, both personally and professionally. When Don was working on his marvelous book *Thomas Jeffer-*

son and the Stony Mountains (1981), I presumptuously supplied him with some of my doctoral dissertation notes on Jefferson as geographer.[1] Don expanded some of my immature musings and, I would like to think, eventually came to understand Jefferson in much the same way I had—as a geographer by birth, by training, and by inclination. The suggestion is still strong in my mind—a quarter-century after completing my doctoral work—that Thomas Jefferson, like most geographers, was born a geographer as much as he was made a geographer by virtue of training and circumstance. He evidenced, from a very early age and before training and circumstance had a chance to act upon him, a curiosity not just about the elements of nature that surrounded his boyhood home at Shadwell but also the arrangements in space of those elements. The geographer's spatial perspective, an innate sense of place and scale and spatial organization, was early on a vital part of Jefferson's formidable intellectual inventory; it later became what may have been both his most well developed intellectual sense and his most important contribution to the future of his country—the Declaration of Independence notwithstanding.

Nowhere in the heritage that Thomas Jefferson left us do we find greater evidence of his sense of geography than in his writings, particularly those few sections in *Notes on the State of Virginia*[2] that bear on the trans-Appalachian region and the documents related to the Louisiana Purchase and the Lewis and Clark expedition. It is in these writings that Jefferson gives us evidence of his easy mastery of the traditional tools of the geographer's trade—the ability to view the world at different scales and to work easily up and down the hierarchy from the local to the global and back again; the tendency to seek concepts that help make sense of the complicated spatial patterns that make up the world's natural and cultural mosaic; the fascination with maps and the ability to convert the map view to a view of the real world; the understanding that geography is a point of view, a way of looking at things, rather than a study of any particular thing.[3] Most important, in Jefferson's writings on the West, including his only book, *Notes on Virginia,* and four documents written in late 1803 and early 1804,[4] we find evidence of his geographical imagination, of his ability to look beyond the Blue Ridge or Stony Mountains without ever leaving Monticello. Ask any regional geographer practicing his art and science today and you will be told that the imagination is as important for doing regional geography as any of the traditional tools noted above. Some regional geographers are great travelers; others are "armchair specialists." And no professional in the field can tell you which is the more qualified or does the best work. Much has been made of the fact that Jefferson was a "vicarious Westerner," that he never traveled beyond the Blue Ridge. He didn't have to. In addition to actually living farther west than any other major political figure of his time, he lived farther west in his mind.

THE EDUCATION OF A GEOGRAPHER

How did Thomas Jefferson become a geographer?—arguably the most accomplished geographer of his age, save the great Alexander von Humboldt, the father of modern geography and, not so coincidentally, one of Jefferson's most frequent correspondents.[5] Let us begin with his beginning and the assumption that geographers are, at least in part, born. His father, Peter Jefferson, was one of the first of his generation to abandon the worn-out soil of the Tidewater for the new lands of the Piedmont.[6] In sight of the Blue Ridge, Peter Jefferson built Shadwell, where Thomas Jefferson was born in 1743. When the Virginia tobacco culture moved out of the Tidewater and spread west to the base of the Blue Ridge, there was a need for qualified surveyors to establish property boundaries and settle conflicting land claim disputes. It was in this field that Peter Jefferson received his first recognition. Even before he moved west with his family, he had made several trips into and across the Blue Ridge on surveying assignments. In 1746 he was appointed as one of the official surveyors, along with another Piedmont farmer named Joshua Fry, of the limits of the Fairfax grant between the Rappahannock and the Potomac Rivers and extending into the Blue Ridge.[7] The result of the surveying project of Jefferson and Fry was one of the first accurate maps made in the colonies—the 1751 Jefferson-Fry map of the inhabited parts of Virginia.[8] The map was not superseded until 1787 when Peter Jefferson's son used it for a base map and made improvements thereon for the London edition of his *Notes on Virginia*. If there is such a thing as geography genes, Thomas Jefferson possessed them in abundance.

The Jefferson-Fry map of the Fairfax line represented the geography of reality, but other events that occurred while Peter Jefferson was engaged in the Fairfax survey embodied the geography of the imagination. Peter Jefferson found the opportunity to purchase several tracts of land west of the mountains, extending in theory to the banks of the Mississippi.[9] He also acted as an unofficial purchasing agent for other interested Albemarle County residents—including Joshua Fry, Dr. Thomas Walker, and Reverend James Maury—and by 1749 several prominent Albemarle gentlemen had acquired tracts of land beyond the mountains. It is probable that these land purchases were for speculation; late in 1749 a company to be known as "the Loyal Land Company" was chartered for the purpose of "the discovery and sale of western lands."[10] What of Fry and

Walker and Maury and their impact on the budding imagination of a young geographer? To answer that question, we need to go back in time to the early years of the eighteenth century, well before the Loyal Land Company was formed.

As early as the 1720s, British promotional literature on North America had introduced the concept of symmetrical geography—the idea that all major American rivers flowed from a common source area. One of the foremost proponents of the symmetry of American drainage systems was Daniel Coxe, author of the promotional tract *Carolana* and its accompanying map. Coxe described great rivers in the western parts of the continent that flowed from interior mountains "passable by Horse, Foot, or Wagon in less than half a day." West from these mountains of the mind were other rivers "which run into a great lake that empties itself by another great navigable River into the South Sea."[11] The great lake Coxe called "Thoyago," and it existed only in the imagination. The great navigable river flowing into the South Sea or Pacific was also imaginary, but as imaginary geographical features sometimes have a way of doing, it became real in the 1790s with the discovery of the Columbia. Joshua Fry obtained a copy of Coxe's book, and he and Peter Jefferson, Thomas Walker, and James Maury used it to concoct a grand scheme. Maury would write about it years after the fact: "Some persons were to be sent in search of that river Missouri, if that be the right name of it, in order to discover whether it had any communication with the Pacific Ocean: they were to follow the river if they found it, and make exact reports of the country they passed through, the distance they traveled, what worth of navigation those rivers and lakes afforded, &c., &c."[12]

The "grand scheme" (that was Maury's description of it) was based on an idea so ridiculously simple that it is surprising that it had not been suggested before. "When it is considered," wrote Maury,

> how far the eastern branches of that immense river, Mississippi, extend eastward, and how near they come to the navigable, or rather canoeable parts of those rivers which empty themselves into the sea that washes our shores to the east, it seems highly probable that its western branches reach as far the other way, and make as near approaches to rivers emptying themselves into the ocean to the west of us, the Pacific Ocean, across which a short and easy communication, short in comparison with the present route thither, opens itself to the navigator from that shore of the continent unto the Eastern Indies.[13]

Maury had stated the principle of continental symmetry—and its derivative of the Passage to India—as well as anyone had ever stated it.

Dr. Thomas Walker, who had already made one journey west of the Blue Ridge—through the Cumberland Gap and northward to the Shenandoah before returning to Albemarle County—was chosen to make the grand scheme operational. Part of Walker's potential as a leader of an expedition was his field experience west of the Blue Ridge. But also important—especially to a group calling itself the Loyal *Land* Company—was his belief in the interior plains on both sides of the Mississippi River as a veritable garden of fertility, a future pastoral paradise. Such a belief lent credence to the plans of a group of land speculators and seekers after a passage to the Pacific. The bulk of the early-to-mid-eighteenth-century British geographical literature on North America with which the members of the land company could be expected to be familiar either ignores or disparages the agricultural potential of the West. However, the French literature of the same period (with which Walker was apparently reasonably conversant) was enormously enthusiastic about what several early French writers referred to as "the garden of the world."[14] What Daniel Coxe had called "Carolana" the French called "Louisiana," and it was a land of abundance. One French chronicler—whose book appears on Maury's library list and with whom Walker was also apparently familiar—claimed that "the soil is so fertile that, almost without cultivation, it produces European wheat and all kinds of fruit and vegetables which are unknown in France."[15] The Loyal Land Company sought what Meriwether Lewis and William Clark would seek a half century later—a passage through the garden. With the full cooperation of Governor Robert Dinwiddie and the governing council of Virginia, the Walker expedition got as far as the planning stage. Walker drew up "a list of all the necessary implements and apparatus for such an attempt, and an estimate of the expense, and was upon the point of making all proper preparations for setting out, when a sudden stop was put to the further prosecution of the scheme for the present, by a commencement of hostilities between this Colony and the French and their Indians."[16]

It is hard to imagine a bright, lively, and intelligent boy, ten years of age, not knowing about this activity and being impressed by it. We do know, at the very least, that Coxe's book was passed to Peter Jefferson upon Fry's death and, subsequently, was left by Peter Jefferson to his son. We also know that Peter Jefferson's will appointed Thomas Walker as one of the guardians of young Thomas, charged specifically with the duties of educating the boy, fourteen years old on his father's death. And we know that Walker's first step in carrying out this responsibility was to remove young Jefferson from the Latin school where he had been studying for five years and to place him in the school run by James Maury.[17] Here young Thomas received what was probably his only formal geographic education, Maury being a believer in a knowledge of geography as extremely important for the well-rounded young gentleman.[18] And here Jefferson would have learned more about the West, about the principles of symmetrical geography that dominated the thinking of Daniel Coxe and the Loyal Land Company, and about the West as a potential agricultural para-dise—a prominent topic in most of the geography texts on Maury's library list. While there were many other influences on Jefferson's life and intellectual development, I have to believe that the "early associations" played more than a small part. Everything I know about the ways that geographers develop their bent for faraway places with strange-sounding names tells me this was the case.[19] It may have taken years to manifest itself, but the influence of the Loyal Land Company, of Thomas Walker and James Maury, of stories of the Lake of Thoyago and mysterious mountains and great western rivers and fecund inte-rior plains loomed large in the development of Thomas Jefferson's image of western North America.

WRITING AND READING GEOGRAPHY, 1781–1801

The first written evidence we have of Jefferson's developing image of western geography is in his *Notes on Virginia,* a book compiled and written between 1781 and 1785 in response to a questionnaire from François Marbois, first secretary of the French legation to the new United States. During the years between his boyhood and his writing of *Notes on Virginia,* there had been little discernible trace of Jefferson's geographical imagination, little evidence of the latent geographer who "saw his father return bone-weary from journeys across the Blue Ridge, heard Dr. Walker's tales of the Cumberland Gap, and knew that his neighbors dreamed of an expedition to the great South Sea."[20] But *Notes on Virginia* changed all that. Jefferson's book was not, of course, a book on the western parts of North America; it was, more than anything else, a natural and economic and political history of the region between Chesapeake Bay and the Allegheny Plateau. But I do not believe that it was purely acciden-tal that, during the writing of *Notes on Virginia,* Jefferson wrote to several correspondents requesting "information of the country between the Missisipi and the waters of the South Sea" or that, in 1783, he wrote to George Rogers Clark and proposed that Clark lead an American expedition in search of a water route to the Pacific.[21]

If we define *geographical image* as a pattern of beliefs about the nature of a region (principal geographical features such as mountain ranges, lakes, and rivers) and the content of a region (secondary geographical features such as mineral deposits, climate, soil, vegetation, animals, and people), then *Notes on*

Virginia provides at least some evidence of Jefferson's image of the West in the mid-1780s. For example, Jefferson describes the Missouri River as the principal stream of the Mississippi-Missouri system, with a source north of the Mississippi's and west of that of the Rio Grande. He notes that Spanish traders from St. Louis ascend the river two thousand miles, that silver, lead, and salt are available in the Missouri valley, and that the soil and climate are potentially productive. He makes no specific mention of trans-Mississippian mountain ranges in *Notes on Virginia*. He does, however, comment on the mountains east of the Mississippi:

> The mountains of the Blue Ridge . . . are thought to be of a greater height, measured from their base, than any others in our country, and perhaps in North America. . . . [They] are not solitary and scattered confusedly over the face of the country; but that they commence at about 150 miles from the sea-coast, are disposed in ridges one behind another, running nearly parallel with the sea-coast, though rather approaching it as they advance northeastwardly.

He also notes that the courses of great eastern rivers are at right angles to the eastern mountains, and for someone immersed early, as was Jefferson, in the tenets of symmetrical geography, the obvious does not even have to be stated: mountains west of the Mississippi should bear the same relationship to the Mississippi valley and the Pacific coast as the eastern mountains do to the Mississippi valley and the Atlantic coast; western rivers, like eastern rivers, should flow at right angles to the north-south orientation of western ranges, and, in places, burst through the Stony Mountains like the Potomac through the Blue Ridge.[22] If Jefferson did not think of continental symmetry while writing *Notes on Virginia*, I would be very surprised.

Jefferson's geography book (and that is exactly what it was) also addressed the issue of the quality of interior lands west of the Appalachians. They were, Jefferson concluded, lands that were warmer in climate than the Atlantic Seaboard. Having a warmer climate, the interior could form a very suitable place for the expansion of agriculture, particularly the cultivation of those exotic and subtropical crops that could not be grown on the coast.[23] And running through the center of this interior garden were the Mississippi and Missouri rivers—"principal channels of future commerce for the country westward of the Alleghany."[24]

In writing *Notes on Virginia*, Jefferson crossed an intellectual meridian and became a practicing geographer. In addition to textual geographical description, the book contained Jefferson's first and only published map—*A Map of the*

Country between Albemarle Sound, and Lake Erie, Comprehending the whole of Virginia, Maryland, Delaware and Pennsylvania, with Parts of Several Other of the United States of America. Latent geography was becoming kinetic geography; thought would give rise to action and over the next two decades Jefferson's image of the West would expand and grow as he took on, more and more, the role of the young nation's leading geographical authority on the trans-Mississippi West.

The first burst of Jefferson's awakened geographical imagination began at approximately the same time that *Notes on Virginia* was published, stimulated by the writing exercise itself and the opportunity afforded Jefferson by his appointment as U.S. Minister to France in 1784. For a five-year period, Jefferson engaged in a feverish book-buying spree in Europe and, as he would comment later, "purchased everything I could lay my hands on which related to any part of America, and particularly had a pretty full collection of the English, & Spanish authors on the subject of Louisiana."[25] We do not know for certain what works Jefferson possessed prior to this period of acquisition; certainly he had Daniel Coxe's *Carolana,* although that volume had burned, along with his entire library, when Shadwell itself burned in 1770. There is good evidence that between then and 1783, he had replaced Coxe and two other geographically oriented books from the Shadwell library—Thomas Jeffrey's *Natural and Civil History of the French Dominions in America* and Anson's *Voiages to the South Seas*—and had purchased two new works, Baron Lahontan's *New Voyages to North America* and Robert Rogers' *Concise Account of North America.*[26]

The latter two acquisitions were critical. Lahontan's travel account (almost certainly apocryphal) described a journey made in 1689 up "the Long River" that flowed into the Mississippi from the West. At the head of the Long River, Lahontan came upon a large lake, fed by springs that came out of a ridge of mountains, on the other side of which were the headsprings of another great river that flowed west to "a great water"—all of this in a landscape of fertile meadows filled with deer and turkeys, an abundant land that Lahontan described as "the most agreeable in the world."[27] In a few pages, Lahontan conveyed not only the rudiments of symmetrical geography but also the image of the farther West as a garden.

Rogers' account was less bombastic than Lahontan's but, ultimately, only slightly less fanciful. While petitioning Parliament in 1765 for sponsorship of an expedition across the North American continent, Rogers claimed that he had discovered the Northwest Passage by land. That passage lay "toward the Head of the Mississippi, and from thence to a River called by the Indians Ouragan which flows into a Bay that projects North-Eastwardly into the

Country from the Pacific Ocean."[28] Rogers' petition was denied, but he turned to the public for support and, in *A Concise Account*, made the claim that he had unlocked the riddle of the geography of the western interior and, hence, of a route to the Pacific. Rogers' description was the epitome of the British concept of symmetrical geography. Toward the center of the continent was a mountain range that served as a pyramidal height-of-land from which rivers drained in several directions: "by these rivers the continent is divided into so many departments, as it were from a center."[29] Through the writings of Rogers and his lieutenant, Jonathan Carver (more of whom we will learn later), British symmetrical geography and the hypothetical height-of-land were reinforced as geographical concepts in Jefferson's imagination.

The reinforcement continued as Jefferson commenced purchasing books in France and England. A partial listing of the geographical titles acquired would include: Jonathan Carver's *Travels in the Interior of North America*, Pierre F. X. Charlevoix's *Histoire et Description Generale de la Nouvelle France*, Thomas Jeffrey's *American Atlas*, Thomas Hutchins' *A Topographical Description of Louisiana and the Floridas*, Louis Hennepin's *Description of Louisiana*, Dumont de Montigny's *Historical Memoires of Louisiana*, Henri Tonti's *Late Discoveries in North America*, and Antoine Simon Le Page du Pratz's *The History of Louisiana*.[30] From this inventory, Jefferson himself would note the works of Carver, du Pratz, and Hennepin as being "a particularly useful species of reading."[31]

Carver's work was an extension of that of Robert Rogers, whom Carver had served as field lieutenant and cartographer. But Carver's popularity as an author exceeded that of Rogers exponentially—where Rogers had had to publish *A Concise Account* himself, Carver's *Travels in the Interior* went through more than thirty editions after its first English publication in 1788, remaining for most informed people (including America's foremost geographical writer and gazetteer, the Reverend Jedediah Morse) the authoritative source on the interior of the continent. Carver's comments on the content of western geography—on the climate, soil, natives, rivers, and mountains of western North America—became an important part of Thomas Jefferson's imaginary geography. The climate of the lands west of the Mississippi, Carver wrote, was "much more temperate than in those provinces that lie in the same degree of latitude" east of the Mississippi. The soil was fertile, producing mighty forests and a "great deal of land that is free from woods" that promised to "produce a sufficient supply of all the necessaries of life for any number of inhabitants."[32] There were also mountains in the West beyond which could be found

other lakes, rivers, and countries, full fraught with all the necessaries or luxuries of life; and where future generations may find an asylum, whether driven from their country by the ravages of lawless tyrants, or by the religious persecutions, or reluctantly leaving it to remedy the inconveniences arising from a superabundant increase of inhabitants. . . .[33]

Years before anyone had heard of Manifest Destiny or the words *Oregon Country*, Jonathan Carver was expressing thoughts that would find action.

But it is in Carver's thorough descriptions of the nature of western geography that we find what was perhaps his greatest impact on Jefferson. "I have learned," he wrote, "that the four most capital rivers of the Continent of North America, viz., the St. Lawrence, the Mississippie, the River Bourbon, and Oregon or River of the West have their sources in the same neighbourhood."[34] This "neighbourhood" was the highest land in North America, the center of continental geography. "It is," Carver continued, "an instance not to be paralleled on the other three quarters of the globe, that four rivers of such magnitude should take their rise together, and each, after running separate courses, discharge their waters into different oceans at the distance of two thousand miles from their source."[35] He even named the mountains that gave rise to these mighty rivers: they were "the Shining Mountains . . . from an infinite number of chrystal stones, of an amazing size, with which they are covered, and which, when the sun shines full upon them, sparkle so as to be seen at a very great distance." The Shining Mountains they would become for later generations, and Carver, looking beyond his mountains of the mind, had even discovered the passage through them: if one followed a

branch of the river Messorie, till having discovered the source of the Oregan or River of the West, on the other side of the summit of lands that divide the waters which run into the Gulph of Mexico from those that fall into the Pacific Ocean, then he would have sailed down that river to the place where it is said to empty itself near the Straights of Annian.[36]

"The Straits of Anian"—a name out of Renaissance cartography entered American geographical lore and the developing image of Jefferson's West.

Although Jefferson acknowledged the importance of Carver's work for his own ideas on the West, the works of the other two authors—Hennepin and du Pratz—may have been nearly equal in significance because they bore explicitly upon the territory of Louisiana: an area that would soon become American territory and the focus of Jefferson's geography of the imagination. Hennepin was a Recollect father and official historian of La Salle's first expedition to the Mississippi River. Wandering west from the Mississippi in 1680, he sought geographical information from native peoples, and in his reports appeared statements that could be added to those of Coxe, Rogers, Carver, and others as core segments of the emerging Jeffersonian image. Hennepin's West, like Carver's, was a garden "of exceeding great fertility and beauty. . . . There are vast Meadows, which need not to be grubb'd up but are ready for the Plow and Seed; and certainly the soil must be very fruitful."[37] Flowing through this garden was "the River of the Osages and Messorites" and it was formed "from several other Rivers, which spring from a Mountain about twelve days' journey from its Mouth . . . from this Mountains one might see the Sea, and now and then some Great Ships."[38] Hennepin added that by proceeding up the Missouri one might "find some great River running into the Pacifick-Sea, whereby . . . it will be easie to trade and have commerce with China and Japan."[39] The work of du Pratz, the historian of French Louisiana, was also significant.[40] Du Pratz related the story of an Indian with whom he had become acquainted while living in Louisiana. This Indian was a great traveler who had ascended the Mississippi to the mouth of the Illinois River and then overland to the Missouri. Keeping always to the north-northwest, the Indian traveled up the Missouri until he reached its source and there visited several nations "on a neighbouring river, which ran to the opposite direction, since as he judged, it ran from east to west into a sea, of which the Indians did not know the name any more than that of the river."[41] The Indian named the river "the Beautiful River" and he later traveled down it toward the Pacific where he took part in an ambush of white bearded men who dressed like Europeans. The evidence from du Pratz's relation was inescapable and fit the geographic logic of Coxe, Carver, Hennepin, and other authors in Jefferson's growing collection: from some point on the Missouri a traveler had made a crossing between the Missouri and a westward-flowing river that took him eventually to the Sea of the West.

While Jefferson was in residence in France, buying books on the West and other topics, another event transpired that must have bolstered his developing impressions of western geography. He was visited in Paris by an American named John Ledyard, who had served with Captain James Cook during the great navigator's exploration of the Pacific coast of North America. Cook's maps and journals were becoming available, and they portrayed a range of mountains paralleling the Pacific coast and no great distance inland—just as the tenets of symmetrical geography had suggested a century or more earlier. Ledyard proposed to Jefferson a remarkable strategy: Ledyard would leave Paris for Russia, cross Siberia and pick up passage on a Russian fur trading ship for Kamchatka and the Pacific Northwest; here he would locate the Great River of the West and follow it to its source, across the mountains to the Missouri, and down to the Mississippi.[42] It was a remarkable plan that went nowhere but it illustrates the power of the concept of symmetrical geography nearly two decades before the Lewis and Clark expedition would test Jefferson's ultimate imaginary geography.

After returning from Europe, Jefferson continued to purchase books on the West—adding to his library, for example, Alexander Mackenzie's *Voyages from Montreal,* which was to play an important role in shaping his objectives for Lewis and Clark, as well as recent American geographies and the latest French and English histories of Louisiana. When, in 1793, Jefferson (acting on behalf of the American Philosophical Society) drew up a set of instructions for the French botanist André Michaux, who, it was proposed, would make an attempt on locating the connection between Atlantic and Pacific streams, it was clear that Jefferson was relying primarily on his understanding of western geography as derived from source materials as old as Coxe and as recent as Mackenzie. The "fundamental object" of Michaux's proposed travels, noted Jefferson, "and not to be disposed with," was the location of that source region of the upper Missouri where "a river called Oregan interlocked with the Missouri for a considerable distance, & entered the Pacific ocean, not far southward of Nootka sound."[43] In his early years as president, when he began thinking and writing about the West, it was the works of Coxe and Lahontan, of du Pratz and Hennepin, of Carver and Rogers that he would turn to again and again as "a particularly useful species of reading." And when events in 1802–3 transpired so as to make Louisiana Territory a part of the United States, that "useful species of reading" became even more useful as Jefferson prepared to launch the expedition of Lewis and Clark.

THE JEFFERSONIAN IMAGE OF THE WEST

There can be little question that, at the time of the purchase and the expedition, Jefferson was the best informed American on the trans-Mississippi area. He certainly had the most complete library on western subjects. Unfortunately, he never translated all of the information in his possession into a definitive statement of the geography of western North America. He came the closest in four documents written during the latter part of 1803 and the first part of 1804, documents that are—at the same time—remarkable for their lack of speculation yet still fully illustrative of Jefferson's geographic imagination. These documents, in ascending order of their importance rather than their chronology, were: "An examination of the boundaries of Louisiana," "A chronological series of facts relating to Louisiana," "Official account of Louisiana," and Jefferson's instructions to Meriwether Lewis.[44]

The first two of these documents are closely related in that both were drawn almost exclusively from Jefferson's library collection. Neither contains much "hard" geographical information, but inferences can be drawn from both. In "examination into the boundaries of Louisiana," for example, Jefferson's comments on the newly acquired territory's western boundary are instructive of his imaginary geography. The western boundary of Louisiana, he wrote, would be "up the Rio Bravo [by which he meant the Rio Grande] to it's source; thence to the highlands encompassing the waters of the Missisipi, and along those highlands round the heads of the Missouri & Mississippi & their waters."[45] The nature of these highlands is not mentioned, but it is probable that Jefferson saw them as a simple dividing ridge or even just a height-of-land rather than a great mountain range. Most geographical writers of the time (including Jonathan Carver) had described "the mountains of New Mexico" as terminating near the forty-seventh parallel of latitude, and recent evidence from the British fur trade supported that description. Jefferson knew mountains, he had grown up near mountains; if he had meant to describe the divide west of the Mississippi-Missouri system, it is unlikely that he would have used the term *highland* rather than *mountain*. And from "A chronological series of facts about Louisiana," although again we see little real evidence of Jefferson's image of the West, inferences can be made. The sources that Jefferson relied on the most heavily in writing his chronology were Coxe, Hennepin, and du Pratz. It is unlikely that he would have accepted and used their history without accepting and using their geography as well. And in the geography of each, the Missouri heads in mountains or a height-of-land from which there also flows a great river to the Pacific.

In Jefferson's "Official account of Louisiana," presented to Congress in November 1803, there is considerably more "hard" geography, although relatively little of it applies to the farther West and most of that relates to the content of the region rather than its nature. When describing Upper Louisiana (the region north and west of St. Louis), for example, Jefferson notes that the face of the country, although somewhat more broken than the Mississippi valley, was "equally fertile." Furthermore, the area of Upper Louisiana had many advantages that were not normally characteristic of regions in the same latitudinal zone. It was elevated and well watered and had a "variety of large, rapid streams, calculated for mills and other water works." The soil was more fertile than anywhere else in the same latitudes, and the land was said to yield its produce almost without input of human labor. To the north and west, along the Missouri itself, was "one immense prairie" that produced nothing but grass—not because of aridity but because the soil was "too rich for the growth of forest trees." Beauty combined with utility in this land, and the landscape was "carved into various shapes by the hand of nature," presenting the "appearance of a multitude of antique towers." Throughout the western interior, "idealized Rivanna Rivers flowed by future Monticellos."[46] In the "Official account," Jefferson did not speak of the mountains or highlands at the head of the Missouri, and we learn little about his views on the nature of western geography. But he did not have to comment on those broader aspects of the region for us to know what was in his mind: he had, by this time, already presented Meriwether Lewis with his instructions.

From Jefferson's instructions to Meriwether Lewis, we obtain as precise a picture of Jefferson's imaginary western geography as can be had. We can also see the two primary biases—utilitarian and agrarian—that colored Jefferson's thought about the West. In June 1803, Jefferson prepared his instructions, incorporating what was literally a lifetime's worth of imaginary geography, into a document that was remarkable not only for its geographic content but also as a blueprint for exploration.[47] "The object of your mission," wrote Jefferson, "is to explore the Missouri river, & such principal stream of it, as, by it's course and communication with the waters of the Pacific ocean, whether the Columbia, Oregan, Colorado or any other river may offer the most direct & practicable water communication across this continent for the purposes of commerce. . . ."

The first and most obvious thing that strikes us about this passage in Jefferson's instructions to Lewis is that the plan for exploration was virtually identical to that proposed for Dr. Thomas Walker a half-century earlier—up the Missouri to the highlands separating it from a river that would flow to the Great South Sea. The primary objective of exploration? A water passage across the continent for the purposes of commerce—and this, too, is identical to the goals of the Loyal Land Company and illustrates the importance of utilitarian thought in Jefferson's view of the West. Only one river combination on the continent was understood to permit the attainment of this objective, and that was the Missouri and "whatever river heading with it" flowed to the Pacific. For the Loyal Land Company, that river had no name, but they knew it was there; for Thomas Jefferson, the river of the imagination that had been the "Great River of the West" of Daniel Coxe, the "Beautiful River" of du Pratz and Hennepin, and the "Oregan" of Rogers and Carver, was now the "Columbia," a river that existed in the mind well before it existed in what came to be understood as geographic reality.

The utilitarian nature of the connection between the Missouri and the Columbia was reinforced in three subsequent sections of the instructions:

> The interesting points of the portage between the heads of the Missouri, & of the water offering the best communication with the Pacific

ocean, should also be fixed by observation, & the courses of that water to the ocean in the same manner as that of the Missouri. . . .

Should you reach the Pacific ocean, inform yourself of the circumstance which may decide whether the furs of those parts may not be collected as advantageously at the head of the Missouri (convenient as it is supposed to the waters of the Colorado & Oregan or Columbia) as at Nootka sound, or any other point of that coast; and that trade be consequently conducted throughout the Missouri and U.S. more beneficially than by the circumnavigation now practised. . . .

Atho' your route will be along the channel of the Missouri, yet you will endeavor to inform yourself, by enquiry, of the character & extent of the country waters by it's branches, & especially on it's Southern side. The North river or Rio Bravo which runs into the gulph of California, are understood to be the principal streams heading opposite the waters of the Missouri and running Southwardly. Whether the dividing grounds between the Missouri and them are mountains or flat lands, what are their distances from the Missouri, the character of the intermediate country, & the people inhabiting it, are worthy of particular inquiry. The Northern waters of the Missouri are less to be enquired after, because they have been ascertained to a considerable degree, & are still in a course of ascertainment by English traders and travellers. But if you can learn anything of the most Northern source of the Missisipi, & of it's position relatively to the lake of the woods, it will be interesting to us. . . .

What separated the source waters of the Missouri from those of the Columbia and other western streams? Some of Jefferson's literary informants had written of mountains and some of highlands and some of simple heights-of-land as the French fur traders in the Laurentian shield comprehended that term: a low-lying drainage divide affording a portage between two navigable streams. Jefferson himself was less specific on the mountains of the mind than he was on the river systems that rose from them. But from a variety of sources, including a map[48] that was constructed for Meriwether Lewis' use, it can be concluded that Jefferson understood clearly that there were mountains in the vicinity of the headwaters of the Missouri and Columbia. To the north were the mountains crossed by Alexander Mackenzie in 1793 on his way to the Pacific, mountains that had been appearing in British literature and on British maps for a century. To the south were the mountains long known as the "mountains of New

Mexico" that had been described in French and Spanish accounts of Louisiana for a long a period of time. There was nothing in the literature that said the two ranges had to be connected, but Jefferson's imaginary geography was based not just on the literature but upon interpretations of it—and upon experience. Raised on the principles of symmetrical geography and growing up at the base of the Blue Ridge, it is likely that Jefferson envisaged a highland region connecting the Stony Mountains of the North and the New Mexico mountains of the South. This highland region lay no great distance from the sea (as verified by exploration along the Pacific coast in the 1790s), and the source region itself was level enough that the upper Missouri and upper Columbia could be connected with a portage. And from this highland region there probably flowed not only the Missouri and Columbia but other great western rivers—the Rio Grande, the Colorado, and perhaps several others as well—and might they, too, be connected via simple portages? Jefferson was not engaging in metaphysical speculation, he was operating upon his long-standing utilitarian understanding of river systems. If portage connections existed between western rivers—and everything in Jefferson's geographical experience suggested they should—then something else was also possible: canals. Just as Jefferson had proposed connecting the Potomac and the Ohio nearly twenty years earlier,[49] so might he have visualized the development of navigation improvements on western rivers, improvements that might have the ability to "spread the field of our commerce Westwardly and Southwardly beyond any thing ever yet done by man."[50] Jefferson's utilitarian imaginary geography thus afforded connections between the east and west of the continent and between the north and south as well. A transportation nexus would satisfy both Jefferson's imperial ambition and his utilitarian geographical imagination. And what had the Loyal Land Company been if not imperialistic and utilitarian? Small wonder that clarifying the geography of the imagination was so important to the president raised in the shadow of the Blue Ridge. The view beyond the Stony Mountains opened upon the Passage to India.

But Jefferson envisioned more than a simple passage; the other component to his image of the West was the content of the region. Although the primary purpose of Jefferson's expedition was the location of the passage to the Pacific, he gave Lewis other directives that illustrated Jefferson's awareness of the ingredients of western regional geography as they bore upon the agrarian tradition he saw as necessary to the future of the republic. In addition to locating the passage to the Pacific, Lewis was to make careful observations of the character of the native inhabitants of the land through which he would pass, of the botanical and zoological features he would encounter, and of the region's mineral productions of every kind. Second in importance only to locating the passage, Lewis was to make himself fully acquainted with the quality of the lands between the Mississippi and the Pacific and record carefully soil fertility and vegetative and climatic characteristics. Jefferson's imaginary geography was not only utilitarian in a commercial sense; it was also agrarian in a political context. Agriculture was, in his view, not only the most useful of human endeavors, but necessary if the United States were to remain a democracy based on a firm agrarian tradition. Jeffersonian Republicanism made a simple analogy: in Europe the "lands are either cultivated or locked up against the cultivator."[51] In Europe were to be found despotic governments. But in the United States and the remainder of North America, there was "an immensity of land courting the industry of the husbandman."[52] In America was a republican form of government. The availability of land for the yeoman farmer that was the backbone of Jefferson's republic was therefore necessary for the well-being and continuation of that republic. To maintain the republican system, more and more land was necessary in order to maintain the growing population of "those who labor in the earth . . . the chosen people of God, if ever He had a chosen people."[53] Meriwether Lewis was sent westward to find the passage to the Pacific and satisfy Jefferson's utilitarian geography; he was also sent westward to explore that interior garden of Jefferson's agrarian imagination, a garden that was necessary to preserve the republic. "Our governments will remain virtuous for many centuries," Jefferson wrote to James Madison in 1787, "as long as they are chiefly agricultural; and this will be as long as there shall be vacant lands in any part of America."[54]

Thus Thomas Jefferson's imagined West in 1803: a vast and fertile land too rich for the growth of forest trees, bordered by western analogues of the Blue Ridge, and crossed by stately rivers offering unparalleled connections between American civilization and the Orient. It was the realization of the commercial desideratum that had existed since Europeans recognized the presence of a barrier continent barring their way to the riches of Cathay. This was Jefferson's dream, as stated eloquently by James Ronda: "Americans would never be seduced by city lights so long as there was rich land available and reliable sources to world markets. Ouragon could secure the republican dream of simplicity and virtue in a peaceable kingdom."[55] The dream died hard but, as dreams often do, it died fast. Thomas Jefferson thought it would be "a thousand years" before American civilization filled up the great spaces between the Mississippi and the Pacific and the republic was threatened. Could he have foreseen what would happen in one scant century? A Virginian contemporary of Jefferson's, better known for his supposed "give me Liberty or give me death" speech, apparently did when he also said, "The greatest patriot is he who fills gullies." But Patrick Henry was speaking of the worn-out tobacco lands of the Piedmont—not the Garden of the World. No, Jefferson could not have known—no one could have known—that the technological revolution just getting underway as Meriwether Lewis and William Clark were wandering the West would transform the face of western America in less than a century. Jefferson's mighty rivers were made redundant by rivers of steel carrying enormous cargoes on the back of steam and extracting enormous environmental costs. Jefferson's fertile lands were transformed to near desert by the vision of public land policy, rapid immigration, and greed-induced agricultural practices.[56] The Passage to India and the Garden of the World was a dream in the mind of a Virginian who imagined beyond the Blue Ridge of his boyhood. The impact of that dream, particularly for the environment of the American West, was a curve that was hyperbolic when plotted against the two centuries that followed.

NOTES

1. John Logan Allen, "The Geographical Images of the American Northwest, 1673–1806: A Historical Geosophy" (Ph.D. diss., Clark University, Worcester, Mass., 1969).

2. Thomas Jefferson, *Notes on the State of Virginia* (London: John Stockdale, 1787). Unless otherwise indicated, the copy of *Notes on Virginia* consulted for this paper is Jefferson's own copy in the McGregor Rare Book and Manuscript Collection of the Alderman Library of the University of Virginia. This copy carries a number of significant marginal notations in Jefferson's hand.

3. See Donald W. Meinig, "A Life of Learning," Charles Homer Haskins Lecture, American Council of Learned Societies, Occasional Paper No. 19, 1992, for a contemporary geographer's viewpoint on "the geographer's perspective."

4. The four documents are: "A chronological series of facts relating to Louisiana," Jefferson Papers, Library of Congress, vol. 139, fol. 24017-19; "An examination of the boundaries of Louisiana," ibid., vol. 136, fol. 23692–93; "Official Account of Louisiana." ibid., vol. 126, fol. 23535, printed in *American State Papers,* vol. 20 ("Miscellaneous," vol. 1, doc. 164, 8th Cong., 1st sess., 344–56); and Jefferson's instructions to Meriwether Lewis, dated June 20, 1803, copies in the Jefferson Papers of the Library of Congress and elsewhere and also published in a number of sources, including Donald Jackson, *Letters of the Lewis and Clark Expedition with Related Documents* (Urbana: University of Illinois Press, 1962), 61–66.

5. Helmut De Terra, "Alexander von Humboldt's Correspondence with Jefferson, Madison, and Gallatin," *Proceedings of the American Philosophical Society* 103 (1959), 783–806; see also Jefferson Papers, Library of Congress, and Julian Boyd, ed., *The Papers of Thomas Jefferson* (Princeton: Princeton University Press 1950–).

6. Most of what we know of Peter Jefferson comes from Thomas Jefferson's "Autobiography" (New York: G. Putnam and Sons, 1959). An excellent source for the influence of Peter Jefferson on his son is the first two chapters in John Dos Passos, *The Head and Heart of Thomas Jefferson* (Garden City, N.Y.: Doubleday, 1954).

7. Thomas J. Lewis, "Diary of the Fairfax-line Surveys" (Charlottesville, Va.: Albemarle County Historical Society, 1934).

8. *The Fry and Jefferson Map of Virginia and Maryland: Facsimiles of the 1754 and 1794 Printings* (Charlottesville: University of Virginia Press, 1966).

9. In the records of Albemarle County, the copy of Peter Jefferson's will ("1757 July 13-filed. Albemarle County Courthouse. Probated 13 October 1757, John Nicholas, Clerk") notes that a tract of land of unspecified size and location but "on the Missisipi river" was left to Thomas Jefferson.

10. A photostat copy of the charter of the Loyal Land Company is in the rare manuscript collection of the McGregor Collection, Alderman Library, University of Virginia.

11. Daniel Coxe, *A Description of the English Province of Carolana by Spaniards Call'd Florida and by the French la Louisiane*, 2d ed. (London, 1741).

12. "The Letters of James Maury" [letter of January 10, 1756], in Ann Maury, *Memoirs of a Hugenot Family* (New York: G. P. Putnam's and Sons, 1912), 391.

13. Ibid., 388. Maury cited Coxe as the source of his geographical information and noted that he had seen Coxe's book at Joshua Fry's house (389–90).

14. See Thomas Walker, *Journal of an Exploration in the Spring of the Year 1750* (Boston: Little, Brown and Co., 1888).

15. Jean Bernard Bossu, *Travels through That Part of North American Formerly Called Louisiana* (London, 1771), 131.

16. Ibid., 391.

17. This information is from Peter Jefferson's will (see note 9 above) and from Thomas Jefferson's "Autobiography," in Adrienne Koch and William Peden, eds., *The Life and Selected Writings of Thomas Jefferson* (New York: Random House, 1944).

18. See Maury's "Treatise on Practical Education" (ms. in Maury Papers, Manuscript Division, Alderman Library, University of Virginia). Richard Beale Davis, in *Intellectual Life in Jefferson's Virginia* (Chapel Hill: University of North Carolina Press, 1964), describes the traditional type of education that a young man in colonial Virginia might have received (5–14).

19. For an opposing viewpoint, see Donald Jackson, *Thomas Jefferson and the Stony Mountains: The West from Monticello* (Urbana: University of Illinois Press, 1981), which claims that "none of these early associations with geographers, land speculators, and would-be discoverers played more than a small part in the early orientation of young Thomas Jefferson" (12). Don and I disagreed on very little, but we agreed to disagree on this point.

20. Jackson, *Jefferson and the Stony Mountains,* 21.

21. Boyd, ed., *Papers of Thomas Jefferson,* 6:204, 301.

22. Thomas Jefferson, *Notes on the State of Virginia,* ed. William Peden (Chapel Hill: University of North Carolina Press, 1955), 20; see also Jackson, *Jefferson and the Stony Mountains,* 37.

23. Jefferson, *Notes on Virginia,* 75.

24. Ibid., 7.

25. Jefferson to William Dunbar, March 13, 1804, Jefferson Papers, Library of Congress, vol. 139, fol. 24017.

26. In 1771, after the Shadwell plantation burned, Jefferson sent a friend a list of 150 books that approximated his destroyed library; Coxe, Jeffreys, and Anson were included in that list (Boyd, *Papers of Thomas Jefferson*, 1:76–81). In 1783, when asked to provide a book list for a prospective national library, Jefferson included Lahontan and Rogers, both authors who seem to have been included in his personal library (ibid., 6:216).

27. The English edition of Lahontan's account, and the one apparently owned by Jefferson, was Louis Armand de Lom d'Arce, Baron de Lahontan, *New Voyages to North America*, 2 vols. (London: H. Benwicke, 1703).

28. Cited in David Lavender, *Westward Vision* (New York: McGraw-Hill, 1963), 52.

29. Robert Rogers, *A Concise Account of North America* (London: published by the author, 1765), 153–54.

30. Ms. catalogue of Jefferson's library purchases, with notes by Stephen T. Riley, Jefferson Collection, Massachusetts Historical Society.

31. Boyd, ed., *Papers of Thomas Jefferson*, 8:411.

32. Jonathan Carver, *Travels through the Interior Parts of North America in the Years 1766, 1767, and 1768*, 3d ed. (London, 1781), 533–36.

33. Ibid., 121–22.

34. Ibid., 75–76.

35. Ibid., 76–77.

36. Ibid., 542.

37. Louis Hennepin, *Nouvelle Decouverte, A New Discovery of a Vast Country in America*, trans. and ed., Reuben Gold Thwaites (Chicago: A. C. McClurg and Co.), 213.

38. Ibid., 188.

39. Ibid., 373.

40. Antoine Simon le Page du Pratz, *The History of Louisiana, or the Western Parts of Virginia and Carolana . . .*, 2 vols. (London, 1763).

41. The version of this tale cited here is found in Benjamin French, ed., *Historical Collections of Louisiana* (New York: Lamport, Blakeman and Law, 1955), 5:123–24.

42. John Ledyard to Jefferson, August 16, 1786, in Boyd, ed., *Papers of Thomas Jefferson*, 10:259.

43. Jackson, *Letters of the Lewis and Clark Expedition*, 669–72.

44. See note 4 above for bibliographic information on these source materials.

45. Ms. copy, Alderman Library, University of Virginia, 12.

46. Charles A. Miller, *Jefferson and Nature: An Interpretation* (Baltimore: Johns Hopkins University Press, 1988), 241.

47. My discussion of Jefferson's instructions to Lewis is based upon a similar discussion in John Logan Allen, *Passage through the Garden: Lewis and Clark and the Image of the American Northwest* (New York: Dover, 1991), 106–8.

48. This was the Nicholas King map of 1803, manuscript in the Geography and Map Division, Library of Congress. For an extended discussion of this cartographic document, see *Passage through the Garden*, 74–103 (reproduction of the map, 100–101).

49. Boyd, ed., *Papers of Thomas Jefferson*, 6:548.

50. Ibid., 7:558.

51. Jefferson, *Notes on Virginia,* 289.

52. Ibid., 290.

53. Ibid.

54. Boyd, ed., *Papers of Thomas Jefferson,* 12:442.

55. James P. Ronda, "Calculating Ouragon," *Oregon Historical Quarterly* 94 (Summer/Fall, 1993), 125.

56. An intriguing summary of American environmental history may be found in John Steele Gordon, "The American Environment," *American Heritage,* October, 1993, 30–51.

CHAPTER TWO

"THE OBTAINING LANDS"

Thomas Jefferson and the Native Americans

ANTHONY F. C. WALLACE

In his relations with the Native Americans, Thomas Jefferson has been viewed as a well-intentioned statesman who brought philanthropy and science to bear on Indian affairs. His image differs sharply from that of Andrew Jackson, who has usually been seen as the impetuous frontiersman who advocated removal—i.e., ethnic cleansing—as the final solution to the Indian problem. But the two men agreed on one essential thing, a policy that united their administrations in a common purpose: the necessity of acquiring Indian lands for a growing white population. As early as February 16, 1803, before the Louisiana Purchase and while the struggle for the trans-Appalachian Old West was still going on, Jefferson as president wrote to Jackson as general of the Tennessee Militia, succinctly stating his administration's official policy toward the American Indians. "Two objects are principally in view," he told Jackson: "1. The preservation of peace; 2. The obtaining lands." He assured Jackson, "I am myself alive to the obtaining lands from the Indians by all honest and peaceable means." He went on to explain how Indian lands were actually to be obtained; we shall take up that question later.[1]

In this essay, I shall not be able to attend properly to Jeffersonian philanthropy, which has been so ably dealt with by Bernard Sheehan, or with Jefferson's interests in archaeology, linguistics, and ethnology, which have been described by James Ronda and others, including Jefferson himself in *Notes on the State of Virginia*. Instead, I shall be looking most closely at Jefferson's statements and actions in acquiring land from Native Americans for settlement by immigrant Europeans.

The President of Virginia's Provincial Council, Thomas Lee, in 1750 declared that, based on the Royal Charter of 1609, Virginia's western boundary was the

"South Sea" [i.e., the Pacific Ocean] and included California.[2] Thomas Jefferson grew up among Virginia gentlemen who shared this imperial vision. By the early 1740s, English settlements had pushed to the foothills of the Appalachians in Pennsylvania, Virginia, and in parts of the Carolinas and Georgia. Virginia took the lead in efforts to cross the Appalachian barrier by attempting to purchase lands from the supposed Indian proprietors and, beginning in 1745, by chartering land companies, which were authorized to explore, survey, and sell to settlers huge tracts of land across the mountains. The most aggressive, and best known, of these Virginia land companies was the Ohio Company, which in 1749 was granted a total of 500,000 acres on the Allegheny River. The Ohio Company was required within seven years to build a fort, garrison it, and settle on their lands at least one hundred families, an effort that challenged French pretensions in the Ohio Valley and precipitated the French and Indian War.[3]

One of the Virginia gentlemen of imperial vision was Thomas Jefferson's father, Peter Jefferson. Another was Colonel Joshua Fry, a friend, fellow surveyor and mapmaker, and neighbor of the Jeffersons. In 1749 Fry and Peter Jefferson worked together to survey an extension of the boundary line between Virginia and North Carolina, and in 1751 the Fry and Jefferson map of Virginia was published; it remained a standard map of the state through the colonial period. Fry was the initial commander of the relief expedition to the Ohio Company's fort (before his death en route) that Washington led on to surrender at Fort Necessity.[4]

Fry and Peter Jefferson had another connection, however, that is more to the point of land and Indians. They were both charter members of another Virginia land company, the Loyal Land Company. The Loyal Company was also chartered in 1749; its grant was for 800,000 acres of land bounded on the south by the North Carolina-Virginia line and running thence west and north. Another member of the Loyal Company, and its chief agent and surveyor, was Dr. Thomas Walker, also a friend and neighbor of the Jeffersons. In 1750, on behalf of the company, Walker crossed the Appalachian Mountains and explored some western foothills in parts of the intended tract, becoming the first white explorer to enter what later became the state of Kentucky. Lamentably for the Loyal Company, he failed to extend his survey to the Blue Grass country farther west.

The Jefferson connection with the Loyal Land Company had still another corollary. Of the five executors and guardians appointed in his father's will, three were members of the company: Thomas Walker, John Harvie (or Harvey), an attorney, and Thomas Turpin, a surveyor and Peter Jefferson's brother-in-law.[5]

Dr. Walker attended Peter Jefferson in his last illness in the summer of 1757. Upon his father's death, Thomas Jefferson and his brother and sisters inherited his share (one of a total of forty shares) in the Loyal Company. During the Indian wars, however, the company was unable to exploit its grant, beyond surveying and selling about a thousand lots east of the mountains, amounting to some 200,000 acres. The titles were not completed until after the Revolution, and the affairs of the company were still not resolved at the time of Walker's death in 1794. Litigation concerning the affairs of the company continued well into the nineteenth century; the last suit was not settled until 1872.[6]

In later years, Jefferson in official capacities expressed an unfavorable view of speculative land companies as a vehicle for the surveying and settlement of lands acquired from the Indians, and was sensitive to rumors about his own participation in such ventures. In a letter to James Madison in 1784, he protested his innocence in a somewhat defensive passage. Except for the Loyal Company share and a couple of other short-lived investments, he declared, "I never was nor am now interested in one foot of land on earth, off of the waters of James river."[7]

It would be interesting but time-consuming to track down all of the other original shareholders in the Loyal Company in order to discover their possible direct involvement in transactions with the Indians and personal connection with Jefferson, or to recount the adventures of the Vandalia Company and the Transylvania Company, whose claims Jefferson vigorously and successfully opposed in the Virginia House of Burgesses. (But the claims of the Loyal Company were approved.) It is enough to say that the young Jefferson was surrounded by people passionately concerned with the subject of Indian lands. Of these, Thomas Walker was probably the most influential. He was a veteran treaty commissioner and served as Jefferson's early mentor on Indian affairs; to him, among others, Jefferson turned in 1783 for advice on Indian matters while editing his manuscript of *Notes on Virginia*. "If you could be as pointed as possible as to those circumstances relating to the Indians I should be much obliged to you," he wrote in a note accompanying a copy of relevant parts of the work.[8]

Not only did Jefferson grow up among Virginia gentlemen passionately interested in Indian lands, but he also grew up among Indian fighters, men who battled the Native Americans for control of the Old West during the French and Indian War, Lord Dunmore's War, and the early days of the War of Independence. Young Jefferson undoubtedly read and heard about Indian atrocities upon hapless frontier families during these wars. By the time of the Revolution, he had developed a deep rage at the Indians' "uncivilized" meth-

ods of warfare and at the British Crown's seeming indulgence of native resistance to Virginia's expansion into the Ohio valley.

To my knowledge, Jefferson's opinion of Indians during the Revolution was
first expressed in writing in the bill of particulars against George III that serves
as preamble to, and justification for, the Declaration of Independence. He
accused the king of endeavoring to bring down upon the frontier inhabitants
"the merciless Indian Savages, whose known rule of warfare is, an undis-
tinguished destruction of all ages, sexes, and conditions." He also protested
against the Crown's policy of prohibiting land purchases and settlements beyond the Proclamation Line that ran down the ridge of the Appalachians. And
during the war, he was distressed by news of Indians attacking white settlements in the South and the North, and as burgess and then governor was in
part responsible for the military defense of the frontiers and for the successful
expeditions of John Sevier and George Rogers Clark. His brutal incarceration
of British Governor Henry Hamilton, the accused "hair-buyer" of white scalps,
reflects Jefferson's horror and rage at the methods of guerrilla warfare practiced
by Native American warriors.

Jefferson began writing *Notes on Virginia* in 1781 while still wartime governor.[9] But as regards the Indians, the benign, if somewhat funereal, tone of the
Notes on Virginia, and its attention to native character and intelligence, rhetorical skills, language, and origins, contrast sharply with the shrill rage of the
Declaration. In the discussion of the "Productions Mineral, Vegetable, and
Animal," he took issue with the charge by the French naturalist Buffon that the
aborigines of the continent, like its other productions, were degenerate and
inferior in comparison with European men. Jefferson indignantly rejected this
claim. They were, Comte de Buffon to the contrary notwithstanding, as virile
as whites, as brave, and as intelligent: "They are formed in mind as well as in
body, on the same module with the Homo sapiens Europaeus." He declared
further that in oratory they were equal, if not superior, to the best Europe had
to offer, including Demosthenes and Cicero. To demonstrate native eloquence,
Jefferson introduced the speech of Logan, "The Great Mingo," delivered at the
conclusion of Lord Dunmore's War in 1774. The sad lament, and its lugubrious
last words, "Who is there to mourn for Logan?—Not one," became famous as a
kind of epitaph for a doomed race. It was reprinted countless times, and has
been learned by rote and recited by generations of schoolchildren.

Jefferson also wrote a chapter entitled "Aborigines." So few Native Americans still remained in that part of Virginia east of the mountains that his
account of them amounted to little more than a recital of the names of extinct
tribes and confederacies. There followed a description of his excavation of an
Indian burial mound along the Rivanna River, near Monticello. Following this

archaeological report, Jefferson went on to consider the question of the origin of the native peoples of America. Noting the physical similarities between the "red men of America" and the peoples of Asia, he assumed a common origin. But where? He turned to linguistic research as potentially providing the answer. Noting that the number of linguistic stocks in the New World seemed to outnumber those in the Old by a ratio of twenty to one, and assuming that the degree of divergence from a common ancestor was correlated with the passage of time, he concluded that the Indians were of greater antiquity than the Asiatics, and thus that the migration of the race had proceeded from America to Asia across the Bering Strait. Although Jefferson was mistaken about the direction of the migration and the relative antiquity of the peopling of Asia and the Americas, he deserves credit for suggesting that "vocabularies [be] formed of all the languages spoken in North and South America" and lamenting "that we have suffered so many of the Indian tribes already to extinguish, without our having previously collected and deposited in the records of literature, the general rudiments at least of the languages they spoke." Jefferson himself collected Indian vocabularies and promoted such collection by the correspondents of the American Philosophical Society and the Lewis and Clark expedition.

The section on aborigines concludes with a census and gazetteer of the Indian tribes, not of eastern Virginia (whom he does not list) but of the whole United States. This census, arranged in tabular form, reproduces the numbers contained in several reports by well-known authorities. The original lists, however, gave only warrior counts, not total population figures, a fact that Jefferson's list as published does not point out; he leaves the impression that this is the total population, by introducing the list as a statement of "the nations and numbers of the Aborigines which still exist in a respectable and independent form." Worse, his omission of the Virginia Indians from the table implied that they were extinct; actually, several hundred survived on small reservations as late as the 1830s, and some are still resident in Virginia today.

In his letter to Andrew Jackson, already quoted, Jefferson stated his theory of how the Indians could "honestly" be persuaded to part with their lands:

> We consider the leading the Indians to agriculture as the principal means from which we can expect much effect in the future. When they shall cultivate small spots of earth, and see how useless their extensive forests are they will sell, from time to time, to help out their personal labor in stocking their farms, and procuring clothes and comforts from our trading houses. . . . I believe that the honest and peaceable means adopted by us will obtain them as fast as the expansion of our settlements, with due

regard to compactness, will require. The war department, charged with Indian affairs, is under the impression of these principles, and will second my views with sincerity.[10]

Two days later Jefferson wrote to his old friend Colonel Benjamin Hawkins, Superintendent of Indian Affairs for the tribes south of the Ohio River (and about whose devotion to "the obtaining lands" policy Jackson had expressed doubts) explaining his views in somewhat more detail; a week later he wrote to William H. Harrison, governor of Indiana Territory and Superintendent of Indian Affairs for the tribes north of the Ohio, urging Harrison, as he had Hawkins, to promote agriculture and the cession of land. In his letter to Harrison (but not in the one to Hawkins, who was perhaps deemed too solicitous of the Indians' welfare to condone the suggestion) he proposed that the federally supported trading houses see to it that "the good and influential individuals among them run in debt, because we observe that when these debts get beyond what the individuals can pay, they become willing to lop them off by a cession of lands."[11] Apparently, Jefferson took a hands-on role in carrying out the debt-and-cession strategy. In 1806 he personally told a prospective keeper of the federal store among the Cherokees to get them to run a debt in the amount of ten or twelve thousand dollars. "That is the way I intend to git there countrey," he is reported to have said; "to git them to run in debt to the publick store and they will have to give there lands in payment." The suggestion outraged the storekeeper, who replied, "If that is your Deturmeanation you must git some other person to keep the store."[12]

In the letters to Hawkins and Harrison, Jefferson painted a future for the Indians as a people doomed to extinction—not to biological extinction, but to cultural extinction as "a separate people."[13] "The ultimate point of rest and happiness for them is to let our settlements and theirs meet and blend together, to intermix, and become one people. Incorporating themselves with us as citizens of the United States" will be the best way "in which their history may terminate." But he also envisioned other futures if the tribes refused to "incorporate with us as citizens of the United States." One was for them to "remove beyond the Mississippi"; if any tribe should be so foolhardy as to take up the hatchet, he proposed "seizing the whole country of that tribe, and driving them across the Mississippi, as the only condition of peace." This would be "an example to others, and a furtherance of our final consolidation."

But this view of the ultimate result of continuous cessions of land, he believed, would upset the Indians if known to them. He therefore urged both Hawkins and Harrison not even to "hint" to Indians of his plans for them, "to keep it for your own reflection," "how improper to be understood by the

Indians." The Indians should be made to believe that the actions of the United States proceeded "from motives of pure humanity only."

But the civilization policy was essentially irrelevant to the actual process of obtaining Indian lands. Jefferson had other criteria for deciding when and where to purchase. First, he wished to secure safe routes for inland trade and military transport, particularly along the Ohio and Mississippi Rivers, which should be just as free to American shipping as the open seas. Certain overland rights-of-way were also to be acquired. Second, he wished to plant American settlements close to threatened borders, so as to provide militia for defense. And third, he wanted to consolidate settlements, advancing the nation westward in a compact body, rather than pursuing the old hop-scotch pattern of the eighteenth-century land companies. The "civilization" (in the European sense) of the Native Americans played no real part in establishing priorities, let alone methods, for acquisition.

The obtaining of lands began in the Old Northwest, where extensive purchases had already been made during Washington's and Adams' presidencies. In his letter of instruction to Harrison in February 1803, Jefferson noted that "a favorable opening" for purchase existed in his superintendency. "The Kaskaskias, being reduced to a few families, I presume we may purchase their whole country for what would place every individual of them at his ease, and be a small price to us." He proposed to allot these families as much acreage of "rich land" as they could cultivate, enclose the whole "in a single fence," and add sufficient annuities to "place them in happiness." It was so done. In August of the same year, the Kaskaskia ceded to the United States most of central Illinois, from the Ohio north nearly to Chicago, including the east bank of the Mississippi from Cairo to St. Louis. They retained two and one-half square miles for their own use.

In the same letter, Jefferson urged Harrison to "soothe and conciliate" the Kickapoos and Potawatomies in preparation for a cession. An agent should be sent to live in the village of the leader, Decoigne, "as if on other business, and to sound him and introduce the subject [of a cession] by degrees." The next purchase, however, was made instead in 1804 along the Ohio in southern Indiana, from the Delawares and Piankeshaws (one of the Miami group). This purchase, together with another Piankeshaws cession in 1805 and a cession from the Delawares, Potawatomies, Miami, Eel River, and Wea in the same year, gave the United States possession of the land on the north side of the river Ohio from its confluence with the Mississippi all the way up the forks at Pittsburgh.[14] Jefferson expressed his satisfaction with this accomplishment in his fifth annual message to Congress in December 1805. The last purchase (from the Piankeshaws) "completes our possession of the whole of both banks of the Ohio and the navigation of that river is thereby rendered forever safe to our citizens settled and settling on it's extensive waters."[15]

The civilization policy had nothing to do with those cessions and the others that followed in the Northwest Territory. By 1809, when Jefferson left the presidency, Harrison had secured most of the remaining land in Ohio, Indiana, and Illinois, except for a substantial reservation in the northwest corner of Ohio, and another in Indiana. But his strong-arm methods, including bribery and offers of land west of the Mississippi as an inducement to escape from harassment by settlers and whiskey sellers, had thoroughly antagonized the Indians who remained. A religious prophet emerged among the Shawnees in 1805. Tenskwatawa, a brother of Tecumseh who was popularly known as "the Prophet," preached against land sales and the white man's civilization. Jefferson rejected suggestions that the Prophet be seized and jailed as "not in the character of our government," but he intimated that he would not object if the Indians were to deal with him "in their own way."[16] Despite Jefferson's threats, the Prophet's message was effective: land cessions ceased in 1809, both north and south of the Ohio, and did not resume until 1814, after the Indian forces whom the Prophet and Tecumseh had inspired were finally defeated in the War of 1812.

One of the major Jeffersonian land purchases north of the Ohio had an especially tragic dénouement. In 1804, shortly after the Louisiana Purchase had been effected, the Sac and Fox tribes, who were primarily resident west of the Mississippi in Iowa and Missouri but who also claimed lands east of the river, entered into a treaty with the United States under the aegis of William Henry Harrison. The Sac and Fox sold to the United States an immense tract on both sides of the Mississippi, from the Missouri River north nearly to Prairie du Chien in southern Wisconsin, embracing lands in northern Missouri, Illinois, and Wisconsin. The circumstances under which this treaty was held were not pleasant. A Sac hunting party had killed some white settlers trespassing on Indian lands in Missouri. Harrison (temporarily governor of Upper Louisiana) demanded in "strong language" that the Sac chiefs attend a council in St. Louis at which the murderers were to be surrendered. When the Indians arrived with one of the alleged murderers, whom they gave up to the whites, they were confronted with a demand for a cession of land; under the implied threat of force, they complied. The alleged murderer was pardoned, but unfortunately the pardon arrived after he had been shot "while attempting to make his escape." Some Fox and Sac never accepted the treaty as legitimate. Among them was Black Hawk, who, in 1832, inspired by another Indian prophet, led a band of men, women, and children into Illinois to reclaim their lands about

Rock River. In the ensuing debacle of the Black Hawk War, hundreds of the doomed Indians were killed.[17]

South of the Ohio, Jefferson's Indian policy was less successful. Virtually all of the Indians of that part of the Northwest Territory lying south of the Great Lakes were emigrants from land cessions farther east; they were a tattered remnant, a few thousand survivors of the almost incessant warfare that had raged in the trans-Appalachian region from the 1740s on. However, the four major tribal groups of the Old Southwest—the Cherokees, Creeks, Chickasaws, and Choctaws—were living on their native soil, the land of their ancestors, and despite their own wars were still populous, numbering upwards of seventy-five thousand souls. When Jefferson assumed the presidency in 1801, Native Americans still held title to lands in western Kentucky; most of Tennessee was in the possession of the Cherokees, to the east, and Chickasaws, to the west; most of Georgia and all of Alabama were occupied by the Creeks; and the Choctaws and Chickasaws possessed Mississippi, except for a tract at Natchez. In fact, the entire east bank of the Mississippi River above the Natchez tract was in the possession of Native Americans, a situation that raised foreboding in Jefferson's mind, always fearful of the machinations of European powers on America's borders who seemed ready to subvert the Indians and invite the "merciless savages" to war upon innocent farm families.

Nevertheless, Jefferson had high hopes for treaties of cession, and the Creek agent continued to encourage these hopes with reports of the progress the southern Indians, particularly the Creeks and Cherokees, were making toward civilization. But Hawkins' timetable was a more relaxed one; he expected that it would require "ten or twenty years ... to perfect our plan of civilization," and he did not think Georgia would require more land for that period of time after the small cession by the Creeks in 1802 of certain lands between the Oconee and Okmulgee Rivers.[18] Under Georgia's prodding, another cession was secured in 1805, completing the purchase of the Oconee-Okmulgee region. The Choctaws in 1801, 1802, and 1805 were persuaded to cede a district north of Louisiana and east of Natchez, in the southwestern corner of Mississippi, and a few moved west of the river. And the Cherokees in 1805 and 1806 sold a pair of adjoining tracts north of the Tennessee and Clinch Rivers in southern Tennessee and northern Alabama. However, these cessions were marginal, leaving intact in 1809 a central core of Indian-owned territory from the Mississippi north of Natchez eastward across most of Mississippi, Alabama, and Georgia. Still, the United States was able to establish boundaries and secure the right to create roads across Indian territory, such as the important trace from Nashville to Natchez.[19]

The reluctance of the southern Indians to sell lands was particularly galling to Jefferson when it applied to the east bank of the Mississippi. Hearing that the Choctaw hunters were deeply in debt to "certain mercantile characters" and that the chiefs were desirous of paying off the creditors by a sale of lands, in 1805 commissioners were appointed to negotiate a treaty of cession, "with instructions to purchase only on the Mississippi." But the chiefs refused to part with the lands along the river and offered instead some lands in the interior. Jefferson, annoyed, refused even to submit the treaty to the Senate for ratification. But as United States relations with Spanish authorities in Florida and Texas became tense, the desirability of obtaining a "footing for a strong settlement of militia" who would establish "a barrier of separation between the Indians and our Southern neighbors" became apparent. Jefferson eventually submitted the treaty to the Senate in 1808.[20]

It is clear that the civilization policy was really irrelevant to the purchase policy both north and south of the Ohio. Where the Indians were unable or unwilling to embark on the difficult and divisive path of emulating the white agricultural economy, Jefferson's agents nevertheless pressed for cessions of land, land needed not only for settlers but also for strategic purposes, such as national defense or commercial traffic. And even where some of the Indians were committing themselves to herding, plowing, spinning, and weaving, they still obstinately refused to sell their hunting grounds. Why should they? Hunting was still a productive enterprise; and anyway, the chiefs might argue, if their population did increase with the progress of white-style agriculture, they would need the lands themselves for future expansion—a possibility that Jefferson seems not to have considered. Twenty years later, it became clear, at least to Andrew Jackson and many southern whites, that the more "civilized" the Indians became, the less likely they were to want either to move or to sell.

As a device for persuading Native Americans to sell their land, the civilization policy was a failure, and, as Bernard Sheehan has forcefully pointed out, it was not much of a success in promoting civilization either.

The Louisiana Purchase confronted Jefferson with a new and little-known population of Indians. He had for years sought to acquire for the United States more information about Spain's, and later France's, vast domain west of the Mississippi. Part of the interest, as always with Jefferson, was strategic: to draw the tribes on America's borders away from menacing alliances with her real or potential enemies, particularly the British. One of the means for counteracting foreign influence was to open up trade with these Indians, hopefully weaning them from English traders from Canada; plans for the Lewis and Clark expedition were being made well before news of the purchase reached Washington.

Jefferson had apparently not expected to acquire, at that time, all the lands drained by the western tributaries of the Mississippi; the negotiations in Paris were aimed at obtaining New Orleans and adjoining tracts in order to secure American navigation down the Mississippi to New Orleans and the Gulf of Mexico.

Lewis and Clark were sent out with instructions to invite the Indian tribes along the Missouri to peace, friendship, and mutually profitable relations with American fur traders. They were also to gather information about the location, numbers, languages, customs, history, and intergroup relations of the Native Americans. Some of these Indians were reasonably well known to the Chouteau brothers and their trading organization in St. Louis, and to various other French, Spanish, and British traders, but they were an unknown quantity to Jefferson. They were, in fact, occupants of several different culture areas, ranging from the village-dwelling, corn-growing Osages, Mandans, Omahas, and others along the Missouri River, to the more mobile hunting bands of Yankton and Teton Sioux now encroaching on the plains, to the Indians of the traditional horse-stealing and buffalo-hunting "wild Indians" like the Pawnees, to the hunters and gatherers of the Great Basin and Plateau. These were not like the relatively sedentary—and by now harried and depopulated—village dwellers of the East; whites of the eastern seaboard, who had dealt with the eastern Indians for two centuries, were not familiar with their customs, their politics, their intertribal alliances and hostilities. James Ronda has carefully described the diplomatic difficulties and successes of the Corps of Discovery as they patiently muddled through to the Pacific and back to St. Louis, wisely following Jefferson's sage advice to avoid confrontation, offer the hand of peace and friendship, and pass out the Jefferson medals so thoughtfully struck in 1801.[21]

Jefferson's initial policy toward these western Indians was in a theoretical way very different from his policy toward his eastern neighbors. There would be no thought of "obtaining land" here; the goal was obtaining trade. Although some day in the future, these Indians too would have to give up their lands, abandon the hunt, and become civilized, for now the new Louisiana Territory would be, as Peterson has expressed it, "a great Indian reserve," closed to all settlers and governed by the military. But traders, both well-established firms like the Chouteaus' and new ones such as John Jacob Astor's, were strongly encouraged to establish trading posts at suitable locations.[22] Astor's American Fur Company, of course, went on to virtually dominate the fur trade in the West.

There were two major exceptions to the "trade only, no cessions" policy, however, that presaged the early application of the "obtaining lands" policy west of the Mississippi. As we noted earlier, in their 1804 cession the Sac and

Fox gave up, in addition to their claims in Illinois and Wisconsin, a substantial tract in northeastern Missouri; and in 1808 the Osages sold a vast extent of land, including the half of Arkansas north of the Arkansas River and almost all of Missouri south of the Missouri River.[23] The Osages, traditional proprietors of the lands between the Arkansas and the Missouri, were now chronically engaged in border skirmishes with intruding white settlers and also with Indians removed from the east, including Shawnees, Delawares, and Kickapoos from the northwest and Choctaws, Chickasaws, and Cherokees from the south. These clashes angered Governor Lewis and General Clark, and they threatened the Osages with retaliation by tribal enemies and an embargo on trade. These measures were specifically approved by Jefferson.[24] The cession also provided for a U.S. military post (Fort Osage) on the lower Missouri near some of their villages, and a U.S. trade factory there to supply the Osages and other tribes.

Possession of the lands in Arkansas and Missouri reinvigorated Jefferson's old removal notions. In January 1809 he urged a Cherokee delegation to send an exploring party to the lands between the Arkansas and White Rivers; the exploring party came back with a favorable report, and soon over a thousand Cherokees were said to be prepared to remove.[25] Jefferson had already, as early as 1803, come to think of Indian removal to the Louisiana Territory as an alternative to civilization. Writing to William Claiborne, governor of the Mississippi Territory and temporarily of the Louisiana Territory, Jefferson advised the governor to give the southern tribes guns, ammunition, and other essentials for removal, so as "to prepare in time an eligible retreat for the whole."[26] And in 1776 (in the heat of war, to be sure), he had declared that the Cherokees and all other hostile tribes ought to be forced across the Mississippi. In 1803, he even proposed a constitutional amendment that would reserve all of the Louisiana Purchase Territory north of the thirty-first parallel (which bisects the present state of Louisiana) as a home for the eastern tribes, who would relinquish their lands and remove to the west. White settlers west of the river would in turn give up their western lands and return east (an extraordinary fantasy!).[27] The proposed amendment to the Constitution was not approved, and Jefferson's other plans for removal of the southern Indians failed also, except for the Cherokees; a large number of them did emigrate to Arkansas, to be joined over the years by a trickle of others dissatisfied with conditions in the East.

The second administration was darkened by clouds of war on the horizon. To the north, in Jefferson's opinion, British troops lay in wait, covertly preparing the Indians to attack when the time was ripe. To the east, the British navy prowled; their interference with American shipping resulted in the Embargo Act, which unintendedly interfered with the fur trade and thus with the Indians' ability to pay their debts to the traders. To the south and west were

Spanish domains, still threatening, in Jefferson's view, to subvert the southern and western Indians.

Back east, meanwhile, the Jeffersonian land-cessions-and-civilization policy was producing deep resentment among many Native Americans. As I noted earlier, in November 1805 a religious prophet, Tenskwatawa, arose among the Shawnees in Ohio. Jefferson had saluted the Iroquois prophet Handsome Lake a few years earlier, but Handsome Lake's people had sold almost all their land, and he was advocating a civilization program under Quaker tutelage and government endorsement. The Shawnee prophet's message of rejection of white ways boldly contradicted Jefferson's policy. Jefferson reacted with the same rage that he expressed at the "merciless savages," allies of the British, who threatened the colonies at the outset of the Revolution. In 1807, learning of a meeting of the governor of Canada with the Indians in the Prophet's quarter, he decided "that we should immediately prepare for war." He ordered the governors of Michigan, Ohio, and Indiana to put their militia on the alert and to collect sufficient supplies for "any expedition." The Indians should be advised not to intervene on either side in the anticipated war with the British, and they should also be told "that if ever we are constrained to lift the hatchet against any tribe, we will never lay it down till that tribe is exterminated, or driven beyond the Mississippi. . . . In war, they will kill some of us; we shall destroy all of them." And he threatened not to wait, "if any tribe means to strike us," but to "anticipate by giving the first blow."[28]

Of the Prophet personally, Jefferson was contemptuous. At first he thought Tenskwatawa was "a visionary, enveloped in the clouds of their antiquities, and vainly endeavoring to lead back his brethren to the fancied beatitudes of their golden age." The Indians would never give up the "habits and comforts they had learned from the whites [for] the hardships and privations of savagism."[29] But later, he suggested bribing him; he was "no doubt a scoundrel, and only needs his price."[30]

After Jefferson left the presidency, General Harrison did in fact "anticipate" the armed uprising of the Prophet's followers by his attack on the Prophet's village at Tippecanoe, Indiana, in November 1811. By this time, Tecumseh was traveling among the southern tribes, mobilizing support for a great Indian confederacy that would drive back the Americans. His followers among the Creeks were especially enthusiastic, and with the onset of the War of 1812, led by their own prophets, the Red Sticks, the anti-civilization faction once more attacked the frontiers. The Creeks were defeated by General Andrew Jackson in a bloody war that made Jackson's reputation.[31] Jefferson, at the onset of this war, was again beset by rage at the merciless savages. He regretted that he had let the Prophet "go on . . . unmolested" in his early, apparently visionary days before the British "found him corruptible." Now that war with the "backward" tribes of the Northwest had come, "We shall be obliged to drive them, with the beasts of the forest into the Stony mountains."[32]

In evaluating Thomas Jefferson's relationships with the American Indians, it is necessary to keep in mind that for most of his life he was a public man who was, first as a Virginian and then as president of the United States, deeply committed to the purchase and settlement of Indian lands in the Old West between the Appalachian Mountains and the Mississippi. But he brought to this almost sacred cause a geopolitical mind that viewed places and events around the world in the light of a vision of American destiny. In 1801, a few months after taking office as president, he wrote to James Monroe, then governor of Virginia, outlining his dream. American white settlers, sturdy yeomen, would increase in numbers and eventually would "cover the whole northern, if not southern continent, with a people speaking the same language, governed in similar forms, and by similar laws; nor can we contemplate with satisfaction either blot or mixture in that surface."[33]

This was a geopolitical vision not so much of an empire that embraced a diversity of nations, races, and cultures as of an ethnic homeland, European in origin and spirit, agrarian in economy, governed by republican institutions derived from old Anglo-Saxon and even pre-imperial Roman models. People of Indian ancestry could "incorporate with us" if they chose to accept "civilization." Those who preferred the hunter's life and the ways of their ancestors would inevitably have to withdraw to the west, beyond the Mississippi, as game was depleted and hunting grounds were sold in the east. Eventually, they too would have to adopt civilization or perish as the Louisiana Purchase itself and the lands beyond were overrun and settled.

But there was a darker side to the geopolitical vision. Always, in Jefferson's thought (and to a great degree in reality), there were enemies—always the British, at times the French and Spanish—just outside the expanding circle of the American nation, threatening to block that "final consolidation" of the American world he sought to achieve. And all too often, allied with them as spoilers of the American dream were the Indians, the "merciless savages" who had fought throughout his lifetime to block the westward march of the American folk. This image of the Indian as savage murderer of innocent frontier farm families undoubtedly was implanted in his youth and was responsible for that chronic rage that boiled up into belligerence whenever Indians resisted his plans or threatened to break the peace.

Thus there was a degree of ruthlessness in Jefferson's dealings with the

Indians, the ruthlessness of a benevolent zealot who would do virtually anything to ensure that his new, free American republic survived and grew. As president of an expanding nation and as one personally committed to the purchase of Indian land, he knew from the Iroquois example that the civilization of the Indians would follow, not precede, the sale of hunting grounds. These hunting grounds already provided the cash crop—skins and furs—with which the men could purchase necessary hardware and dry goods. So the effective methods for inducing the Indians to sell were actually five other procedures: first, run the hunters into debt, then threaten to cut off their supplies unless the debts were paid out of the proceeds of a land cession; second, bribe influential chiefs with money and private reservations; third, select and invite friendly leaders to Washington to visit, and negotiate, with the president after being overawed by the evident power of the United States; fourth, permit white trespassers on Indian lands to remain long enough to provoke the Indian owners to harass intruding families, steal horses, and murder a few hunters; and fifth, war, in case a hostile tribe had to be driven westward. Jefferson was no doubt doing what he felt he had to do in the public interest: obtain lands by all means short of unprovoked wars of conquest.

Perhaps *duplicity* is too strong a word to characterize the contrast between Jefferson's actual methods of obtaining lands and the publicly announced civilization policy, which every year he assured Congress was proceeding smoothly; the contrast between the bellicose Jefferson threatening to "exterminate" unfriendly tribes and the gentle scholar nostalgically excavating Indian mounds, celebrating Logan's rhetoric, praising Indian intelligence and egalitarianism, and patiently collecting vocabularies. As Gilbert Chinard observed, "theory never seemed to have interfered with his practices."[34] If it was duplicity, it was duplicity that, like his ruthlessness, was a weapon in the struggle to ensure the survival of his United States. The civilization policy, originally formulated by Federalists, was probably sincerely intended by Jefferson, but it also functioned as a public relations device that provided a moral justification for purchases. Similarly, the scholarly exercises displayed in *Notes on Virginia* and supported at his urging by the American Philosophical Society, while they were certainly the product of genuine intellectual curiosity, also served a public relations function: to convince Europeans that Americans were already civilized, were capable of a parting salute to a race doomed to cultural, if not physical, extinction, a generous obituary from a compassionate American people.

But this was an obituary that, like Mark Twain's, was "greatly exaggerated." Native American people still survive and in a few cases thrive, in both the Old and the New West.

NOTES

1. Jefferson to Andrew Jackson, February 16, 1803, in Andrew A. Lipscomb and Albert Ellery Bergh, eds., *The Writings of Thomas Jefferson*, 20 vols. (Washington, D.C.: Thomas Jefferson Memorial Association of the United States, 1903–04), 10:357.

2. Quoted in Lawrence H. Gipson, *The Southern Plantations* (Caldwell, Idaho: Caxton Printers, 1936), 4.

3. See Gipson, *Southern Plantations,* and Lois Mulkearn, ed., *George Mercer Papers* (Pittsburgh: University of Pittsburgh Press, 1954) for details relating to the Ohio Company and other land companies of the period.

4. See Phillip Slaughter, *Memoir of Col. Joshua Fry* (n.p., n.d.), for an account of Fry's career.

5. Dumas Malone, *Jefferson the Virginian* (Boston: Little, Brown, 1948), 438.

6. For accounts of Walker's career, see Archibald Henderson, "Dr. Thomas Walker and the Loyal Company of Virginia," *Proceedings of the American Antiquarian Society*, n.s., 41 (1931): 77–178, and J. Stoddard Johnston, *Doctor Thomas Walker's Journal,* Filson Club Explorations Series, vol. 13 (Louisville, Ky.: Filson Club, 1898).

7. Julian P. Boyd, ed., *The Papers of Thomas Jefferson* (Princeton: Princeton University Press, 1950–), 7:503–4.

8. Ibid., 6:340.

9. The following discussion of Jefferson's *Notes on the State of Virginia* relies on the edition of William Peden (Chapel Hill: University of North Carolina Press, 1955).

10. Jefferson to Andrew Jackson, February 16, 1803, in Lipscomb and Bergh, ed., *Writings of Thomas Jefferson,* 10:357–59.

11. Jefferson to William Henry Harrison, in ibid., 370.

12. Quoted in R. S. Cotterill, *The Southern Indians before Removal* (Norman: University of Oklahoma Press, 1954), 140.

13. For the quotations that follow, see Jefferson to Benjamin Hawkins, February 18, 1803, and Jefferson to William Henry Harrison, February 27, 1803, in Lipscomb and Bergh, ed., *Writings of Thomas Jefferson,* 10:360–65, and 368–73, respectively.

14. Charles C. Royce, *Indian Land Cessions in the United States* (Washington, D.C.: U.S. Government Printing Office, 1899) gives details of this and other land purchases during Jefferson's presidency.

15. James D. Richardson, ed., *Messages and Papers of the Presidents* (Washington: Bureau of National Literature, 1969), 1:375.

16. Jefferson to Henry Dearborn, August 12, 1807, in Lipscomb and Bergh, ed., *The Writings of Thomas Jefferson,* 11:325.

17. See Anthony F. C. Wallace, *Prelude to Disaster: The Course of Indian-White Relations Which Led to the Black Hawk War of 1832* (Springfield: Illinois State Historical Library, 1970) for an account of the 1804 treaty and its aftermath.

18. C. L. Grant, ed., *Letters, Journals, and Writings of Benjamin Hawkins* (Savannah, Ga.: The Beehive Press, 1980), 2:456.

19. See Royce, *Indian Land Cessions in the United States.*

20. Richardson, ed., *Messages and Papers of the Presidents*, 1:422–26.

21. See James P. Ronda, *Lewis and Clark among the Indians* (Lincoln: University of Nebraska Press, 1984) for a thoughtful and detailed account of Lewis and Clark's encounters with the Indians.

22. Jefferson to John Jacob Astor, April 13, 1808, in Lipscomb and Bergh, eds., *Writings of Thomas Jefferson*, 12:28.

23. See Royce, *Indian Land Cessions in the United States*.

24. Jefferson to Henry Dearborn, August 20, 1808, in Lipscomb and Bergh, eds., *Writings of Thomas Jefferson*, 12:139.

25. Cotterill, *Southern Indians before Removal*, 159.

26. Quoted in Richard Drinnon, *Facing West: The Metaphysics of Indian-Hating and Empire Building* (New York: Schocken, 1990), 87.

27. See Bernard W. Sheehan, *Seeds of Extinction: Jeffersonian Philanthropy and the American Indian* (New York: Norton, 1974) for discussion of early Jeffersonian ideas about removal as well as civilization. The amendment proposals are printed in Paul L. Ford, ed., *The Writings of Thomas Jefferson* (New York: 1892–99), 8:241.

28. Jefferson to Henry Dearborn, August 28, 1807, in Lipscomb and Bergh, eds., *Writings of Thomas Jefferson*, 11:342–46.

29. Jefferson to John Adams, April 20, 1812, quoted in Sheehan, *Seeds of Extinction*, 217.

30. Jefferson to Henry Dearborn, August 12, 1807, in Lipscomb and Bergh, eds., *Writings of Thomas Jefferson*, 11:325.

31. See Robert V. Remini, *The Life of Andrew Jackson* (New York: Harper & Row, 1988) for an account of the Creek War.

32. Jefferson to John Adams, June 11, 1812, quoted in Drinnon, *Facing West*, 97.

33. Jefferson to James Monroe, November 24, 1801, in Lipscomb and Bergh, eds., *Writings of Thomas Jefferson*, 11:296.

34. Quoted in Merrill D. Peterson, *The Jefferson Image in the American Mind* (New York: Oxford University Press, 1960), 415.

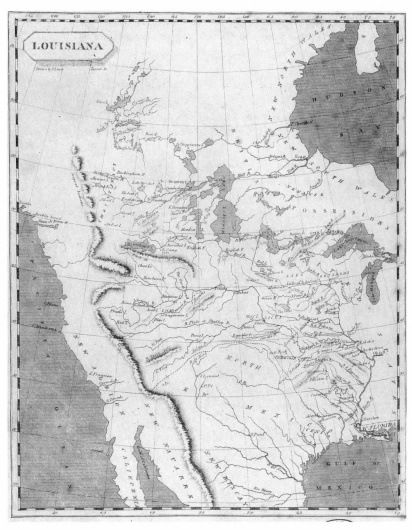

MAP 2. "LOUISIANA." BY S[AMUEL] LEWIS, 1804.
MISSOURI HISTORICAL SOCIETY LIBRARY MAP COLLECTION.

No map better portrays the Anglo-American vision of the West on the eve of the Lewis and Clark expedition than Samuel Lewis' "Louisiana." Drawing on generations of speculation about the geographic character of the West, Lewis sketched the lands west of the Mississippi in their barest essentials. By erasing native people and all but the simplest terrain features, Lewis made his West ready to be Jefferson's garden.

CHAPTER THREE

THOMAS JEFFERSON
Indigenous American Storyteller

ROBERT A. WILLIAMS, JR.

WHAT'S THE USE?

Writing as a Native American scholar, I wish to ask in this essay what use
Indian peoples of the changing, twenty-first century American West can find
for Thomas Jefferson's eighteenth-century vision of America. Having previously studied Jefferson's writings on Indians,[1] I knew from the start that this
would be a difficult task to carry out.

When you get right down to it, Thomas Jefferson didn't have much use for
Indians in his vision of America; at least not the tribal kind. We know he
studied tribal Indians closely in his *Notes on the State of Virginia*,[2] and speculated that they were "formed in mind as well as in body, on the same model" as
Europeans.[3] He was singularly active among his contemporaries in collecting
Indian word lists and promoting the study of American Indian linguistics in
his country.[4] In addition, we have his carefully drawn set of instructions to
Lewis and Clark in 1803 for collecting as much information as humanly possible on the Indians they encountered on their expedition of the newly acquired
western country under the Louisiana Purchase.[5]

When examined closely, however, the bulk of Jefferson's writings on Indians
generally reflect either his characteristically dogged pursuit of a research agenda
devoted to the study of North America and its natural history, or his prudent
efforts to gather facts as this country's first great armchair empire builder.
Stated simply, Jefferson's interest in Indians was always secondary to some
larger purpose he had in mind.

As for how Indians fit into his research agenda on North America, we have his famous refutation of the great French intellectual the Comte de Buffon. Buffon had cast serious doubt on the potentiality of the New World by pointing to the existing accounts of the Indians and their numerous deficiencies. Small and feeble, sexually impotent, near-hairless, unintelligent, cowardly: in Buffon's depiction, the Indians of the New World were a little race of ardorless souls, abusive of their women and possessed of none of the qualities that makes for anything good in life.[6]

Jefferson and his American contemporaries were understandably incensed by Buffon's picture of the Indian and the implications it held for the New World's potentiality. The European world trading system had emerged in robust, vigorous form by Jefferson's time. Countries like England, France, Spain, and Portugal were colonizing the lands of little nonwhite races of peoples all over the world. Buffon's theory, if allowed to stand, was seen as depressing America's rising stock in this emerging world system. America's underlying assets, as measured by the Indians' deficiencies, were of uncertain value. The best and wisest investments in this system—investments of capital, of talents, in the refinements of civilization—would always be found in Europe. Some French philosophers took this theory so closely to heart that they declared colonies to be expensive diversions; at best, a passing fad that, with hope, might disappear like the latest seasonal Parisian fashion.[7]

In his *Notes on Virginia*, Jefferson launched into Buffon's accounts of the Indians as being based on fables, no more true than those of Aesop and not even to be honored "with the appellation of knowledge" (210). The Indian, Jefferson says, "is neither more defective in ardor, nor more impotent with his female, than the white reduced to the same diet and exercise; . . . will defend himself against a host of enemies . . . meets death with deliberation . . . is affectionate to his children . . . his friendships are strong . . . his sensibility is keen . . . his vivacity and activity of mind is equal to ours in the same situation. . . ." As for the "drudgery" endured by Indian women, Jefferson supposed this "the case with every barbarous people," and so he wasn't going to get too upset about it (210–11).

Reading Jefferson's point-by-point refutation of Buffon, it is apparent that this is no case of some Enlightenment philosopher's effort to situate the Indian as next in line for the Rights of Man and a universal equality that was the privilege of every citizen of the republic. No, Jefferson's careful scrutiny of the Indian's character was solely for the purpose of gathering enough facts on the "barbarous peoples" of North America to explain that the circumstances of their inferiority to European civilization had nothing to do with the potentiality of the American environment. The Indians themselves were really to blame; or, more accurately, the "savage" character of their society explained their deficiencies.

Jefferson's refutation of Buffon appears in the section of *Notes on Virginia* entitled "A Notice of the mines and other subterraneous riches; its trees, plants, fruits, etc." When I read this section (and much of Jefferson's other writings on the Indian), I always have the feeling that I'm being led on a "flora and fauna"-type tour of the "essential" nature of the barbarous peoples of America. Even Jefferson's careful study of native languages on the continent reflected a strong didactic desire to isolate the Indian's origins, and thereby more precisely situate the savages of North America in the story of humankind's course of civilized development.

Reading Jefferson, I find no evidence that his varied intellectual interests in Indians ever reflected a desire to integrate Indian tribalism into his future vision of America. His commitment was to integrating Indians into the social evolutionary theories mapped out by the then-fashionable eighteenth-century Scottish school on human civilization's progress, from its "rude" hunter state to its highest form of achievement in the civilization of Western Europe.[8] All that Jefferson really wanted to establish by his research agenda on the Indian was that the American savage's retrograde form of cultural organization had nothing to do with America's potentiality for surpassing Europe.

As for how Indians occupied the interests of Jefferson, the armchair empire builder, it is useful to recall the reasons why Jefferson had called on Lewis and Clark to launch their famous expedition.[9] As the president who had acquired the Louisiana Territory, Jefferson had an obvious strategic purpose in mind in collecting information on the then-present occupants of the lands he had just purchased for Anglo-American settlement. He spoke to this purpose in his inaugural address of his second term as president, wherein he discussed the fate of the Indians in the context of the vast new lands opened for American settlement by virtue of his Louisiana Purchase. Making his always obligatory concession to the Indians' essential equality with Europeans and commending their noble set of primitive virtues, he ruminated on the savage's primitive social state as follows:

> Endowed with the faculties and the rights of men, breathing an ardent love of liberty and independence, and occupying a country which left them no desire but to be undisturbed, the stream of overflowing population drenched itself on these shores, without power to divert, or habits to contend against, they have been overwhelmed by the current, or driven before it."[10]

The problem of policy that Jefferson sought to address in his second inaugural speech was what to do with the Indians who had been "driven before" the "stream of overflowing population" and now resided in the western frontier regions of the continent. To deny white Americans the right to occupy the lands of the West held claim by roving bands of Indians would be detrimental to the national interest, and in any event, the facts were that the territory of the Indians was growing smaller every day.

The recent acquisition of Louisiana, Jefferson stated, would make the western lands available for expansion by Americans. This meant that the Indians would not be able to roam freely much longer. They were now, according to Jefferson at least, "reduced within limits too narrow for the hunter's state." Their only chance was to submit to new economic conditions and become farmers. The government's duty toward them was simple: "to encourage them to that industry which alone can enable them to maintain their place in existence, and to prepare them in time for that state of society, which to bodily comforts adds the improvement of mind and morals." In Jefferson's view of the Indians, there was no room for "a sanctimonious reverence for the customs of their ancestors." Their duty was not "to remain as their Creator made them." It was to follow the dictates of reason and abandon their inferior cultural state of existence, or else become extinct as a race with no one but themselves to blame.[11]

Indians had only one role to play in Jefferson's vision of America. They were to get out of the way of the white people he saw as destined to tame this virgin wilderness and redeem it from its savage state. Other than this, Jefferson had little use for Indians.

As elegantly explained in Roy Harvey Pearce's classic 1953 study on the American Indian and the European-derived idea of civilization, *The Savages of America*, "the American theory of the savage takes its clearest and most definite origins in Jefferson's thinking."[12] For Jefferson, both his intellectual and political agendas determined Indian tribalism's role as an inassimilable and inferior form of social organization on the North American continent that had to yield to a superior race of European cultivators.

WOULD THE DALAI LAMA READ CHAIRMAN MAO
FOR HIS DAILY MEDITATION?

Given his antiquated eighteenth-century views on tribal Indians as an inferior race doomed for extinction, why should Indians in the changing American West of the twenty-first century expect to find anything useful in Thomas

Jefferson's writings and thoughts? The Indians are still among us. As far as they are concerned, Jefferson was a false prophet when it came to predicting their role in the future of America.

For Indians, however, the fact that a Euro-American essentially despised their cultures does not automatically disqualify that individual as a source of useful information. In fact, anyone who is at all familiar with Indians and their centuries-long struggle with the supposedly superior race of European-derived peoples who invaded their continent knows that tribalism's continuing survival in the United States can be attributed to the one true virtue that characterizes most tribal peoples in our country: Indians are the Great American Utilitarians. They are continually taking the meager scraps left over on the Great American Banquet Table of Opportunity and trying to make a meal out of them.

The Indians' unique ability to survive by taking the cultural products of other peoples and combining these with their own traditions and customs to make something better, something unique, something of impeccable value— this adaptive capacity is a primary reason why Indian tribalism has continued to perpetuate itself on the land of America. Through forms of cultural expression that are both wondrous and strange, and which Jefferson would likely find inexplicable, Indians have managed to persist in America.

The Indians' ability to borrow, take, and adapt explains why Indian tribes have been able to develop and sustain peculiar niche economies on their reservations through marginal and even submarginal enterprises like cigarette smoke shops, gaming, and bingo parlors. Consider the dynamic level of cultural adaptivity necessary to sustain a tribe like the twentieth-century Mescalero Apaches, who feel confident they can manage a high-level nuclear-waste storage facility on their New Mexico reservation. Consider the achievements of the Navajo Supreme Court in adapting the case method of the Anglo-American common law tradition to perpetuate Navajo traditions. Consider the ridiculous price you would pay for an R. C. Gorman original painting on display in any contemporary American art gallery in Scottsdale, Santa Fe, Los Angeles, or San Francisco.

The Indians' ability to survive and perpetuate tribal culture, tribal traditions, and tribal thought and expression through whatever outlets are made available by the dominant white society explains syncretistic religious phenomena like the Yaqui Deer Dance, or the peyote rituals of the Native American Church. Tribal promotion of Indian reservations as tourist destinations, and the new Cadillac that might be found parked outside the hogan of an elderly Navajo rugweaver, provide evidence that Indians can adapt to the white man's ways through methods that are both jarring and subtle. The reason

Jefferson was wrong about the Indians was that he never understood this unique capacity of Indian peoples to survive by making use of whatever is available in the white world for their own purposes, whether that be slot machines, the Anglo-American legal system, or the writings of an eighteenth-century dead white European-derived male cultural imperialist.

I grew up in an Indian family where elders would look at me sternly at the dinner table and interrogate me with the loaded question, "What have you done for your people today?" For me, that was a personal injunction to take something from the white man's world—his knowledge, his tools, whatever—and use it to make life better for our people, the Lumbees. That is why for me the highest honor I ever receive is when an Indian elder comes up to me after a talk and tells me, "That was useful information, young man." Jefferson, who did not really understand the utilitarian cast of mind carried around by Indian tribal people in their daily lives, missed this aspect of the Indian's potentiality in his future vision of America. Factually speaking, his political philosophy, at least when it came to Indians, was most incorrect.

STORIES MAKE THINGS HAPPEN

If you look at the Indian presence on the contemporary American cultural landscape, particularly in the changing American West, where states like Arizona, New Mexico, California, Nevada, and Washington can have up to twenty Indian reservations within their borders, it is strikingly evident that what Indian people need today is useful information for carrying out a de-colonization struggle. The bingo parlors; the tribal leaders in three-piece suits negotiating joint venture deals with multinational corporations; the renais-sance of tribal art, literature, and dance; the demands for jurisdictional control over reservation lands; the revival of tribal languages—all of these phenomena are related aspects of the contemporary American Indian struggle for self-determination. It is a struggle which is dramatically altering the cultural land-scape of the western United States.

As Indian tribes seek to redefine their status from colonized peoples to decolonized peoples, as they move forward with this process of redefining their role in the changing American West of the twenty-first century, as they begin to confront the challenge of transforming the dominant society's conceptions of their rights under United States law, they will find that there is a great deal of useful information in Jefferson's thinking. Jefferson, after all, was the intellec-tual leader of the West's first great decolonizing, redefining, transformational struggle—the American Revolution. Any Indian who reads Jefferson closely—

not just Jefferson on Indians, but Jefferson on liberty and democracy, on basic human rights, on the principle that consent of the governed is the legitimating foundation of all government-derived power—will quickly come to appreciate that there is much that can be made useful in Jefferson's thought by contemporary American Indians.

The method I propose for retrieving this useful information from the catalog of Jeffersonian thought is one which Indian people would find congenial to their own traditions, and of which Jefferson himself I think would approve. I propose viewing Jefferson as the Great Indigenous American Storyteller. Some of the stories Jefferson tells will have great use to American Indians in understanding and conveying the nature of the challenges that confront their contemporary decolonization struggles. Others won't. According to Indian traditions of storytelling, we decide to retell those stories which we find useful, and to forget those we don't. Being the empiricist that he was, Jefferson, I believe, would heartily approve of this approach.

Many non-Indians may not fully appreciate the special significance attached to my proposal that Indians adopt Thomas Jefferson as an indigenous American storyteller. The storyteller holds a particularly honored role in American Indian culture. In Indian culture, to be known as a storyteller is to be known "as one who participates, in a communally sanctioned manner, in sustaining the group."[13]

In the western world, of course, it has been quite some time since individuals could find any special or recognized honor in their society by being assigned the role of storyteller. Storytelling these days is something yuppie parents do out of a book like "The Berenstain Bears Buy a Minivan" to model good reading habits for their children in later life. Danielle Steele, Stephen King, or even Stephen Spielberg might qualify as "storytellers" in our culture (which tells you a lot about our culture), but we don't think of these individuals as occupying or performing a clear and critically regarded role in a society such as ours. If there's an art to the stories they tell, it's the art of the deal, or the type of art to which Oscar Wilde must have been referring a century ago when he declared that all art is quite useless.

In the Western World, to paraphrase the dead white European male poet Auden in his famous requiem for the dead white European male poet Yeats, stories make nothing happen. That's not the way it is for Indians, however. For Indians, a storyteller is one who fulfills a most important and vital role in the group. Indians believe, unlike writers in the western tradition, that stories have great utility. "[S]tories—both the mythic traditional tales passed down among the people and the day-to-day narrations of events—do make things happen," writes Arnold Krupat.[14] Stories have a capacity to produce material effects.

Here would appear to be the major difficulty you would expect Indians to encounter in trying to adapt Jefferson as an indigenous American storyteller to their purposes. How can Native Americans appropriate Jefferson as a storyteller, given that his thought and policies on Indians were focused not on sustaining Indian tribalism, but on destroying it? The Jefferson narrative on Indians produced material effects that today would meet the modern definition of ethnocide.

If you understand Indian character, however, even just a tad better than Jefferson did, you should recognize that Indians would find no difficulty in finding something useful in Jefferson's thought and writings. Native Americans, being judicious utilitarians, are extremely selective in terms of the stories they appropriate:

> Traditional Native American literary forms were not—and, in their contemporary manifestations, usually are not—as concerned about keeping fiction and fact or poetry and prose distinct from one another. It is the distinction between truth and error rather than between fact and fiction that seems more interesting to native expression.[15]

Prior to the seventeenth century, of course, the line between history and myth was not very clearly marked in western thought either. "But that," as Krupat remarks, "is the way things have always been for Native American literature."[16]

A Native American approach to viewing Thomas Jefferson as a storyteller would adopt and reinvent only those stories that Jefferson tells which remain true. As for the stories that, as shown by the present undeniable reality of tribalism's persistence on the American cultural landscape, are demonstrably false, these stories are simply not *useful* to Native Americans. These Jeffersonian stories will, in effect, be lost in the retellings.

This Native American idea of narrative as continually reinvented or lost is wonderfully illustrated by Leslie Marmon Silko, the brilliant Laguna Pueblo writer. Silko dedicates her appropriately titled autobiography, *Storyteller*, "to the storytellers as far back as memory goes and to the telling which continues and through which they all live and we with them."[17] The storyteller, in other words, is situated in a "tradition of tellings." Our individual speech is a product of many tellings.[18]

Silko speaks in her autobiography of her storyteller aunts, Aunt Susie and Aunt Alice, "who would tell me stories they had told before but with changes in details or descriptions. . . . There were even stories about the different versions of stories and how they imagined these differing versions came to be."[19]

From an Indian perspective, understanding Jefferson as a Great Indigenous American Storyteller is simply to recognize the power of certain Jeffersonian narratives to "make things happen." Through indigenous American tellings and retellings, Jeffersonian narratives can be used to further the American Indian's struggle for decolonization.

"A COMPILATION OF COMMONPLACES"

To commence this process of situating Jefferson as a storyteller in the narrative tradition of Indian tribalism's struggle for decolonization, we must first perform a cleansing ritual. We must assess Jefferson's understanding of the American Indian's essentially negative role in his future vision of America.

Like all great storytellers, Jefferson's narratives are not originary of the mythos they sustain. As a storyteller, Jefferson continually reinvented the familiar narratives that sustained the group-image Americans of the Revolutionary era held of themselves.

Here, after all, is the man who conceded that the text of the Declaration of Independence that he drafted contained not a single new idea. It merely represented, in his words, "a compilation of commonplaces." What authority it possessed, he acknowledged, derived from "the harmonizing sentiments of the day."[20] Yet if Jefferson, as a storyteller, proceeds in *medias res* in weaving together the narrative strands that comprise our American mythology, he stands out as a singular figure in shaping the basic fabric of our national character through his stories.

So many of our national narratives are continually reinvented upon Jeffersonian themes. It was Jefferson, after all, who, by his Louisiana Purchase in 1803, inaugurated the century-long period of expansion across the North American continent that became the defining force in the consolidation of our national mythology. The conquest of the western frontier—the generative source of the mythic narratives that have defined how we envision ourselves as a people since the earliest days of the republic—is a Jefferson-inspired epic. The idealized images of a virgin land untainted by Old World corruptions, of yeoman farmers transformed into "Americans" by the frontier experience, of civilization's steady march of progress across the western plains: these are the stories that converge in our national mythology of nineteenth-century continental expansion. And all of these stories are found in their most quintessential American tellings and retellings in the writings of Thomas Jefferson.

As a people, we find ourselves continually renewing the narrative traditions that converge so powerfully in the Jefferson creation epic of American frontier conquest. To the extent that the mythos weaved out of these narratives serves us, to borrow from the anthropologist Bronislaw Malinowski, as a "warrant, a charter, and often even a practical guide"[21] for our activities as a people, we have Jefferson, the American myth-weaver extraordinaire, to blame or to thank. It was Jefferson who brought coherence of vision to our disaggregated narratives of who we were as we confronted our destiny in the American West at the beginning of the nineteenth century.

Jefferson's vision of the American cultural landscape was an amalgam of commonplace idioms and hopes that had been absorbed into the language of post-Revolutionary America's public rhetoric. Leo Marx has identified the important role played by the pastoral ideal in Jefferson's writings on the American landscape. The classical Roman Virgilian motif of withdrawing from the Great World and beginning a new life in a fresh, green landscape was a staple of the colonial-era literature on America's uniqueness in the world.[22] Jefferson, however, translated this motif into a compelling political vision of America's potentiality as a Garden of the World where an agrarian Republic of Liberty would blossom. "Those who labor in the earth," Jefferson wrote, "are the chosen people, whose breasts He has made His peculiar deposit for substantial and genuine virtue" (*Notes*, 280). Henry Nash Smith has written that the mythic Jeffersonian landscape of a peaceable agricultural nation taming a virgin wilderness into a garden helped further a mode of belief that "defined the promise of American life."[23] It must be recognized, of course, that the promise could only be redeemed by removing the Indian as an obstacle to this Jeffersonian vision.

For Jefferson, America's destiny was to be populated by virtuous yeomen farmers. Conquest of a wilderness occupied by wandering hoards of uncivilized savages would provide the material foundation for perpetuating republican virtue, not only within the borders of this redeemer nation, but beyond as well. The "fee simple empire," a phrase selected by Smith as emblematic of the mythic narratives of the nineteenth-century farming West,[24] originates in Jefferson's vision of a Republic of Liberty emerging out of the North American wilderness. Upon the virgin lands of the frontier, human nature, according to the Jeffersonian mythology, could finally escape the conditions of dependence bred in the workshops in the Old World. "Subservience and venality," which work to suffocate the "germ of virtue" in a republic, Jefferson once wrote, could never take root in a nation where the lands are not "locked up against the cultivator" as in Europe, and the "industry of the husbandman" is employed in the improvement of the soil (*Notes*, 280).

Here, of course, in the "horror of closure," to use Michael Rogin's term,[25] we begin to develop a much firmer sense of the role of Indians in Jefferson's North American empire of expansion. In the Jefferson mythology, Indians were fated to the role of being removable obstacles to white expansion. Their very presence on the continent only got in the way of what Jefferson and his contemporaries saw as the absolutely necessary work of maintaining America's future virtue. America, Jefferson once wrote James Madison, would only remain virtuous "while there remain vacant lands." Conquest of the frontier was essential to what America must become. "When we get piled together upon one another in large cities, as in Europe, we shall," he warned Madison, "go to eating one another, as they do there."[26]

Better to eat the Indians, at least according to the Jeffersonian vision of America. They were destined, by virtue of their savage nature, to disappear before the march of white civilization onto the frontier anyway. That unfortunate destiny nicely complemented the Jeffersonian challenge laid down to white Americans on the continent, who, to remain virtuous and unthreatened by corruption, had to continually expand their Empire of Liberty into Indian-occupied territories.

An "unofficial and private" letter written by Jefferson in 1803 to Indiana's territorial governor and famous Indian fighter William Henry Harrison shows clearly that Jefferson thought in terms of a just war for the North American continent between the Indian and white races, a war which the Indian race was destined to lose. Articulating his long-term strategy for solving the nation's Indian problem, Jefferson related to Governor Harrison the inevitable choice confronting the Indian tribes that still remained east of the Mississippi River:

> [O]ur settlements will gradually circumscribe and approach the Indians and they will in time either incorporate with us as citizens of the United States, or remove beyond the Mississippi. . . . As to their fear, we presume that our strength and their weakness is now so visible that they must see we have only to shut our hand to crush them, and that all our liberalities to them proceed from motives of pure humanity only. Should any tribe be foolhardy enough to take up the hatchet at any time, the seizing of the whole country of that tribe, and driving them across the Mississippi, as the only condition of peace, would be an example to others, and a furtherance of our final consolidation. . . .[27]

Of course, in Jeffersonian thought, even the Indian's retreat across the Mississippi would only be a temporary interlude in tribalism's ultimate disappearance from North America. The "horror of closure" would impel Anglo-

American civilization into those regions eventually as well.[28] The destiny of the American national character and experience was thus tied to national conquest of all the lands occupied by Indians on the continent. A civilized race of cultivators needed all of Indian North America to sustain its virtue.

"A FIERCE RACE OF SAVAGES"

Frederick Jackson Turner, the "American Isaiah" who announced the closing of the western frontier in 1893,[29] was really only retelling a familiar Jeffersonian story from his particular vantage point in time when he wrote what he thought was the closing chapter on our national creation myth: "vast forests blocked the way; mountainous ramparts interposed; desolate grass-clad prairies, barren oceans of rolling plains, arid deserts, and a fierce race of savages, all had to be met and defeated."[30] Turner was writing from within a long-standing Jeffersonian tradition on the American Indian.

It is hard to believe that the anachronistic racist and genocidal language that Jeffersonian thought draws on in constructing its narrative of Indian tribalism as an obstacle to national destiny would continue to have any vitality at all in defining the role of Indian peoples in the contemporary American experience. Yet it does. Many of our present-day understandings about the role of American Indians in our history can be traced directly to our unconscious assimilation of the Jeffersonian-inspired mythology of western frontier conquest. The Indian as foil, the savage contrast to pioneer values, the stubborn red-skinned obstacle to white civilization's dynamic westward march, the vanquished warrior at the end of the trail: these are, at base, Jeffersonian images that the American mind calls up whenever it situates the Indian within the national experience.

The long-unassailable paradigms of American historical scholarship are not the only or most pernicious causes of blame for the unquestioning perpetuation of this Jeffersonian myth of the Indian as inassimilable other. Dime novels, Hollywood westerns, and national politicians have all actively perpetuated the Jeffersonian mythology of the Indian in the stream of narratives capturing an Anglo-American nation's self-absorbed conversation with itself about itself.

Consider the rich diversity and perversity of the contemporary cultural translations of the mythology: the tomahawk chops and sports team mascots that sustain the stereotyped image of the Indian as a "savage" warrior; *Dances With Wolves;* New Age white-male religionists beating Indian drums in solar powered sweatlodges. These cultural constructions of the otherness of the

Indian and Indian culture flourish throughout our public discourses as a testament to the continuing vitality of the Jeffersonian myth in our national experience.

Ronald Reagan, the Great American Communicator himself, frequently demonstrated the undissipated potential of the Jeffersonian mythos in our public discourses throughout his presidency. In 1988, he sounded positively Jeffersonian in explaining the present-day role of the American Indian on the American cultural landscape. Speaking to a group of Moscow University students in the then-Soviet Union, Reagan declared:

> Let me tell you just a little something about the American Indian in our land. We have provided millions of acres of land for what are called preservations—or the reservations, I should say.
>
> They, from the beginning, announced that they wanted to maintain their way of life, as they always had lived there in the desert and plains and so forth. And we set up their reservations so they could, and have a Bureau of Indian Affairs to help take care of them.
>
> At the same time, we provide education for them—schools on the reservations. And they're free also to leave the reservations and be American citizens among the rest of us, and many do.
>
> Some still prefer, however, that way of—that early way of life. And we've done everything we can to meet their demands as to what they—how they want to live.
>
> Maybe we made a mistake. Maybe we should not have humored them in that, wanting to stay in that primitive lifestyle. Maybe we should have said, "No, come join us. Be citizens with the rest of us."[31]

AS ANY INDIAN STORYTELLER WILL TELL YOU . . .

As any Indian storyteller will tell you, these continual reiterations, these continual retellings of the myth of the Indian as inassimilable other, do have consequences. In 1955, the year of my birth, the United States Supreme Court denied constitutional protection to Indian peoples' rights of possession in their aboriginally occupied lands by drawing on the Jeffersonian narrative of Indian cultural inferiority. In *Tee-Hit-Ton Indians v. United States*, a group of Alaska Native peoples asked the federal government for compensation for timber taken off of lands they indisputably had occupied from time immemorial. Justice Reed's majority opinion in *Tee-Hit-Ton* explained the reasoning behind the Supreme Court's decision in this landmark case in United States Indian law in the following Jeffersonian terms:

> The line of cases adjudicating Indian rights on American soil leads to the conclusion that Indian occupancy, not specifically recognized as ownership by action as authorized by Congress, may be extinguished by the Government without compensation. Every American schoolboy knows that the savage tribes of this continent were deprived of their ancestral ranges by force and that even when the Indians ceded millions of acres by treaty in return for blankets, food and trinkets, it was not a sale but the conquerors will that deprived them of their land.[32]

Tee-Hit-Ton shows how a twentieth-century court makes an unjust law out of a story told by the Jeffersonian mythology of the American Indian. Indian tribes can be deprived of their ancestral lands in the twentieth century because "the savage tribes of this ancient continent were deprived of their ancestral ranges by force" in past centuries. In actuality, the Tee-Hit-Tons were never conquered by the United States; they never even went to war with the United States. They were, in fact, in peaceable possession of their lands at the time of the U.S. government's decision to seize them. But for the Tee-Hit-Tons at least, the Jeffersonian story of American frontier conquest did make things happen. As every American schoolboy should know, and as any Indian storyteller will tell you, they were Indians, so they lost their land.

Indians have lost more than their lands by perpetuation of the Jeffersonian mythology of the Indian as inassimilable other; they have also lost the ability to control and protect the Indian communities that still live on those reservation lands not yet taken by the United States.

In 1979, the current chief justice of the United States Supreme Court, then-associate justice William Rehnquist, authored the majority opinion for the court in *Oliphant v. Suquamish Indian Tribe*.[33] *Oliphant* is the modern Supreme Court's most important decision on the rights of Indian tribes to control their reservations.[34] The issue in *Oliphant* was whether Indian tribes possessed the inherent sovereign authority to try and punish white people for crimes committed on their reservations.[35]

Rehnquist's opinion for the court held that Indian tribes did not have this basic police power over whites on their reservations. Tribal sovereign powers, Rehnquist reasoned, could not interfere with the interests of United States citizens to be protected from "unwarranted intrusions" on their personal liberty.[36]

Numerous commentators,[37] the U.S. Commission on Civil Rights[38] and even the Supreme Court itself in the body of its opinion[39] recognize that

Oliphant essentially destroys the ability of tribal governments to maintain law and order in Indian communities. Whites cannot be prosecuted by tribes for any crimes they commit on an Indian reservation, no matter how serious and how offensive to the Indian community's sense of justice.

Rehnquist's *Oliphant* opinion justified this race-based restriction on Indian tribes by drawing from the great Jeffersonian narrative on Indian tribalism's cultural inferiority. Quoting from an 1834 House of Representatives' report,[40] Rehnquist declared that the "principle" that tribes, by virtue of their deficiencies, lacked criminal jurisdiction over non-Indians "would have been obvious a century ago when most Indian tribes were characterized by a 'want of fixed laws [and] of competent tribunals of justice.' It should be no less obvious today, even though present-day Indian tribal courts embody dramatic advances over their historical antecedents."[41]

Stories like *Tee-Hit-Ton* and *Oliphant* demonstrate that the Jeffersonian narrative on the Indian as unassimilated other *does* make things happen in contemporary American life. Indian lands and Indian sovereignty are imperiled each time the Jeffersonian story of the Indian is retold.

INDIGENOUS DECOLONIZATION AND THE
JEFFERSONIAN NARRATIVE ON NATURAL RIGHTS

Given its role in marginalizing the Indian from our American experience, how do American Indians make Jeffersonian thought useful to their decolonization struggles in the changing American West of the twenty-first century? Indian peoples will likely find little use in the Jeffersonian stories that deny them any role to play in the contemporary American experience. But there are other Jeffersonian narratives that speak directly to the major issues confronting Indian tribalism today in this country. Take for example, the Jeffersonian narrative on natural rights.

Paramount to the Jeffersonian conception of natural rights is its humanistic embrace of a theory of governmental legitimacy grounded upon consent of the governed. The classic statement of the theory, of course, is contained in the American Declaration of Independence of 1776:

We hold these truths to be self-evident, that all men are created equal, that they are endowed by the Creator with certain inalienable rights, that among these are life, liberty, and the pursuit of happiness. That to secure these rights, governments are instituted among men, deriving their just powers from the consent of the governed.

Borrowed and adapted from European Enlightenment-era philosophers such as Hobbes, Locke, and Rousseau, this consensual, contractual theme appears throughout Jefferson's writings on governmental legitimacy. In his 1792 letter to Gouverneur Morris, American minister to France, Jefferson stated flatly: "We surely cannot deny to any nation that right whereon our own government is founded, that every one may govern itself under whatever form it pleases, and change these forms at its own will. . . . The will of the nation is the only thing essential to be regarded."[42]

There is great use that can be made by American Indians of the Jeffersonian narrative on natural rights and the consensual legitimacy of governmental power. In fact, this Jeffersonian narrative tradition speaks directly to the decolonization struggles of indigenous tribal peoples in all the western settler-state constitutional democracies. Indigenous tribal peoples in countries such as the United States, Canada, Australia, and New Zealand never consented to relinquish their distinct group identities as self-defined indigenous nations, and they were never freely incorporated within the western settler-state polities. These types of embarrassing facts enable these indigenous groups to frame a compelling case for recognition of their self-determining rights in terms that a western constitutional democracy, by its own sustaining Jeffersonian-inspired political and legal ideology, is obliged to respect and entertain.

Of course, even without self-consciously relying on any Jeffersonian narrative, indigenous tribal peoples have increasingly gained the attention of western settler-state governments during the past several decades.[43] Nonetheless, it is still useful to note that virtually all of the contemporary demands for self-determination that have been made by indigenous peoples are supported by the most basic of Jeffersonian principles.

Most indigenous demands for self-determination seek a power for tribal communities to resume living by laws of their own unfettered choosing and creation. Indigenous peoples demand this power, which the legal philosopher Robert Cover has called the power of "jurisgenesis,"[44] even when their laws are opposed to the majority society's laws.[45] It is a power, incidentally, that Jefferson saw as inherent in every self-constituted community of rational individuals.

The increasing attentiveness of western settler-state governments to the jurisgenerative claims of indigenous tribal peoples underscores the deep resonances evoked in the western legal tradition by a people's simple assertion of a fundamental human right to self-determination. It would be very useful, therefore, for American Indians to develop a better conscious understanding of how Jefferson himself, as the Great Indigenous American Storyteller, sought to capture these resonances in his own, very successful narrative on natural rights that he told in support of America's decolonization struggles.

THE NORMAN YOKE IN A POSTMODERN WORLD

A subtle appreciation of historical context is crucial to an understanding of the rhetorical force and power of the Jeffersonian narrative on natural rights in the American imagination. When Jefferson's narrative first emerged in American public rhetoric, it strongly appealed to how Americans during the Revolutionary era envisioned themselves as a people.

As was characteristic of his integrative method as a storyteller, Jefferson's first public translation on the European Enlightenment-era discourse of natural rights was grafted upon a narrative tradition that the American imagination of the Revolutionary era found highly endearing: the tradition of the noble race of freedom-loving Anglo-Saxons opposing the tyranny of the Norman Yoke.[46]

The image of an alien, Norman king's usurpation of the natural rights of true Englishmen was one of the most powerful and conceptually integrated expressions of radical resistance during the American Revolutionary era. As early as 1764, James Otis, the great harbinger of American Revolutionary spirit, had drawn upon the symbology of the "Norman Yoke" oppressing the ancestors of the true English people, the freedom-loving Saxons, in his pamphlet calling for resistance against British tyranny, *The Rights of the British Colonies Asserted and Proved.*[47] "Liberty," Otis proclaimed, "was better understood, and more fully enjoyed by our ancestors, before the coming in of the first Norman tyrants than ever after, 'till was found necessary, for the salvation of the kingdom, to counter the arbitrary and wicked proceedings of the Stuarts."[48]

As the English historian Christopher Hill has observed, the second half of the eighteenth century witnessed revivals of the "Norman Yoke" discourse by radicals in England as well as America.[49] Intended to reprise the spirit of resistance of England's Glorious Revolution of 1688–89 and the peaceful overthrow of the tyrannically regarded Stuart dynasty, the theory of the Norman Yoke boiled down to the opinion that before 1066, the Anglo-Saxon tribes of England lived as free and equal citizens under a form of representative government that was inspired by divine principles of natural law and the common rights of all individuals. The Norman Conquest in 1066, however, had destroyed this true Saxon model of government.[50]

Many of Jefferson's contemporaries were alert to the strategic connections between the situation in colonial North America and the situation of the freedom-loving Saxons oppressed by Norman tyranny in jolly old England. American radicals were able to rescript the Norman Yoke discourse according to a cyclic concept of political time that saw English history as a continual struggle by true Englishmen to re-establish their revered and ancient Saxon rights and liberty.[51] Thus John Adams, the Boston revolutionary, sensed providence at work in the settlement of America and the realization of a pure English-Saxon centered constitution that was to be achieved by the colonists: "It was this great struggle that peopled America. . . . [A] love of universal liberty, and a hatred, a dread, a horror, of the infernal confederacy [by temporal and spiritual tyranny] projected, conducted, and accomplished the settlement of America."[52]

While writers like Adams got close, it was Thomas Jefferson, alone among his Revolutionary-era contemporaries, who was able to collect the "harmonizing sentiments of the day" and squarely situate the continuation of the Saxon struggle for liberty upon the American frontier wilderness. With his characteristically dogged habits of research, Jefferson painstakingly collected every scrap of evidence to reconstruct the history of his "Saxon Ancestors,"[53] producing one of the most influential and popular pamphlets published during the Revolutionary era, *A Summary View of the Rights of British America* (1774).[54] In many ways, *A Summary View* can be read as the narrative elaboration of many of the more concisely stated expressions of the American Revolutionary spirit later proclaimed by Jefferson in the Declaration of Independence. The pamphlet is singularly emblematic of Jefferson's unique gifts as an indigenous American storyteller.

Written on the eve of the first Continental Congress, Jefferson's *Summary View* launched the by-now familiar attack on the Crown's tyrannical usurpation of Anglo-American rights and liberties according to the revolutionary thematics of the Norman Yoke. But Jefferson's construction of this mythology focused particularly on its meanings for the Anglo-American experience in the New World. His story of the colonists' natural rights commences "from the origins and the first settlement of these countries":

> [O]ur ancestors, before their emigration to America, were the free inhabitants of the British dominions in Europe, and possessed a right which nature had given to all men, of departing from the country which chance not choice, has placed them, of going in quest of new habitations, and of there establishing new societies, under such laws and regulations as to them shall seem most likely to promote the public happiness.[55]

It was at this critical point in his account of America's first settlement by natural rights-bearing Englishmen that Jefferson digressed backwards into history, drawing the mythology of the freedom-loving Saxons into his narrative on America's destiny. The Saxons had similarly emigrated from Northern Europe eons ago, and had "possessed themselves" of England, "less charged with inhabitants." Once settled there, they established "that system of laws which has so long been the glory and protection of Great Britain."[56]

The lords whom the Saxons had left behind in Northern Europe, according to Jefferson, did not dare to claim "superiority" over those freedom-seeking sojourners of Europe's Dark Ages who migrated to the British Isles. That noble race had "too firm a feeling" of their rights ever to bow down to such distant, "visionary pretensions" of sovereignty.[57]

Having demonstrated that the Saxons had rightly earned their independence by emigrating to England and establishing a polity there many centuries before, Jefferson performed a remarkable narrative manipulation of political time: he boldly extended the trajectory of the parallel implications of his Saxon history to the English who had emigrated to the New World to found colonies. No circumstances have occurred, he argued, to distinguish materially the British from the Saxon emigration. "America was conquered, and her settlements made, and firmly established at the expense of individuals, and not of the British public. Their own blood was spilt in acquiring lands for their settlement, their own fortunes expended in making that settlement effectual; for themselves alone they have a right to hold."[58]

America, Jefferson declared in his pamphlet, was not conquered by William the Norman, nor its land surrendered to him, or any of his successors. Thus, according to Jefferson, the King of England's Norman-derived feudal prerogatives did not apply in America:

> It is time, therefore, for us to lay this matter before his Majesty, and to declare that he has no right to grant lands of himself [in America]. From the nature and purpose of civic institutions, all the lands within the limits which any particular society has circumscribed around itself are assumed by that society and subject to their allotment only. This may be done by themselves, assembled collectively, or by their legislature, to whom they may have delegated sovereign authority; and if they are allotted in either of these ways, each individual of the society may appropriate to himself such lands as he finds vacant, and occupancy will give him title.[59]

Jefferson's story of the Norman Yoke told in *A Summary View* reminds us of the quite important fact that our own decolonization struggle as a nation is inspired by a natural rights-based theory of consent of the governed. But what use can American Indian people make of the Jeffersonian narrative of the Norman Yoke in their contemporary decolonization struggles? Like the freedom-loving Revolutionary-era descendants of the noble Saxons, American Indians never consented to their colonial domination by a foreign-born race of invaders. By suggesting the historical parallels between the Indian struggle for self-determination in the contemporary United States and our own Revolutionary epic, a retelling of this Jeffersonian narrative can be made to speak endearingly to the vision that a western constitutional democracy such as the United States holds of itself in a changing postmodern world.

The postmodern world, as penetratingly described by the poet and statesman Vaclav Havel, is the world that has emerged out of the two most important political events in the second half of the twentieth century: the collapse of colonial hegemony and the fall of communism.[60] The postmodern world, in other words, is a decolonized world, and therefore is a world most congenial to the Jeffersonian narrative on natural rights.

The United States, along with the other western constitutional democracies that continue to exercise colonial forms of control over indigenous tribal peoples, is a participant in the consolidation of the postmodern world legal system.[61] Briefly, by the term *postmodern world legal system*, I refer to an evolving, globalized system of law and authoritative decision making that has emerged in the postmodern world. This system addresses itself to the central, critical task of our era. It seeks to link the various nation-states, international and regional organizations, informal trading blocs, institutionalized efforts toward economic integration, nongovernmental organizations, and other nonstate actors—including transnational corporations and multilateral lending institutions of the postmodern world—through a diversity of overlapping and ever-expanding relationships of interdependence and mutual accommodation.[62]

The struggle for self-determination carried on by American Indian peoples in the United States, and by indigenous tribal peoples around the world, takes place within the larger, interactive context of the emergent postmodern world legal system and its developing norms and monitoring processes and institutions. That indigenous peoples have increasingly turned to this system for assistance over the past several decades in their human rights struggles and decolonization efforts makes strategically good sense. The genesis of the postmodern world legal system is intimately related to the emergence of international human rights norms as an integrative, progressive force in the postmodern world and the decolonization processes spawned in dialectical reaction to western colonial expansion in the second half of the twentieth century.[63]

INDIGENOUS HUMAN RIGHTS AND JEFFERSONIAN NARRATIVES

The emergence of international human rights discourse is one of the most important and revolutionary developments in the evolving postmodern world legal system. International human rights law has proven itself capable and effective in directly and indirectly influencing the domestic laws and policies of those states that desire acceptance and integration into the postmodern world legal system. By the sheer force of its consolidating vision of universal norms sanctioning a government's conduct toward its citizens, international human rights discourse seeks to expand the competency of international law over spheres previously reserved to the asserted prerogatives of the sovereign nation-state.

The primary reasons that the contemporary discourse of international human rights has assumed an increasingly influential role in regulating instances of egregious state conduct against human rights are relatively simple and easy to grasp. The major participants in the postmodern world legal system rely heavily on domestic and regional stability and international and multilateral harmonization of interests and goals. Human rights law has had "a socializing impact on the human community"[64] because governments, particularly powerful western ones, increasingly take human rights considerations into account in developing their foreign policy. Diplomats as well as multinational corporations have no trouble in recognizing that a nation's oppression of its own people is a sign of weakness and instability. More and more, the benefits of political and economic linkages with other countries are determined according to a calculus that includes the critical dimension of human rights:

> Governments now know that there is a political and economic price to be paid for large-scale violations of human rights. That knowledge affects their conduct, not because they have suddenly become good or altruistic, but because they need foreign investment or trade, economic or military aid, or because their political power base will be seriously weakened by international condemnation.[65]

Indigenous peoples, in the United States and elsewhere around the world, have been quick to seize upon the significance of international human rights discourse as an integrative, progressive force in the postmodern world legal order. Since the 1970s, indigenous peoples have found a number of important international forums to generate dialogue on their demands for decolonization and expanded rights of self-determination.

One of the more important forums in the international legal system devoted to issues of indigenous peoples' rights is the United Nations Working Group on Indigenous Populations.[66] The Working Group is a unique body within the institutional human rights structure of the United Nations. It was created by the U.N. Economic and Social Council (ECOSOC) in 1982. Its mandate as a forum devoted exclusively to the survival of indigenous peoples includes the important task of developing international legal standards for the protection of indigenous peoples' human rights.

The information gathered through more than a decade of appearances before the Working Group by indigenous peoples who have expressed their vision of the human rights they want protected by the postmodern world legal system has evolved into a Draft Universal Declaration on the Rights of Indigenous Peoples.[67] The Working Group's Draft Declaration is intended to be forwarded ultimately to the U.N. General Assembly for ratification. Once so ratified, the Universal Declaration on Indigenous Rights would assume its place among other authoritative international human rights instruments as declarative of the international community's minimum legal standards for the protection of indigenous peoples' human rights to survival.

Eventual adoption by the U.N. General Assembly of the Working Group's Draft Declaration could provide a unique stimulus to the contemporary global movement for recognition, protection, and promotion of indigenous peoples' human rights. The draft's broad scope of recognition for indigenous human rights specifically addresses many of the most serious concerns raised by indigenous peoples during the course of their interventions to the U.N. Working Group since 1982.[68] In its present form, the draft expressly recognizes the unique nature of indigenous peoples' collective rights, the centrality of indigenous peoples' territorial rights to indigenous survival, indigenous peoples' rights to attain a measure of self-determining autonomy, and the need to provide effective mechanisms for international legal protection of indigenous rights.[69] While the present draft will most certainly undergo substantive revisions and refinements of terms as it progresses through the institutional standard-setting machinery of the U.N. human rights process, it will most certainly serve to increase and focus the attention of the postmodern world legal system on the necessity of an international legal instrument devoted to the protection of indigenous peoples' survival.[70]

The emerging global discourse of indigenous human rights in contemporary international law and standard-setting activities is thus one of the most significant developments in the decolonization struggles of indigenous peoples in the postmodern world legal system. The United States and other settler-state governments are principal supporters as well as beneficiaries of the economic, cultural, and strategic relationships that arise out of the postmodern world legal system and its integrating constellation of human rights norms. In the postmodern world, western constitutional democracies like the United States pursue a vision of themselves as leaders in the international movement for broadened recognition of human rights. The domestic policies and judge-made law of the western settler-state governments toward indigenous peoples, therefore, are particularly amenable to the progressive, ameliorating influences of the international human rights process and its developing norms on indigenous rights.[71] In turn, legal developments in these advanced democracies, because of the interlinked nature of the postmodern world legal system, can produce ameliorating effects in the laws and policies regarding indigenous peoples in other countries. It is foreseeable, therefore, that the principles contained in the Draft Universal Declaration on the Rights of Indigenous Peoples and other developing international norms on indigenous rights[72] will come to assume a more authoritative and at times even constraining role on western settler-state policies and judicial decisions affecting indigenous peoples' rights and in other countries with indigenous tribal populations as well.

The emerging discourse of indigenous human rights is still only in its gestational stage, however, and is subject to the myriad forces and powerful interests that vie for recognition and legitimacy in the postmodern world legal system. While indigenous peoples certainly cannot hope to control these centrifugal forces and interests, they must confront the challenge of at least influencing them, so that the postmodern world legal system sustains its focus on the promotion and advancement of the decolonization and self-determination efforts of indigenous peoples. It is here that the Jeffersonian narrative on natural rights can be of significant use to indigenous peoples in meeting this challenge by helping us transcend our ordinary ways of thinking about the role of indigenous tribal peoples in America and the postmodern world.[73] For example, imagine a retelling of the Jeffersonian story of the Norman Yoke in the context of the contemporary human rights struggles of American Indian peoples. Such a retelling could make things happen by focusing American public discourse on the contemporary parallels between the Revolutionary-era descendants of the freedom-loving Saxons and American Indian peoples who today live under a legal system that denies them ultimate sovereignty and the right of self-determination in their lands. As we have seen, under court cases like *Tee-Hit-Hon* and *Oliphant*, the United States asserts ultimate sovereignty over the lands occupied by Indian nations, and can unilaterally strike down the exercise by tribes of even the most pedestrian forms of self-government. No other citizens under our Constitution have such restrictions placed upon their rights or their lands. No other citizens find their human rights still denied by the feudal vestiges of the Norman Yoke.

A Jeffersonian retelling of the story of the contemporary Indian decolonization struggle would tell of modern-day Indian tribes that have sought to realize their own vision of a pure, indigenous American form of self-determination, unencumbered by the tyranny of their Norman-derived status as conquered peoples. In this Jeffersonian-racist narrative, tribal efforts to exercise criminal jurisdiction and civil regulatory authority over non-Indians on their reservations would be seen as expressing basic Jeffersonian values, indigenous to our American way of life. From a Jeffersonian perspective, tribal demands for autonomy in managing Indian water and other natural resources, and in defining what economic development means from an Indian perspective, are seen not as obstacles to our prosperity as a nation, but as basic human rights belonging to America's indigenous tribal peoples.

Ironically, the Jeffersonian narrative of the Norman Yoke can be used to underscore the embarrassing fact that the colonial power exercised over Indian peoples today under outmoded Jeffersonian narratives on Indian cultural inferiority denies Indian peoples their basic Jeffersonian-understood natural rights. Like the ancient tribal Saxons, Indians today find themselves appealing the right of an alien conqueror to exercise power over them without their consent. Such appeals, when effectively grounded in a Jeffersonian narrative on natural rights, even the conqueror's courts will find difficult to deny.

The Jeffersonian narrative on the Norman Yoke can also be used to develop the decolonization potential of the treaties that Indian Nations negotiated with the United States. From a Jeffersonian prospective, the treaties between Indian tribes and the United States are not at all unlike the great documents, such as the *Magna Carta* of the British constitutional tradition, by which a tribal people sought to preserve their ancient liberties and self-determining rights against an invading tyrant. Seen from a Jeffersonian perspective, the history of Indian treaty rights under United States law has been one of constant and unjust attacks by an alien sovereign authority upon the charter-guaranteed liberties of American Indians.

These are just some of the uses American Indian peoples can find in Jefferson's story of the Norman Yoke. There is likely much more that Indians will find of great use in Thomas Jefferson's vision of a pure Saxon constitution and his revolutionary denouncement of the Norman Yoke as applied to America. The notion that a people's control over its own lands also implies control over its own destiny was a principal guiding theme in the Jeffersonian Revolutionary narrative. It was to make the relation between property and self-determination more explicit and secure that the Jeffersonian generation in fact declared its independence from the Norman Yoke and established its own, more pure form of a constitution based on natural rights.[74]

As we have now passed the 250th anniversary of the birth of that Great Indigenous American Storyteller, Thomas Jefferson, is it not the proper time to recognize the historical parallels between today's seemingly revolutionary discourses calling for broader recognition of basic Indian human rights of self-determination and control of treaty-guaranteed property, and the Jeffersonian discourses of natural rights that inspired the Revolutionary era? Jefferson's philosophically incorrect judgment on the Indian's role in his future vision of America neglected to include all of America's peoples in the story of the de-colonization struggle that made us one people. Now is the time to renew the Jeffersonian narrative for a changing American West of the twenty-first cen-tury, by removing the final vestiges of colonial oppression corrupting Jefferson's purer vision of an America freed from the tyranny of the Norman Yoke.

NOTES

1. See, for example, Robert A. Williams, Jr., "Jefferson, the Norman Yoke, and American Indian Lands," *Arizona Law Review* 29, no. 2 (1987): 165–94, which discusses Jefferson's Revolutionary-era pamphlet, *A Summary View*, in the context of American Indian land rights.

2. The edition of *Notes on the State of Virginia* cited in this essay can be found in Adrienne Koch and William Peden, eds., *The Life and Selected Writings of Thomas Jefferson* (New York: Random House, 1944), 187–288. Further page references to this edition of *Notes on Virginia* will be cited parenthetically in the text.

3. Quoted in Roy Harvey Pearce, *The Savages of America,* rev. ed. (Berkeley: University of California Press, 1965), 94.

4. "[I]t is Jefferson from whom our science of Indian linguistics primarily descends. He was particularly active, collecting Indian word-lists himself and encouraging others to too so. . . ." (ibid., 80).

5. Nicholas Biddle, *History of the Expedition Under the Command of Lewis and Clark,* Elliott Coues, ed. (1814; reprint, Francis P. Harper, 1893), 1:xxvi–xxviii.

6. Bernard W. Sheehan, *Seeds of Extinction: Jeffersonian Philanthropy and the American Indian* (New York: Norton, 1974), 66–69.

7. Ibid., 67–71.

8. The works of eighteenth-century Scottish Enlightenment writers on society were a critical source of ideas about the American Indian for Jefferson's era. Several of these writers drew on the fantastic narratives of American Indians by early European explorers to develop a broad range of sociological speculations on the progress of history, "from barbarism to civilization, from a warrior society marked by primitive virtue toward a state of commerce, refinement, and humanity" (J. G. A. Pocock, *The Machiavellian Moment: Florentine Politi-cal Thought and the Atlantic Republican Tradition* [Princeton: Princeton University Press, 1975], 499).

The broad intention of the Scottish school, which included Francis Hutcheson, Thomas Reid, Adam Ferguson, Lord Kames, and William Robertson, was to construct a historical analysis of social progress. To these writers, man's "original nature" was unchanging, "yet obeyed discernible laws of development intrinsic to itself" (Pearce, *Savages of America,* 82–83). The development of human institutions and customs "was judged to be progressive, of the nature of a continuous movement with no breaks, as growth has no breaks, a movement directed by Nature" (Gladys Bryson, *Man and Society: The Scottish Inquiry of the Eighteenth Century* [Princeton: Princeton University Press, 1945], 242–43). The study of "primitive peoples," particularly the American Indian, therefore, provided grist for the mill of a school of thought that sought to understand the processes by which human beings, their institutions, and their customs developed and evolved.

Adam Ferguson's *Essay on the History of Civil Society* (1767; reprint, Edinburgh: Edinburgh University Press, 1966) is regarded as one of the classic sociological texts of the eighteenth-century Scottish school. Ferguson's *Essay* is a "natural history" of man from his "rude" to "polished" state. Throughout his text, Ferguson frequently cites the "savage nations" of America as examples of "rude nations prior to the establishment of property." See, for example, Ferguson, *Essay on the History of Civil Society*, 81–82.

Property, in particular landed property, assumes the crucial role in Ferguson's sociological history of humankind's progress from its "rude state" to its most civilized achievements:

> It must appear very evident, that property is a matter of progress. It requires among other particulars which are the effects of time, some method of defining possession. The very desire of it proceeds from experience; and the industry by which it is gained, or improved, requires such a habit of acting with a view to distant objects, as may overcome the present disposition with the sloth or to enjoyment. This habit is slowly acquired, and is in reality a principal distinction of nations in the advanced state of mechanic and commercial arts (Ferguson, *Essay on the History of Civil Society*, 82).

Thus, according to Ferguson, property was "the principal distinction" between "rude" nations, such as those "in most parts of America," and "advanced" or "polished" nations. The savage nations, while mixing "with the practice of hunting some species of rude agriculture," did not recognize individual property rights in the crops their labor had created, but rather, according to Ferguson, "enjoy the fruits of the harvest in common" (82).

Ferguson's *Essay* sought to demonstrate that savage nations, lacking in the advantages bestowed upon society by the institution of property, inevitably yielded to more advanced nations:

> For want of these advantages, rude nations in general, though they are patient of hardship and fatigue, though they are addicted to war, and are qualified by their stratagem and valor to throw terror into the armies of a more regular enemy; yet, in the course of a continued struggle, always yield to the superior arts, and the discipline of more civilized nations. Hence the Romans were able to over-run the provinces of Gaul, Germany, and Britain: and hence the Europeans have a growing ascendancy over the nations of Africa and America (Ferguson, *Essay on the History of Civil Society*, 95).

For Ferguson, though savage peoples possessed a set of noble virtues, "the love of society, friendship, and public affection, penetration, eloquence, and courage," they were virtues regarded as inherent in man's "original" nature. Such admirable qualities were "not the subsequent effects of device or invention," and must be nurtured in "high civilization" (94). Only private property and the division of labor can achieve this goal. See Pearce, *Savages of America,* 85.

This focus on individual property as a distinguishing norm between "civilized" and "savage" peoples was a prominent feature in the work of other Scottish-school writers. Adam Smith's *Wealth of Nations* (1776), another treatise that was highly regarded during Jefferson's era, asserted that private property and the division of labor accounted for the superior affluence and abundance commonly possessed even by the most despised and lowly member of civilized society, compared with what the most respected and active savage can even hope to attain to.

9. See Biddle, *History of the Expedition Under the Command of Lewis and Clark,* 1:1–2

10. Jefferson's Second Inaugural Address, March 4, 1805, in Davis Newton, ed., *The Inaugural Addresses of the American Presidents: From Washington to Kennedy* (New York: Holt, Rinehart, and Winston, 1961), 20.

11. Ibid., 20–21.

12. Pearce, *Savages of America,* 95–96.

13. Arnold Krupat, "The Dialogic of Silko's *Storyteller,*" in Gerald Vizenor, ed., *Narrative Chance: Postmodern Discourse on Native American Literatures* (Norman: University of Oklahoma Press, 1993), 59.

14. Ibid., 63.

15. Ibid., 59.

16. Ibid.

17. Quoted in ibid., 60.

18. Ibid.

19. Leslie Marmon Silko, *Storyteller* (New York: Seaver Books, 1981), 227.

20. See Jurgen Habermas, *Theory and Practice,* trans. John Viertel (Boston: Beacon Press, 1973), 87–88.

21. Bronislaw Malinowski, *Magic, Science and Religion and Other Essays,* ed. Robert Redfield (Boston: Beacon Press, 1948), 85.

22. See Leo Marx, *The Machine in the Garden* (New York: Oxford University Press, 1964), 3.

23. Henry Nash Smith, *Virgin Land: The American West as Symbol and Myth* (Cambridge: Harvard University Press, 1950), 123.

24. See ibid., chapter 12.

25. Michael Rogin, *"Ronald Reagan," the Movie, and Other Episodes in Political Demonology* (Berkeley: University of California Press, 1987, 1990), 180.

26. Quoted in ibid.

27. Jefferson to William Henry Harrison, February 27, 1803, in Francis P. Prucha, ed., *Documents of United States Indian Policy* (Lincoln: University of Nebraska Press, 1990), 22–23. Jefferson's secret instructions to his military commands on the frontier in this letter reflected the tactical thinking of an armchair empire-builder, unconstrained by the politician's usual need for discretion:

... from the Secretary of War you receive from time to time information and instructions as to our Indian affairs. These communications being for the public records, are restrained always to particular objects and occasions; but this letter being unofficial and private, I may with safety give you a more extensive view of our policy respecting the Indians, that you may be the better comprehend the parts dealt out to you in detail through the official channel, and observing the system of which they make a part, conduct yourself in unison with it in cases where you are obligated to act without instruction (ibid., 22).

Jefferson's basic policy on Indians was widely shared by his fellow members of the Revolutionary-era generation. Benjamin Lincoln, the Revolutionary War hero and general, projected the geographical trajectory of the ultimate solution to tribalism's destiny on the North American continent—if it was ever to have one—in a 1793 journal entry as follows:

[T]o people fully this earth was in the original plan of the benevolent Deity. I am confident that sooner or later there will be full accomplishment of the original system; and that no men will be suffered to live by hunting on lands capable of improvement, which would support more people under a state of cultivation. So that if the savages cannot be civilized and quit their present pursuits, they will, in consequence of their stubbornness, dwindle and molder away, from causes perhaps imperceptive to us, until the whole race shall become extinct, or they shall have reached those climes about the great lakes, where, from the rocks and mountainous ties, the footsteps of the husbandman will not be seen (quoted in Pearce, *Savages of America*, 68 n. 3).

28. On this point, see Jefferson's second inaugural address, discussed in text on page oo, above.

29. For Turner as the "American Isaiah," see Pocock, *Machiavellian Moment*, 544. In his *Significance of the Frontier in American History* (New York: Ungar, 1963), Turner wrote: "[F]our centuries from the discovery of America, at the end of a hundred years of life under the Constitution, the frontier has gone, and with its going has closed the first period of American history" (58).

30. Turner, *Significance of the Frontier in American History*, 269 n. 1.

31. Quoted in David H. Getches, Charles F. Wilkinson, and Robert A. Williams, Jr., eds., *Federal Indian Law: Cases and Materials*, 3d ed. (New York: Association on American Indian Affairs, 1993), 277–78.

32. *Tee-Hit-Ton Indians v. United States* 348 U.S., 272 (1955).

33. *Oliphant v. Suquamish Indian Tribe*, 435 U.S., 210.

34. See Robert A. Williams, "The Algebra of Federal Indian Law: The Hard Trail of Decolonizing and Americanizing the White Man's Indian Jurisprudence," *Wisconsin Law Review* 1986, no. 2 (1986): 219–99.

35. *Oliphant v. Suquamish Indian Tribe*, 435 U.S., 210.

36. Ibid.

37. See, for example, Williams, "Algebra of Federal Indian Law," 267–74; Russel Barsh

and James Youngblood Henderson, "The Betrayal: *Oliphant v. Suquamish Indian Tribe* and the Hunting of the Shark," *Minnesota Law Review* 63, no. 4 (April 1979): 610–13.

38. U.S. Commission on Civil Rights, "Indian Tribes: A Continuing Quest for Survival" (1981), 165–87.

39. *Oliphant v. Suquamish Indian Tribe,* 435 U.S., 272.

40. Ibid., 210 (quoting H.R. Rep. No. 474, 23d Cong., 1st sess., 18.

41. Ibid.

42. Quoted in Gilbert Chinard, *Thomas Jefferson, the Apostle of Americanism* (Boston: Little, Brown and Company, 1939), 286–87.

43. See Robert A. Williams, Jr., "Encounters on the Frontiers of International Human Rights Law: Redefining the Terms of Indigenous Peoples' Survival in the World," *Duke Law Journal* 1990, no. 4 (September 1990): 660–704.

44. See Robert M. Cover, "*Nomos* and Narrative," *Harvard Law Review* 97, no. 1 (1983): 4–68.

45. See J. G. A. Pocock, "Sovereignty and History in a Divided Culture: The Case of New Zealand and the Treaty of Waitangi," in Getches, Wilkinson, and Williams, eds., *Federal Indian Law,* 998–1005.

46. See Robert A. Williams, *The American Indian in Western Legal Thought: The Discourses of Conquest* (New York: Oxford University Press, 1990), 251–71.

47. Reprinted in Merrill Jensen, ed., *Tracts of the American Revolution, 1763–1776* (Indianapolis: Bobbs-Merrill, 1967), 20.

48. Ibid., 20–21.

49. Christopher Hill, *Puritanism and Revolution: Studies in Interpretation of the English Revolution of the Seventeenth Century* (London: Secker and Warburg, 1958), 94. See also Pocock, *Machiavellian Moment,* 506–52.

50. Hill, *Puritanism and Revolution,* 95.

51. See Williams, *American Indian in Western Legal Thought,* 253–55.

52. Quoted in Bernard Bailyn, *The Ideological Origins of the American Revolution* (Cambridge: Belknap Press of Harvard University Press, 1967), 82–83.

53. Hill, *Puritanism and Revolution,* 94.

54. Reprinted in Jensen, ed., *Tracts of the American Revolution,* 256.

55. Ibid., 258.

56. Ibid., 258–59.

57. Ibid., 259.

58. Ibid.

59. Ibid., 273.

60. Vaclav Havel, "Postmodern World Needs New Principle," *The (Tucson) Arizona Daily Star,* Friday, July 8, 1994, sec. A, p.13 (containing excerpts from the address of Vaclav Havel, president of the Czech Republic, on the occasion of receiving the Liberty Medal on July 4, 1994, at Independence Hall in Philadelphia).

61. My use of the term *postmodern world legal system* to describe an increasingly globalized system of law and authoritative decision making in which indigenous peoples assert their rights to self-determination borrows from and extends a concept elaborated by the historian

Immanuel Wallerstein. In his pioneering book *The Modern World-System I: Capitalist Agriculture and the Origins of the European World Economy in the Sixteenth Century* (New York: Academic Press, 1974), Wallerstein contends that the modern world system has boundaries, structures, member groups, rules of legitimation, and coherence. Its life is made up of the conflicting forces that hold it together by tension, and tear it apart as each group seeks eternally to remold it to its advantage (347).

Wallerstein's book focuses on articulating the functioning of the modern world system that emerged out of the European world economy in the sixteenth century. I have borrowed and built upon his concept to describe the functioning of a distended byproduct of this same system, a postmodern world legal system.

The philosopher Jean-François Lyotard uses the word *postmodern* to describe "the condition of knowledge in the most highly developed societies." The "postmodern" condition, writes Lyotard, designates "the state of our culture following the transformations which, since the end of the nineteenth century, have altered the game rules for science, literature and the arts" (Lyotard, *The Postmodern Condition: A Report on Knowledge* [Minneapolis: University of Minnesota Press, 1984], xxiii). The "crisis of narratives" out of which these transformations are generated applies equally to the narratives of law in a postmodern world. See Cover, "*Nomos* and Narrative," 4–11.

62. The developing legal system that seeks to nurture the complex networks of economic, cultural, social, and strategic cooperation characterizing the postmodern world is sustained by ever-improving communications technologies and media penetration around the world. It is accompanied by a historical shift in global rationality and relationality potentially every bit as significant as was the Industrial Revolution in shaping human consciousness. On this newly emergent plural legal order, see Sally Engle Merry, "Legal Pluralism," *Law & Society Review* 22 (1988): 869, and Abdullahi Ahmed An-Na Im, ed., *Human Rights in Cross-Cultural Perspectives: A Quest for Consensus* (Philadelphia: University of Pennsylvania Press, 1992), 1–15. Domestic law and legislation; international law and standard-setting activities; global and regional trade agreements, treaties, tariffs and accords; and other multiple sources of law, together with formal as well as informal sanctioning authority, function and intersect in myriad ways. The overarching goal of this emerging legal order is to connect the various actors engaged in the system into ever-expanding networks of relationships defined according to consensually agreed-upon legal modalities and norms. Processes of mediation and negotiation are widely institutionalized throughout the system. But normative linkages also arise ad hoc out of complex relational structures designed to encourage participation according to sophisticated calculations of self-interest advanced through the mutualization and integration of political, social, and economic goals and agendas on a broadened, globally defined scale. See S. James Anaya, "The Rights of Indigenous Peoples and International Law in Historical and Contemporary Perspective," *Harvard Indian Law Symposium 1989* (1990): 211–12 , and Williams, "Encounters on the Frontiers," 682–84.

63. See Williams, "Encounters on the Frontiers," 672–80.

64. See Thomas Burgenthal, "The Rights Revolution," in Anthony D'Amato, ed., *International Law Anthology* (Cincinnati: Anderson Publishing Company, 1994), 205–6.

65. Ibid.

66. On the Working Group's history and institutional structure, see Williams, "Encounters on the Frontiers," 676–82. The five members of the Working Group are drawn from the select group of international law experts sitting on the U.N. Sub-Commission on the Prevention of Discrimination and Protection of Minorities. With its global agenda and expert membership, the Working Group represents the single most important initiative ever undertaken on behalf of indigenous peoples' rights by the institutional standard-setting machinery of the international human rights process.

67. See U.N. Draft Declaration on the Rights of Indigenous Peoples, U.N. DOC.E.CN. 4/sub. 2/1993/29 (August 23, 1993) (hereafter: U.N. Draft).

68. Ibid.

69. See ibid.

70. The adoption of a Universal Declaration on the Rights of Indigenous Peoples would be an important factor favoring indigenous peoples in their decolonization efforts. As a standard-setting instrument for international law purposes, its alternative vision of indigenous human rights could be employed in international legal and political forums around the world, whether in the U.N. Human Rights Commission, on the floor of the U.N. General Assembly, or in regional bodies such as the Inter-American Commission on Human Rights. Not only could a United Nations Universal Declaration speaking to indigenous human rights be cited as authority in the international legal system, it would also command attention and response in many domestic political and legal arenas. Its prescriptions could be used in a variety of highly publicized forums by any number of indigenous and nonindigenous groups and individuals to challenge state action threatening the survival of indigenous peoples. Perhaps the greatest significance of a U.N. Universal Declaration on the Rights of Indigenous Peoples in fact would be its capacity to translate indigenous people's vision of the human rights they want protected into terms that settler-state governments, particularly in the West, will listen to seriously.

71. Those who might doubt the ability of international human rights law to influence indigenous rights policies and judge-made law in the United States or other western settler-states (see, e.g., Robert Lawrence, "Learning to Live with the Plenary Power of Congress over Indian Nations," *Arizona Law Review* 30, no. 3 [1988]: 428) should consider the example set by the Australian High Court's landmark decision in *Mabo v. Queensland* (107 A.C.R. 1 [1992]), which overturned centuries of racist policies and law denying basic human rights to aboriginal peoples under the *terra nullius* principle derived from the Doctrine of Discovery. Justice Brennan's *Mabo* opinion declared:

> The fiction by which the rights and interests of indigenous inhabitant in land were treated as nonexistent was justified by a policy which has no place in the contemporary law of this country. . . . Whatever the justification advanced in earlier days for refusing to recognize the rights and interest in land of the indigenous inhabitants of settled colonies, an unjustified discriminatory doctrine of that kind can no longer be accepted. The expectations of the international community accord in this respect with the contemporary values of the Australian people. The opening up of international remedies to individuals pursuant to Australia's accession to the [United Nations]

Optional Protocol to the International Covenant on Civil and Political Rights . . . brings to bear on the common law the powerful influence of the Covenant and the international law it imports. The common law does not necessarily conform with international law, but international law is a legitimate and important influence on the development of the common law, especially when international law declares the existence of international human rights. A common law doctrine founded on unjust discrimination in the enjoyment of civil and political rights demands reconsideration. It is contrary both to international standards and to the fundamental values of our common law to entrench a discriminatory rule which, because of the supposed position on the scale of social organization of the indigenous inhabitants of a settled colony, denies them a right to occupy their traditional lands.

72. One source for these developing norms on indigenous rights will most certainly be *The 1989 International Labor Conference Convention 169, Concerning Indigenous and Tribal Peoples in Independent Countries.* See Russel Barsh, "An Advocate's Guide to the Convention on Indigenous and Tribal Peoples," *Oklahoma City University Law Review* 15, no. 1 (1990): 209–36.

73. Several significant factors explain why indigenous peoples have turned to international human rights laws in trying to meet the challenge of achieving their decolonization and self-determination goals in the postmodern world. Because the postmodern world is characterized by ever-increasing interdependencies, ever-improving communications technology, and burgeoning international institutions, the domestic policies and judge-made law of the western settler-states regarding indigenous peoples is increasingly influenced by what Professor S. James Anaya describes as a "multifactorial process of *authoritative* and *controlling* decision[s] operating across national frontiers" (Anaya, "Rights of Indigenous Peoples," 212). In the postmodern world legal system, states with indigenous tribal populations, as well as states without, and nonstate actors, including transnational corporations, international lending institutions, international nongovernmental organizations, and even liberation movements, are all capable of exerting influence on western settler-states' policies and judicial decision-making process regarding indigenous peoples' rights.

74. See Williams, *American Indian in Western Legal Thought,* 241–80.

CHAPTER FOUR

REINVENTING PLACE
Community and Conflict in a Changing West

ROBERT GOTTLIEB

Entering the Pico Farmers' Market in Santa Monica—an experience similar to that available at any of the nearly three dozen farmers' markets spread throughout urban Southern California[1]—is one way to step into the complex, diverse world and shifting landscapes of one part of the American West. Guatemalan instruments greet the buyer with the soft, sensual music of Chiapas, while the explosion of colors, from sunflowers to azaleas to flowering cacti grown in the semidesert of eastern San Diego County by immigrants from the Mexican state of Monterrey, provide a visual entry into what has become both a cultural and literal feast of opportunities and products. Oden melons from the Great Mojave Desert; hot habanera peppers that can burn your lips if you taste them; green and red bell peppers from Vista; peaches and plums and four-inch organically grown grapes from Dinuba (Walter Goldschmidt's classic democratic rural community surviving the agro-industrial onslaught in the southern San Joaquin[2]); honey sticks for the kids in a panoply of flavors and colors; fish caught that morning in the Channel Islands; bagels grown without preservatives; nopaleas grown in the Imperial Valley and sold in numerous bodegas; persian limes (popular with the large Iranian population of west-side Los Angeles); corn, grown on farms without imported labor, that birds have pecked because it still provides the experience of sweet corn; tomatoes from Oxnard that taste like tomatoes; baby bok choy and Japanese eggplant and Chinese cabbage and the array of Asian vegetables that are also a Southern California staple: for all these experiences and more, the Pico Market is an articulation of contemporary urban Southern California.

Such markets define a new urban landscape. They are cultural as well as economic meeting grounds, providing a distinctive sense of place. As meeting grounds, they also contrast with the atomized concept of place associated with the increasing privatization of landscape and cityspace that prevails in areas like urban Southern California. It is here, in a global city like Los Angeles, where one also finds food megastores, built with ten-foot fences and police substations, and where cultural diversity is represented as ethnic gangs, guns, danger, and separation.[3]

I've introduced the experience of the Pico Market as one way to rethink how the West and its many communities and sites and sounds are characterized and analyzed. But describing this region as in transition or in evolution becomes itself problematic, given that the West is such an elusive term to begin with, and that the field of western history, as Patricia Limerick reminds us, is in such "a constant crisis of definition."[4]

As historians have argued, the West can be defined as a region or as a set of regions, or as a shifting frontier (at least the residual idea of frontier that survives as part of the popular imagination in theme parks or other cultural representations).[5] For some, the West consists of borderlands that are permeable to the flow of capital and of labor and, increasingly, of pollution as well as cultural identities.[6] Yet this notion of open border or recirculating border has also vitiated a peculiar western nativism, a nativism reflected both in California's mean-spirited and convulsive Proposition 187, which seeks to purify our public schools by nativist cleansing, and in those self-defined Aryan movements of the Pacific Northwest. For the Aryans, "westerness" is an invented Americanism, purified by Anglo hardiness as well as by race, religion, and creed.[7]

For those who focus on resources and landscape, the West is "rural," a set of discrete communities whose livelihood today is being threatened by the restructuring of the resource economies.[8] It is in relation to this conception of a rural West where the counteroffensive by the Wise Use Movement seeks (often successfully) to pit a notion of community (represented by the survival of the resource-based industries and their jobs) against the concept of protected nature (represented by the big-city, backpacking, enviro-recreationists).[9] But is the West predominantly rural, as measured by jobs, population, or industry activities, or is it urban, as defined by those same variables? Isn't it more accurate to see the West as a collection of powerful and expanding metropolitan areas; areas that not only demonstrate the expanding reach of the urban spaces of the West, but also influence, if not dominate, extraurban life and therefore the region as a whole, as many western historians are now prepared to argue?[10]

Similarly, there are arguments about how to define environment, a term so often associated with the West. In fact, some historians see the West as the birthplace of the environmental movement. In this setting, the West becomes distinctive Nature, a wilderness without people, or at least a place where people encounter a natural environment of large, open spaces.[11] For those advocates of wilderness, the western environment becomes a place to preserve, to set apart from human contact and daily life. Others (myself included) have argued, however, that the concept of environment needs to be bounded to daily life experiences, western or otherwise, and that natural environments and human environments—or "first nature" and "second nature," to borrow from William Cronon borrowing from Hegel and Marx—are not divisible.

And, finally, for purposes of this discussion, there is the compelling concept of the West transformed from resource colony to empire, with its ever-expanding physical—as well as economic, political, and cultural—boundaries. The West as Empire has multiple reference points, whether situated as the resource economy of the trans-Mississippi West, specifically constructed beyond the ninety-eighth or one hundredth meridian;[13] the Empire of the Pacific Basin, recognized for its central role within the global economy; the major urban centers that have dominated a series of intersecting regions;[14] or the military economy that exploded in size and reach during World War II, and, subsequently, during the Cold War.[15]

Each of these themes—resource economy, Pacific Basin, major urban centers, and military presence—were developed by Peter Wiley and myself more than a dozen years ago in *Empires in the Sun,* our book about the contemporary West in the post–World War II years, and in our weekly "Points West" newspaper column, which Peter and I sent out to about thirty-five papers during the early 1980s. (I might note that Peter and I sought to identify a kind of western regional identity in our Points West column. We had argued, in our discussions with a number of western newspaper editors, that an understanding of the West as Region—and of the West as Empire—would be of interest to their readers. The editors claimed, however, partly on the basis of newspaper column economics, that their pages had to be almost entirely devoted to their national [read: Washington, D.C.-based] syndicated columnists, with an occasional local piece by a local author. With the exception at that time of the Boise (Idaho) Statesman—where an op-ed editor loyally published our column every week until he departed Boise by mutual consent with his superiors—our most frequent publication was in the Chicago Tribune, which had its own journalistic and marketing interest in looking westward for commentary in its pages).

In *Empires in the Sun* and in our Points West columns, the theme of the West shifting from colony to empire (or into evolving, intersecting empires) served as our point of departure in characterizing and situating western regions in the twentieth century. Our theme was elaborated by analyzing the massive infrastructure of water development projects; power plants; metal mining, fossil fuel, and timber operations; and an industrializing agriculture. These developments, in turn, constituted the West's expanding resource economy, which consisted of projects whose backers were seeking in part to establish a western autonomy, to become more independent from Wall Street and other, nonwestern financial centers. And while western resource development remained dependent on Washington for funding and a wealth of subsidies (reinforcing that well-known, well-worn western expectation of federal largesse that would simultaneously breed political resentment), the resource economy also became locally constructed. This became apparent even to the extent that those same federal bureaucracies—whether through the regional offices of the Bureau of Reclamation or the Forest Service or the cooperative management agreements of the Bureau of Land Management or the field offices of the USDA—came to be viewed during much of the twentieth century as extensions of locally derived power.[16]

Western water policy perhaps best exemplifies the intricate patterns of local and federal power and, in particular, the crucial role of local interests (both irrigated agriculture and urban development) in establishing a continuing cycle of water development and expansion characteristic of those relationships and the policies they became responsible for. By the turn of the century, the federal role, centered around a newly formed Reclamation Service (later named the Bureau of Reclamation, or BuRec), was deemed essential for building, financing, and subsequently subsidizing the massive infrastructure of projects and facilities that dotted the seventeen western states served by BuRec. But BuRec/local relations, modeled to a certain extent on the Army Corps of Engineers' pervasive "iron triangle" set of relationships between executive branch agency, Congress, and local interests, were predicated not on management or planning or even equity considerations (a mission that fully eroded during BuRec's heyday in the post-World War II period), but on considerations of local agricultural or urban development. Lobbying and trade organizations, such as the National Water Resources Association (NWRA), became both the occasion for, and the manifestation of, such federal/local relationships, the meeting ground for what came to be called the water industry. Organized around the integration of public agencies and private interests, of local and federal players, and of agricultural and urban representation, the western water industry established its own domain of water policy decision making outside public scrutiny. At the same time, the water industry successfully captured the capital and resources necessary to put in place the BuRec's elaborate infrastructure for development.[17]

So many of these developments in the post–World War II era, it also turned out, involved the kinds of massive projects and massive plans worthy of the assumptions of empire. And what plans they were! They included, among others, the myriad of deals for the Upper Basin authorized through the Colorado River Storage Project;[18] the distributive politics associated with the Central Arizona Project;[19] the monumental and much-hyped Pacific Southwest Water Plan; and the North American Water and Power Alliance's monstrous extravaganza of five-hundred-mile trenches carrying water from the outer reaches of British Columbia to the Mexican border to the south and the Great Lakes to the east ("And it will take forty years to do an EIR [Environmental Impact Report]!" quipped Colorado's water czar).[20] Aside from the activities of the western water industry, these schemes also involved other public/private, federal/local relationships and megadeals, such as the "Grand Plan" of the southwest/California/northwest power grid, based on coal-fired plants, nuclear plants, and big hydro projects;[21] the massive land grabs and market dominance of California's agro-industrial entities and chemical manufacturers;[22] and, perhaps most extravagant of all, Exxon's plans (instantly designed and as rapidly abandoned) to build six huge oil-shale pits in western Colorado, each measuring a half-mile deep, 3.5 miles long, and 1.7 miles wide, with enough rock excavated each day to carve out an entire Panama Canal.[23] This, indeed, was the stuff of empire.

The rapid emergence of these contemporary resource developments, it should be noted, was not wholly unanticipated, given earlier cycles of boom and bust in resource extraction and in the resource dependencies of the West. But it was the breadth and scale of such projects, spanning the relatively short period of the 1930s through the 1970s, that distinguished for Wiley and I this era of western empire building. At the same time, this nexus of resource developments coincided with the era of the Cold War and its enormous and far-reaching impact on both resource activities and the economy, the environment, and the politics and culture of the West. In fact, it has become increasingly commonplace for contemporary historians to say that the politics and economy of the West, in the postwar, expansionary years, were embedded in a Cold War praxis. By the building, testing, and storage of bombs and missiles; by the mining and milling of uranium and yellow cake; by the production of plutonium; by the construction of arsenals, bases, research labs, and experimental facilities; by the presence of massive aerospace companies and their thousands of subcontractors; and, perhaps most pervasively, by the culture of the Cold War, much of the West, from Mormon Utah to suburban Southern California, was clearly and deeply affected.[24]

Similar to the example of resource development, the western economies had long been influenced by, and frequently depended upon, the federal government's military activities. Yet the post–World War II period, as with the "Grand Plans" of regional resource development, was different for the West; the scale of the projects, and, perhaps most perniciously, the establishment of expectations of permanent boom in California, the Northwest, and parts of the Southwest and Intermountain West made it so.[25] The militarization of the western economy was integral to its expansion. Among other noteworthy influences, it involved the creation of new communities and urban growth, the transformation of rural areas, the influx of a new population as immigrants came in search of jobs, the utilization of this cheap immigrant labor at the interstices of military production, and the evolution of small companies and start-up firms into massive entities constructed out of federal contracts to build missiles, planes, bombs, or other nuclear-era devices. Writing in 1967, James Clayton calculated that fully one-fourth of all Department of Defense (DOD) military and civilian personnel and one-third of all military prime contract awards (including one-half of all DOD research and development contracts and two-thirds of all missile awards) were let to companies and organizations located in thirteen western states, creating a new type of dependency/expansionary cycle.[26]

These huge federal expenditures dwarfed even the resource megaprojects, and were sometimes responsible for those same resource developments. Take, for example, the influence of the Navy's huge base of operations in the San Diego area. It was the Navy, primarily, that induced the Metropolitan Water District of Southern California to expand into the San Diego region by guaranteeing a continual, imported water supply in exchange for annexation and a monopoly over those same imported water sources.[27] San Diego, in fact, was one of those "instant cities" that have dotted contemporary western history, though in this case the city should be viewed primarily as a military creation, its naval base the key actor in stimulating an infrastructure for future growth and development. Indeed, already by 1960, San Diego had become what one observer characterized as a "metropolitan-military complex."[28]

The Cold War's influence in the West was framed in part by the significant shift westward, toward the Pacific, of the country's military, economic, and political interests, a process that was significantly heightened during World War II. *In Empires in the Sun,* Wiley and I documented how the Six Companies—the consortium of California and Intermountain West companies that captured the federal contract to build the Hoover Dam and subsequently helped lay the groundwork for an emergent western region-based capitalism—became powerful players in the new, post-WWII/Cold War economy.[29] They achieved this in part by winning an additional set of contracts to build some of the major military or military-related industrial facilities aimed at the Pacific during World War II, an arrangement that became a mobile, expansive capitalism in its most militarized form. An executive of the Six Companies put it this way: "A [military] contractor has to set up a tremendous organization where nothing exists, house and feed thousands of workers, establish his own communications. That is what an army does. In both instances you have to move into the 'enemy's' territory, destroy him, then clear out and set yourself up somewhere else."[30]

It was these new western-region capitalists—engineering and construction firms such as Kaiser, Bechtel (one of the Six Companies, Kaiser, Bechtel eventually spawned both the Fluor and Ralph M. Parsons Companies), Utah International, and Morrison-Knudsen, as well as the big aerospace giants like Lockheed, Boeing, and General Dynamics—who collectively presided over the great military-induced expansions of the regional economies of the West in the forties, fifties, and sixties. At the same time, these companies grew rapidly by developing their Pacific Basin ties. Consequently, in the Cold War era they emerged as major multinational players, achieving a kind of a quasi-military or "national security" status in international, primarily Pacific Basin, arenas.[31]

This was also the era of Pacific Basin megadeals, the modern Pacific version of the old Atlantic-triangle trade policies. It was in this setting that new trade and material flows were established and multiplied. For example, iron ore mined in Peru would be shipped on a fleet of convertible ore carriers (built in San Diego) to Japan, unload, and then sail on to Indonesia, where they would pick up crude oil for shipment to refineries on the West Coast.[32] Fossil fuel development could also flow both ways. The much-hyped Japanese market for low-sulfur coal in the 1970s and early 1980s, as another example, induced all kinds of convulsive activities in the West associated with the coal trade. This included new pressures for mining in Utah, plans to build slurry lines through the Interior West, and proposals for West Coast dredging and port expansion in places like Seattle and Long Beach. All of these were based on the premise that the Pacific Basin geopolitical and resource economy ties were worth the environmental costs, the push for low-wage jobs, and the heavy subsidies required.[33] These, in turn, became indicative of how the West was becoming both newly dependent on, as well as exploitative of, its Pacific Basin ties.

The "empire" message was partly a matter of scale: companies (and regions) that "Think Big" could undertake megaprojects that were unprecedented in their restructuring impact, whether in terms of resource use, industrial expansion, population growth, or extension of the boundaries of what the *Los Angeles Times* liked to call "the Pacific Littoral."[34] "Thinking Big," the motto of the *Times,* as well as the philosophy of some of the other promoters of western regional expansion such as the Denver Post and the Arizona Republic, was also the mantra of the big western engineering and construction firms. These companies, tied into both the military economy and the Pacific Basin nexus of trade and resource flows, were instrumental in designing and promoting some of the big resource projects characteristic of the post–World War II era. It was Bechtel in the 1960s, for example, that pushed the concept of a coastal, nuclear-powered desalting plant that would enable the Metropolitan Water District to provide endless water supplies for the endless urban expansion and population growth of its six-county megaregion, which stretched from the desert to the sea.[35] The Southern California-based Ralph M. Parsons Company outdid even its northern California rival with its $200 billion (original cost estimates that continued to ratchet up another $100 billion each decade!) North American Water and Power Alliance (NAWAPA) scheme. For some, like the state of Washington's Senator Henry M. "Scoop" Jackson, NAWAPA was a serious threat, and analysts like Marc Reisner have elevated the plan as a major controversy in the western resource policy debates. But NAWAPA never really had a significant chance for approval. Indeed, for Parsons, NAWAPA was a device, a way to demonstrate that Parsons can "think big." "If you don't think big," Army Corps of Engineers Colonel Robert W. Reiner said in support of NAWAPA, "you don't accomplish big things." And Parsons' strategy in touting its proposal was aimed as much at its Pacific Basin clients as the water agencies, Bureau of Reclamation officials, or politicians like L.A. County Supervisor Kenneth Hahn, who would trot out NAWAPA every chance he could get and thereby create all kinds of regional fears that once again an insatiable urban southern California was coveting those distant imported water sources.[36]

So much of the "thinking big" philosophy associated with western empire building was urban based, with Los Angeles (the "supercity," as its business leaders liked to proclaim) both symbol and substance of this expansionary model of development. Water availability in arid environments like Phoenix, Las Vegas, San Diego, and, of course, Los Angeles, was one part of that model. These were cities that extended Lewis Mumford's concept of urban ecological imbalance in ever more pronounced ways.[37] In the urban West, regional centers of power became increasingly dependent on distant sources for their water, energy, food, and, in reversing the flow, for disposing of wastes or spreading pollutant emissions into faraway, nonurban spaces. The Grand Canyon and the Kaiparowtz Plateau not only came to be located within the urban orbits of Los Angeles and Phoenix because of their coveted resources and energy-generating potential, but because they could also serve as a depository for the unwanted byproducts of urban expansion. All too often, dirty air became synonymous with "place" in the West.

Western cities were also expressions of directed military spending and launching pads for the new Pacific Basin forms of global economy and exchange. The "global cities" concept was the visible, prominent side of the flow of capital and labor.[38] On the other hand, communities of multiple languages, ethnic underclasses, toxic hot spots, food insecurity and homelessness, and creative immigrant energies establishing new cultural, linguistic, and urban landscape hybrids were the darker, often more complex side of the environments of those same cities. Place in the urban West was becoming multiethnic and multidimensional. These were locations constituting a more idiosyncratic melting pot than the imagined unidimensional, frontier-like West settled by sturdy Anglo stock who were presumed to have shaped the region's character of democratic individualism.[39]

Today, it has become clear that the West as Empire image—whether of the global city facing the Pacific, the resource megaproject, the huge military expenditure, or the continuing cycle of expansion in urban growth or resource use—is dated, at best, and perhaps misleading when exploring these historical shifts in regions and places. The 1960s and 1970s, which for many signified an era of continuing expansion, gave way to the 1980s, the new "Morning in America" epoch launched by our most western and empire-conscious of contemporary presidents, Ronald Reagan.

Empires in the Sun concluded with a snapshot of the transition to the Reagan presidency, with the interest groups of the West and other regions lined up at the White House door. The Reagan years were to be a period marked by the anticipation of a signal expansion of that characteristic western mix of government largesse and free market deregulation. It was also a moment of great expectations about renewed empire building as well. These expectations were heightened in the 1980s, given that expansionary plans in the West during the 1970s had been challenged, sometimes suspended, and even derailed. Big water projects were no longer being built. Pacific Basin ties were no longer being singularly directed from our shores. Even the military economy seemed vulnerable in the wake of that extraordinary Pacific Basin debacle, the Vietnam War. Ronald Reagan, the empire-oriented interest groups assumed, would turn it around. The new president would open the West for land grabs ("I am a part of the Sagebrush Rebellion," his newly appointed secretary of the interior, James Watt, had proclaimed in his confirmation hearings).[40] Reagan would, it was also assumed, push ahead aggressively with vast new sums for the military and its contractors, talk tough with the Japanese, initiate all kinds of new water starts, build new nuclear plants, and renew mining leasing and energy exploration.[41]

But what happened? Where was Ronald Reagan and his emissaries when the empire builders needed them most? The results, interestingly, turned out to be problematic. I recall a meeting I attended in Salt Lake City in 1982 of the National Water Resources Association. The keynote speaker was none other than James Watt, formerly of the Denver–based Mountain States Legal Foundation, a self-proclaimed "public interest" law firm for the empire builders that had also worked closely with western water industry interests.[42] With his appointment as secretary of the interior, Watt, the resource developers assumed, would have the power to make western water and energy development projects a reality once again. Just weeks after his confirmation, Watt had already declared that "no area [of federal lands in the West] should be excluded" from energy exploration.[43] A new Cabinet Council on Natural Resources, headed by Watt and including several cabinet heads (but with no EPA representation), was in fact given the task of setting resource and environmental policy for the administration.[44]

It seemed clear, given his background and his public statements, that Watt saw the task of reorienting western resource policy as his cause célèbre. Indeed, with his lay minister style and hothouse rhetoric, James Watt was the western anti-environmental, antigovernment preacher at his most fulsome.[45] "You know the Enemy," he exhorted his water industry hosts at the NWRA conference, speaking darkly of the Democratic/environmentalist alliance. "You have built the West, made it what it is today, but they want to tear it down," Watt declared, alluding to environmentalist dreams of decommissioned dams and power plants. "Join the crusade," he implored the water delegates. "Be ready for the call!"[46]

But the call to what? In the past, friendly secretaries of the interior would announce, at NWRA gatherings, new water starts, new appropriations for the megaprojects, new ways to protect agriculture or mining or urban water interests. However, Watt wasn't able to announce any new water starts. The budget crunch was also putting a squeeze on Bureau of Reclamation spending.[47] Worse, the new buzzword out of Washington was cost sharing, a term that invariably sent shivers through the subsidy-dependent resource developers. This was no longer the highly contested 10 percent cost-sharing figure of the Carter years. Instead, the Reaganites were declaring the need for 35 percent cost sharing, according to another erstwhile western water industry hero, the Army Corps of Engineers' William Gianelli.[48]

The failure to deliver new projects for the water industry raised a corresponding set of questions about the direction of the Reagan revolution itself. Deregulatory efforts were prominent, though only partially successful, as the environmental movement (among others) effectively used legal action to overturn policies while tapping into widespread proenvironment sentiment—including western sentiment—that helped to place constraints on resource development and continued to elevate environmental concern.[49] Military spending had increased exponentially, maintaining some level of confidence among the empire builders that the expansionary impulse had yet to crest, but even military spending was unpredictable and uneven in its growth impacts.[50] It compounded, along with the uncertainty in resource development, widening gaps within the global cities, as well as huge trade imbalances, exposing the uneven and ephemeral nature of the 1980s boom. Ronald Reagan, the Sagebrush Rebel and Western Cowboy personified, also turned out to be the harbinger of yet another identity for the West: the Empire Under Stress.

In the Reagan, Bush, and Clinton years, "most favored region" status did not prevent the West from experiencing sharp declines in its economy and a continuing crisis in resource management and in landscape and environment, while contending with massive upheavals in its urban, rural, and regional identities. With the end of the Cold War, military spending crashed, and with it crashed assumptions about continuing western expansion. A 1962 article by James Clayton about defense spending in California and the West is revealing in this respect. Clayton argued that the danger of a cyclical turn in military spending was always possible, given previous downswings. What was most feared, however, among military-dependent westerners, was the specter of collapse, caused by significantly diminished military spending. But that, Clayton and others argued, was an implausible outcome, advocated predominantly by "disarmament nuts" who were not to be taken seriously.[51]

But Reagan's military spending gambit—applauded for its role in hastening the disintegration of the Soviet Union and its Eastern European counterparts—created the unintended consequence of western regional economic decline. The aerospace industry was not only downsizing, it was departing and shutting down. Military bases were closing. Weapons production was at a standstill. The Department of Defense and Department of Energy became increasingly known for the number of Superfund sites their facilities had created. The military economy had given way to a mitigation and remediation economy. And although these changes were national in scope, their impact on the West was substantial, if not exceptional, particularly for the ways in which the region now found itself vulnerable.

The 1980s and 1990s had brought crucial changes to western cities as well. Homelessness, already entrenched in the East, arrived in the West. The erosion of safety nets, the declining status of the working poor, swings in employment, industry relocation and abandonment—all these had become notable in this region as well. Western cities, with their own patterns of immigration, were becoming a particular variation of a First World/Third World metropolis, where the rich not only got richer and the poor became poorer, but the colors of the residents changed as well.[52]

The rural West was also in turmoil. When Reagan and Bush helped secure increased timber production for a restructuring timber, pulp, and paper industry (and the Clinton administration temporized on some of those same issues, much to the embarrassment of its presumably empowered mainstream environmental supporters), the flow of timber didn't stabilize communities; it went elsewhere, as exports to the Pacific, while jobs went east to the Carolinas.[53] The big fights around grazing—the battleground of Cattle Free in '93—masked the fact that the western cattle industry, including ranchers and meatpackers, had become increasingly whipsawed by the global food economy.[54] The executives of the ConAgras and the Cargills were much more akin to the multinational managers, financiers, and corporate attorneys of the Global City than those much celebrated—and maligned—grizzly westerners who ranched or farmed and who were also finding it increasingly hard to survive.[55]

The evolution of the cattle and meatpacking industry, including changes taking place in the western U.S., have highlighted the differences between regional development and regional identities in contrast with globalization trends. Grazing in the West has become essentially a subset of an intricate system of beef production, marketing, and distribution, characterized, for example, by the emergence of what Steven Sanderson has called the "world steer."[56] In this system, the western U.S.'s part in the making of the world steer was perhaps more directly associated with the use of immigrant labor in huge packing plants, such as Montfort's Greeley, Colorado, facility, than the image of the steak-eating, free and independent cowboy on the range, bringing the cattle home after roaming the open spaces of the West.[57] The restructuring of the meat industry, not environmental claims on grazing lands, were influencing the ranching industry in ways that created stresses on what had been presumed to be a way of life.

This West under Stress (or at least a West whose land, institutions, and urban and rural spaces have been and are still being restructured) is not best understood, I would argue, as a "New West" or a "New New West." Instead, the West remains a continuing and more elaborated battleground over what is meant by "place" in this region, my starting point in this essay. To identify Los Angeles as a "place" in the West, it is no longer adequate to situate it exclusively through the metaphor of the global city or even the expanding metropolis. Los

Angeles is not City Walk, Universal Studio's re-creation of urban space without edges, a community without conflict or divisions, or, perhaps most significantly, a place without colors or languages or the smells and sounds of a complex urban terrain. To see Los Angeles is to see the incredible murals in Estrada Courts in East Los Angeles, where the mural movement was born. It is the view of the Food Court in Koreatown Plaza, where seventy varieties of kimchi can be found. It is the jazz corridor along Central Avenue, where jams at the Dunbar Hotel played to another wave of immigration at another time. And it is back to the Pico Market in Santa Monica, where the sounds and tastes and smells of that other Los Angeles can be found, another kind of place in this semiarid environment where different roots have taken hold.[58]

These different places are urban as well as rural. They are regional in location, or by watershed, or foodshed, or air basin, or land patterns of development. They can signify other, alternative ways of defining what constitutes a place. The practice of exploiting the land, so western in so many ways, for example, can and has given way to a different, more interactive relationship to the land, which is also so western and embedded in the history of the region. This "ethic of place," as Charles Wilkinson has argued, involves different ways to think about a region.[59] It involves, as the Western States Center has sought to implement in its organizing strategies (in part to counter the Wise Use/Resource Development ideologues), a concept of place where community is reconstituted and secured.[60] It is a concept of place where a food system can be defined by "locality and seasonality" within the construct of a regional foodshed rather than by the "distance and durability" factors that characterize the global food system.[61]

Finally, these alternative concepts of place evoke a notion of the West not as empire, but as home. It is here, in this West, where the idea of home or of place offers a connection to the land, to the people, and to the myriad of experiences that survive, stubbornly, outside the orbit of a globalizing, restructuring, reductionist, and, ultimately, disconnected empire.

NOTES

1. For other Southern California farmers' markets, see United States Department of Agriculture, *National Farmers' Market Directory* (Washington, D.C.: USDA Agricultural Marketing Service and Transportation and Marketing Division, March 1994).

2. Walter Goldschmidt, *As You Sow* (New York: Harcourt, Brace, 1947).

3. Andrew Fisher and Robert Gottlieb, *Community Food Security: Policies for a More Sustainable Food System in the Context of the 1995 Farm Bill and Beyond* (Los Angeles: University of California, Lewis Center for Regional Policy Studies, 1995).

4. Patricia N. Limerick, "Making the Most of Words: Verbal Activity and Western America," in William Cronon, George Miles, and Jay Gitlin, eds., *Under an Open Sky: Rethinking America's Western Past* (New York: Norton, 1992).

5. Richard White and Patricia N. Limerick, *The Frontier in American Culture: An Exhibit at the Newberry Library, August 26–November 26, 1994* (Berkeley: University of California Press, 1994).

6. Mario Barrera, *Race and Class in the Southwest: A Theory of Racial Inequality* (Notre Dame: University of Notre Dame Press, 1979); Alan Weisman and Jay Dusard, *La Frontera: The United States Border with Mexico* (San Diego: Harcourt Brace Jovanovich, 1986); Helen Ingram, Leonard Milich, and Robert G. Varady, "Managing Transboundary Resources: Lessons from Ambos Nogales," *Environment* 36, no. 4 (1994): 6–9.

7. For Proposition 187, see Bill Tamayo, "Proposition 187: Racism Leads to Deaths and More Poverty," *Poverty and Race* 4, no. 2 (January–February, 1995). For Aryan movements in the Pacific Northwest, see Philip Weiss, "Off the Grid," *New York Times Sunday Magazine,* January 8, 1995, and Louis Sahagun, "A Wave of Distrust in the West," *Los Angeles Times*, February 3, 1995.

8. Charles F. Wilkinson, *Crossing the Next Meridian: Land, Water, and the Future of the West* (Washington, D.C.: Island Press, 1992).

9. Harvey Jacobs, " 'Wise Use' versus 'The New Feudalism': Social Conflict over Property Rights," Paper Presented to the Thirty-fifth Annual Meeting of the Association of Collegiate Schools of Planning, Philadelphia, October 29–31, 1993; Ron Arnold and Alan Gottlieb, *Trashing the Environment: How Runaway Environmentalism is Wrecking America* (Bellevue, Wash.: Merril Press, 1993); Richard M. Stapleton, "Greed vs. Green," *National Parks* 66 (November/December 1992): 32–37; Michael O'Keefe and Kevin Daley, "Checking the Right: (Conservative Backlash Against the Environmental Movement)," *Buzzworm* 5, no. 3 (May/June 1993): 38–44.

10. See, for example, Carl Abbott, *The Metropolitan Frontier: Cities in the Modern American West* (Tucson: University of Arizona Press, 1993), and Gerald D. Nash, *The American West in the Twentieth Century: A Short History of an Urban Oasis* (Englewood Cliffs, N.J.: Prentice Hall, 1973).

11. Richard White, "American Environmental History: The Development of a New Historical Field," *Pacific Historical Review* 54, no. 3 (August 1985): 297–335.

12. William Cronon, *Nature's Metropolis: Chicago and the Great West* (New York: Norton, 1991), xvii; Robert Gottlieb, *Forcing the Spring: The Transformation of the American Environmental Movement* (Washington, D.C.: Island Press, 1993).

13. Donald Worster, *Rivers of Empire: Water, Aridity, and the Growth of the American West* (New York: Pantheon Books, 1985); Peter Wiley and Robert Gottlieb, *Empires in the Sun: The Rise of the New American West* (New York: Putnam, 1982).

14. Carl Abbott, "The Metropolitan Region: Western Cities in the New Urban Era," in Gerald D. Nash and Richard W. Etulain, eds., *The Twentieth Century West: Historical Interpretations* (Albuquerque: University of New Mexico Press, 1993); Wiley and Gottlieb, *Empires in the Sun.*

15. Gerald D. Nash, *The American West Transformed: The Impact of the Second World War* (Bloomington: Indiana University Press, 1985); Ann Markusen, Peter Hall, Scott Campbell, and Sabina Deitrick, *The Rise of the Gunbelt: The Military Remapping of Industrial America* (New York: Oxford University Press, 1991).

16. Charles F. Wilkinson, *The Eagle Bird: Mapping a New West* (New York: Pantheon Books, 1992); Jeanne Nienaber Clarke and Daniel McCool, *Staking out the Terrain: Power Differentials among Natural Resource Management Agencies* (Albany: State University of New York Press, 1985); Paul J. Culhane, *Public Lands Politics: Interest Group Influence on the Forest Service and the Bureau of Land Management* (Baltimore: Johns Hopkins University Press, 1981); Robert Gottlieb and Margaret FitzSimmons, *Thirst for Growth: Water Agencies as Hidden Government in California* (Tucson: University of Arizona Press, 1991).

17. Helen Ingram, *Water Politics: Continuity and Change* (Albuquerque: University of New Mexico Press, 1990); Gottleib and FitzSimmons, *Thirst for Growth*.

18. United States Congress, *Colorado River Storage Project,* Hearings before the Subcommittee on Irrigation and Reclamation of the Committee on Interior and Insular Affairs, House of Representatives, 83d Cong., 2d sess., on HR 4449, HR 4443, and HR 4463, to authorize the Secretary of Interior to construct, operate, and maintain the Colorado River Storage Project and participating projects and for other purposes (Washington, D.C.: General Printing Office, 1954); Elmo Richardson, *Resource Development and Preservation in the Truman-Eisenhower Era* (Lexington: University Press of Kentucky, 1973).

19. Frank Welsh, *How to Create a Water Crisis* (Boulder, Colo.: Johnson Books, 1985); Rich Johnson, *The Central Arizona Project: 1918–1968* (Tucson: University of Arizona Press, 1977).

20. Nathan W. Snyder, "Water from Alaska," paper presented at the 1977 Irrigation Symposium, November 16, 1977, Fresno, California, and reprinted in *1977 Proceedings of the Irrigation Symposium* (Fresno: California State University and the International Irrigation Association, 1978); Robert Gottlieb, *A Life of Its Own: The Politics and Power of Water* (San Diego: Harcourt Brace Jovanovich, 1989).

21. Wiley and Gottlieb, *Empires in the Sun*.

22. Donald Pisani, *From the Family Farm to Agribusiness: The Irrigation Crusade in California and the West, 1850–1931* (Berkeley and Los Angeles: University of California Press, 1984); Don Villarejo, *New Lands for Agriculture* (Davis, Calif.: California Institute for Rural Studies, 1981).

23. Eleanor J. Tracy, "Exxon Gets Serious about Shale," *Fortune,* May 18, 1981; Bob Anderson, "Oil Shale Future: Jewel or Synfuel?" *High Country News,* April 3, 1981; Karen Tumulty, "Exxon and Tosco Corp. Scrap Shale-Oil Project," *Los Angeles Times,* May 3, 1981.

24. Ann Markusen and Joel Yudken, *Dismantling the Cold War Economy* (New York: Basic Books, 1992).

25. Roger W. Lotchin, *Fortress California: 1910–1961* (New York: Oxford University Press, 1992); Markusen et al., *Rise of the Gunbelt*.

26. James Clayton, "The Impact of the Cold War on the Economies of California and Utah, 1946–1965," *Pacific Historical Review* 36, no. 4 (November 1967): 449–73.

27. Joel Schwarz, *A Water Odyssey: The Story of the Metropolitan Water District of Southern California* (Los Angeles: Metropolitan Water District, 1991); Gottleib and FitzSimmons, *Thirst for Growth.*

28. Lotchin, *Fortress California*, 302.

29. Charles J. Murphy, "The Earth Movers I: Winning the Epic of the Six Companies of the West," *Fortune*, August 1943, 99–107.

30. Charles J. Murphy, "The Earth Movers II: They Turn to Shipbuilding and Change the Face of the West," *Fortune*, September 1943; Wiley and Gottlieb, *Empires in the Sun.*

31. Dan Cordtz, "Bechtel Thrives on Billion-Dollar Jobs," *Fortune*, January 1975, 91–93; Markuson et al., *Rise of the Gun Belt.*

32. Wiley and Gottlieb, *Empires in the Sun.*

33. Western Coal Export Task Force, *Western U.S. Steam Coal Exports to the Pacific Basin*, Summary Report of the Joint Study of the Western Coal Export Task Force and the Working Groups of Japan, The Republic of China, and The Republic of Korea (Denver: Western Governors' Policy Office, 1981); Robert Gottlieb, "The Coal Rush Countdown," *PSA*, June 1982, 79–82.

34. Robert Gottlieb and Irene Wolt, *Thinking Big: The Story of the Los Angeles Times, Its Publishers, and Their Influence on Southern California* (New York: Putnam, 1977).

35. Metropolitan Water District of Southern California, "Contracts for Study of Sea Water Conversion," Twenty-Eighth Annual Report (Los Angeles: Metropolitan Water District of Southern California, 1966), 151–52.

36. Marc Reisner, *Cadillac Desert: The American West and Its Disappearing Water*, (New York: Penguin, 1987); Snyder, "Water from Alaska"; Reed McClure, "Hahn Urges Columbia River Be Tapped to Supply Water," *Los Angeles Daily News*, September 12, 1981.

37. Lewis Mumford, "The Theory and Practice of Regionalism," *Sociological Review* 20, no. 1 (January 1928): 18–33; Carl Sussman, ed., *Planning the Fourth Migration: The Neglected Vision of the Regional Planning Association of America* (Cambridge, Mass.: MIT Press, 1976).

38. Saskia Sassen, *The Global City* (Princeton: Princeton University Press, 1991); John Friedmann and Goetz Wolff, "The World City Hypothesis: An Agenda for Research and Action," *International Journal of Urban and Regional Research* 63 (1982).

39. Abbott, "The Metropolitan Region."

40. Elizabeth Drew, "A Reporter at Large," *New Yorker*, April 4, 1981.

41. Norman Vig and Michael E. Kraft, eds., *Environmental Policy in the 1980s: Reagan's New Agenda* (Washington, D.C.: CQ Press, 1984).

42. Wiley and Gottlieb, *Empires in the Sun.*

43. Rich Jaroslovsky, "Reagan's Drive to Open More Public Land to Energy Firms May Spark Major Battle," *Wall Street Journal*, April 1, 1981.

44. Marc K. Landy, Marc J. Roberts, and Stephen R. Thomas, *The Environmental Protection Agency: Asking the Wrong Questions* (New York: Oxford University Press, 1990).

45. "Interior Department: Religious Fervor," *National Journal*, April 25, 1981, 720–22.

46. Gottlieb, *A Life of Its Own*; Andy Pasztor, "James Watt Tackles Interior Agency Job with Religious Zeal," *Wall Street Journal*, May 5, 1981.

47. Water Information News Service, "Administration Requests Reduced Water Budget" 7, no. 20, February 2, 1983.

48. Western Resources Wrap Up, "Cost Sharing," series 20, no. 48, December 2, 1982; William R. Gianelli, *Water Resources: People and Issues* (Washington, D.C.: U.S. Army Corps of Engineers, EP 870–1–24, August 1985).

49. Andy Pasztor, "Reagan Goal of Easing Environmental Laws Is Largely Unattained," *Wall Street Journal*, February 18, 1983; Jonathan Lash et al., *A Season of Spoils: The Reagan Administration's Attack on the Environment* (New York: Random House, 1984).

50. Markusen and Yudken, *Dismantling the Cold War Economy.*

51. James Clayton, "Defense Spending: Key to California's Economic Growth," *Western Political Quarterly* 15 (June 1962): 280–93.

52. Mike Davis, *City of Quartz: Excavating the Future in Los Angeles* (New York: Vintage Books, 1992).

53. Maureen Smith, *The Paper Industry and Barriers to Recycling: An Environmental Argument for Industrial Restructuring* (Los Angeles: Department of Urban Planning, University of California, Los Angeles).

54. Lourdes Gouveia, "Global Strategies and Local Linkages: The Case of the U.S. Meatpacking Industry," in Alessandro Bonanno, Lawrence Busch, William Friedland, Lourdes Gouveia, and Enzo Mingione, eds., *From Columbus to ConAgra: The Globalization of Agriculture and Food* (Lawrence: University Press of Kansas, 1994).

55. Mustafa Koc, "Globalization as a Discourse," in Bonanno et al., eds., *From Columbus to ConAgra;* Harriet Friedmann, "Distance and Durability: Shaky Foundations of the World Food Economy," in Philip McMichael, ed., *The Globalization of Agro-Food Systems* (Ithaca, N.Y.: Cornell University Press, 1994).

56. Steven E. Sanderson, "The Emergence of the 'World Steer': International and Foreign Domination in Latin American Cattle Production," in F. Lamond Tullis and W. Ladd Hollist, eds., *Food, the State, and International Political Economy* (Lincoln: University of Nebraska Press, 1986).

57. Carol Andreas, *Meatpackers and Beef Barons: Company Town in a Global Economy* (Niwot, Colo.: University Press of Colorado, 1994).

58. Madeline Janis-Aparicio, Gilda Haas, and Robin Cannon, "Sell L.A. in All Its Tastes and Colors," *Los Angeles Times,* March 18, 1994.

59. Wilkinson, *Eagle Bird.*

60. Jeff Malachowski, Western States Center, Personal Communication, 1993.

61. Harriet Friedmann, "After Midas's Feast: Alternative Food Regimes for the Future," in Patricia Allen, ed., *Food for the Future: Conditions and Contradictions of Sustainability* (New York: John Wiley and Sons, 1993).

CHAPTER FIVE

AN "EMPIRE OF LIBERTY"
Thomas Jefferson and Governing Natural Resources in the West

HELEN M. INGRAM AND MARY G. WALLACE

The western United States is central to our notions of democracy in this country. Historically, the West has been viewed not only as a land of limitless opportunities, but also as a fountain of democratic renewal for American society. With its rich natural resources and vast lands, it has been depicted as a place where a man with an independent, self-reliant character and a capacity for hard work could make a good life. The West has been portrayed as the ideal of a democratic society where a man was judged, not by breeding, but by accomplishments.

Thomas Jefferson clearly realized the integral connection between the formation of the American republic and the presence of the western frontier. More than any of the other founders, he was concerned with the settlement of the West, and during his presidency he laid the foundations for western expansion. He also wrote extensively on land policy and the rights of the individual farmer and homesteader. As Henry Nash Smith observes, Jefferson was "clearly the intellectual father of the American advance to the Pacific."[1]

The intent of this essay is to provide a Jeffersonian perspective on democracy and policy and contrast this perspective with the bureaucratic, professionalized, and interest-dominated nature of policies governing western natural resources. The first section examines essential tenets or themes found in Jefferson's ideas about democracy and also looks at his vision of the West, specifically how his appreciation of the western land base shaped his ideas about politics. In contrast, the next section offers an overview of characteristics of western resource policies as they have actually developed. This section includes a discussion of the prevalence of expert bureaucratic decision making in the fate of natural resources and the emergence of a politics of interest in the West. The final section reviews recent efforts to reinvent democracy in the West, particularly the rise of community organizations and the development of partnerships among resource users and government agencies that work to improve the management of natural resources.

ELEMENTS OF JEFFERSONIAN DEMOCRACY

It is not a simple task to delineate the political thought of Thomas Jefferson. He wrote prolifically, with some fifty thousand written items including letters, speeches, articles, and memos currently in circulation. In none of these pieces does Jefferson lay out a coherent and systematic political theory. In fact, the writings of Jefferson, as is true of most political writers grappling with complex political questions, contain contradictions.[2] Nonetheless, strong and consistent themes on democracy can be drawn from Jefferson's writings.

In recent years, Jefferson has become increasingly recognized as one who offers a different type of politics—a radical democratic politics—as an alternative to the traditional view of politics associated with other founding fathers, most notably Madison and Hamilton. For example, Madison's preoccupation was primarily with constructing a government that contained constitutional checks and balances. Hamilton, on the other hand, was concerned with developing a nation of prosperity and power. The central preoccupation of Jefferson, however, was with the people—the citizens of the newly founded republic of America. As Jefferson notes, "I know of no safe depository of the ultimate power of society but the people themselves, and if we think them not enlightened enough to exercise their control with a wholesome discretion, the remedy is not to take it from them, but to inform their discretion."[3]

At least three distinct and complementary themes on democracy run through the writings of Jefferson. These themes include: 1) a belief that people are capable of self-government; 2) a belief in decentralized small governmental units; and 3) a belief in the need for public deliberation and civic education through participation in politics. These beliefs reflect Jefferson's central conviction in the "unfinished revolution," the idea that people would continue to define and reshape society through governmental institutions.[4]

Capacity for Self-Governance

At the core of Jeffersonian thought, and contrary to many other political theorists including Madison, Hobbes, and Locke, is a belief in the human capacity for self-governance. Caldwell observes that Jefferson had "abundant faith in the capacity of the American people to order their affairs to their mutual well-being without the undue aid or interference of self-constituted or even publicly constituted authority."[5] It is this view of human nature—specifically his trust in the people's ability to govern—that distinguishes Jefferson from other writers of his time.

Jefferson shared a belief basic to the eighteenth-century philosophy of the Enlightenment: humans are infinitely perfectible. He therefore believed in human progress. However, like Aristotle, Jefferson saw an integral role for political life in the development of human society. In contrast to Hamilton and Madison, who were firmly rooted in the Anglo-American tradition of possessive individualism, Jefferson saw humans as developing, active, social creatures who define and improve themselves through interactions with others. He believed a sense of mutual responsibility for one another was a necessary feature of self-government. Government must be structured to allow this unfolding of the human spirit.

Decentralized Government

Like many of his contemporaries, Jefferson saw the republic, a form of government that assumes full participation of citizens, as an ideal. Subsequently, he advocated democratic processes with responsibility for governance placed with the citizenry. For Jefferson, Federalism is built from the smallest unit, the level at which citizens conduct their own affairs, up to the national level. In fact, the very foundation of government lies in the right of every citizen to participate in government and to direct his or her own affairs. According to Jefferson, "making every citizen an acting member of the government . . . will attach him by his strongest feelings to the independence of his country, and its republican constitutions."[6]

Jefferson also clearly saw the importance of local communities in how government would ultimately be structured. Although recognizing the importance of national institutions such as the Congress and presidency, Jefferson saw a "true democracy" as one embedded in the full and equal participation of citizens in the governance of their communities. As Jefferson writes, "were we directed from Washington when to sow, and when to reap, we should soon want bread."[7]

Jefferson advocated a decentralized government organized by wards. He contended that citizenship is formed largely through participation in small political units such as town meetings and ward republics. In Jefferson's view:

Where every man is a sharer in the direction of his ward republic, or of some of the higher ones, and feels that he is a participator in the government of affairs, not merely at an election one day in the year, but every day, when there shall not be a man in the state who will not be a member of some one of its councils, great or small, he will let the heart be torn out of his body sooner than his power be wrested from him by a Caesar or a Bonaparte.[8]

Public Deliberation

Jefferson considered politics a daily part of human life, not simply a one-time fulfillment of duty through service in public office. He was as concerned with the means by which public policies were made as with the substance, and he insisted upon the free and equal participation of citizens in public affairs. A key role of government was to provide a place for people to come together to deliberate public affairs. As Jefferson notes, in such a place, "The voice of the whole people would be thus fairly, fully, and peaceably expressed, discussed, and decided by the common reason of society."[9] Without a place for public deliberation to occur, Jefferson believed that government could not effectively function.

From a Jeffersonian perspective, citizens can work out struggles about government through participation in public affairs; the burden of solving public problems rests on the citizenry rather than on the government. As Jefferson writes:

And say, finally, whether peace is best preserved by giving energy to the government or information to the people. This last is the most certain, and the most legitimate engine of government. Educate and inform the whole mass of people. Enable them to see that it is their interest to preserve peace and order, and they will preserve them. They are the only sure reliance for the preservation of our liberty.[10]

Participation in political affairs allows people to look beyond narrow self-interests and reach an understanding of a common good.

Jefferson's faith was in a republican form of government peopled with an informed citizenry capable of exercising good judgment. Further, Jefferson believed that daily participation in politics would act not only as a check to tyranny, but also as a force to encourage each generation to define the terms of government authority and sovereignty. From a Jeffersonian perspective, a key purpose of government is to help people realize connections between political matters and their lives.

Jefferson and the West

These three themes underlying Jeffersonian democracy—capacity for self-government, decentralized government, and active political deliberation—can clearly be seen in Jefferson's writings concerning the West. Jefferson had a long-standing interest in the western territory. Writing in 1786, for example, he noted the importance of the West in absorbing the rapidly expanding population in the original states: "The present population for the inhabited parts of the U.S. is of about 10 to the square mile; and experience has shown that wherever we reach that the inhabitants become uneasy, as too much compressed, and go off in great numbers to search for vacant country. Within 40 years the whole territory will be peopled at that rate."[11] For Jefferson, the western frontier could absorb the inevitable growth that he foresaw and also provide a basis for an open society, based in part on agrarian principles.

However, more significantly for his theories of democracy, Jefferson had a complex understanding of western territorial issues beyond demographics or the abundance of its natural resources. He viewed the existence of the western frontier as integral to the formation of the newly formed nation. During the construction of the U.S. Constitution, much of the debate centered around how power should be dispersed. Most of the framers accepted the idea of a republic, with its concomitant emphasis on citizen participation, in principle only. Instead, a system of constitutional checks and balances was devised to dissipate power among levels of government.

This debate about where power should ultimately be placed was largely framed by Madison's argument in *Federalist* No. 10 that the chief threat to the young country was "the mischiefs of faction."[12] Madison believed that only through a system of checks and balances and the separation of powers could factions could be controlled. In that case, as Lovejoy notes, "no part can dominate the whole, and the result will be the general good" and "ambition must be made to counteract ambition."[13] Madison saw the western frontier as a geographical solution to the problem of factions. He argued: "Extend the sphere and you take in a greater variety of parties and interests; you make it less probable that a majority of the whole will have a common motive to invade the rights of other citizens."[14]

Jefferson, however, had a much different conception of the political implications of the existence of the western frontier. Like Madison, he saw the expanse of the frontier as important to the developing nation, in part because of his long-standing vision of an agricultural life for many Americans. However, Jefferson did not share Madison's conception of a populace composed of a variety of interests whose regulation was the principal task of government.[15]

Instead, he looked to the western frontier as a way to build the "republic" that was guaranteed to the states, even if symbolically, in the Constitution. He envisioned that many of the principles underlying a republican form, particularly interaction among the citizenry, could be realized in the West. As Kemmis observes, this type of government

> was an intensive brand of politics, it was, heart and soul, a politics of engagement. It depended first upon people being deeply engaged with one another ("rejoicing and mourning, laboring and suffering together") and second upon citizens directly and profoundly engaged with working out the solutions to public problems, by formulating and enacting "the common good."[16]

Jefferson saw the western frontier as the best way to introduce these principles of republican government.[17]

As Lynton Caldwell has stated, "Jefferson sought an empire of liberty."[18] He believed that the West, with its vast resources, was the key in building this empire. Jefferson founded his vision of this society on democratic principles such as self-government, small-scale governance, and civic education through participation in politics. It is a society based upon cooperation, with a sense of community and responsibility built as people engage in political life. It is a "politics of engagement" versus a "politics of disengagement" envisioned by Madison.

WESTERN RESOURCE MANAGEMENT

The image of a free and independent life has long been associated with the western United States. It is a life glamorized in print and paint as an ideal of many of the democratic principles associated with Jeffersonian democracy discussed in this essay. "In the imagination of modern America," Richard White observes, "the West has come to stand for independence, self-reliance, and individualism."[19] Through culture, myth, and legal structures, the West has been depicted as a place of unlimited opportunity; settlers were beckoned with promises of tracts of unoccupied land and unfettered opportunities for resource development. The Homestead Acts, the Desert Land Act, the Reclamation Act, and others all held out the promise of a new life. William E. Smythe, an early proponent of agriculture in the West, said of the western settler: "In a way, he is born again. He turns over a new page in his life history. . . . He realizes that his relation to the natural resources of the region is like that enjoyed by the men of a century ago in the place whence he came."[20] The image of this life drew people west as much as the offer of free land.

Connections between democracy and the settlement of the West are clearly illustrated by the Reclamation Act of 1902. The arid nature of the West caused a small but vocal group of people to call for federally subsidized irrigation works. With water, people argued, not only would the desert bloom, but also democracy. Reflecting again the independent character envisioned by Jefferson, a pamphlet written in the early 1880s noted: "There is something fascinating in the idea of every man being his own rain-maker and being independent of shifting clouds and uncertain winds."[21]

Supporters of the Reclamation Act proclaimed it as a way to expand the empire, to provide a land base for a growing population, to preserve democratic institutions, and to mitigate class conflicts.[22] Reclamation of the West was presented as a national interest, one for the entire country to subsidize largely because of its benefits for democracy. As Smythe, one of the most ardent supporters of reclamation, proclaimed: *"The Nation reaches its hand into the Desert,* And lo! private monopoly in water and in land is scourged from that holiest of temples,—the place where men labor and build their homes!"[23] The greatest value of this irrigation society "would be the hundreds of millions of true, loyal American yeoman who would plant that glorious emblem of brotherly love, the stars and stripes, so deep and firm in that irrigated soil . . . secured by a government of the people, by the people and for the people, a true democracy."[24]

Sadly, history has not borne out the promises of these early pioneers of western water policy. The historian Donald Worster has made us aware of the relationship between large-scale irrigation and water supply projects and the concentration of wealth and power in the hands of a few. He argues that the vision of early reclamationists like William Smythe to unlock the stored riches of the centuries through the blessings of irrigation was terribly flawed. Instead of the egalitarian democratic society those who framed the Reclamation Act envisioned, the unequal distribution of the fruits of water has created fragmented bureaucratic structures that overwhelm ordinary citizens through expertise and control of information. Further, the fruits of federal largess have been unequally distributed, creating classes of advantaged citizens who see their exploitation of natural resources as a right, and other classes of people who are bitter and disinherited.

Western water resource development provides a classic example, although much the same story could be told about forests, minerals, and range. The Reclamation Service, an elite cadre of planners and engineers, believed that they could build water projects that would provide the resources fundamental to the small farmer with limited acreage; reclamation backers believed they could create the egalitarian societies of Jefferson's dreams. Once the early projects were built, however, federal officials found they could not hold out against local elites. Acreage limitations were manipulated, ignored, and ultimately greatly increased. Further, the geographic location of later projects increasingly reflected the distribution of political power, not social need or economic efficiency.[25] Fragmented federal water agencies, locked into competition among themselves, sought allies among the Madisonian-type interest groups who came to see government handouts as the spoils of political and economic victory. Rational planning became a rationalization for distributing water to the privileged, which exacerbated rather than narrowed economic and social differences.[26] According to Worster, the West has become a place of concentrated power, "though here, as in other places, power is often hidden behind beguiling masks."[27]

The service of national economic efficiency came to be the primary goal and cost-benefit analysis the necessary test of water projects. Economic benefits replaced any pretense of social or democratic purposes. Those able to produce the most with water, most likely those already able to turn a clear profit, could get into the pipeline for projects while those without the ability to demonstrate economic success could not. Further, economic tests were manipulated. Powerful congressional delegations united with local government officials, cities, and agribusiness to forcefully suggest that projects be redesigned until the numbers came out right.[28]

Expert analysis not only provided the emperors (i.e., the groups that benefited from federal development) with new clothes, it also endowed bureaucracy and professional networks with real power. While it would seem that professionals committed to the tenets of disciplines that include the fair and even-handed application of professional tests would serve as a bulwark against the domination of political power and deal making, professionals and interest groups have collaborated more often than not. In order to reveal their common interests, it is useful to examine first the rise of the bureaucratization, professionalism, and expert networks, then turn to the emergence of a politics of interests in the West.

Bureaucratization, Professionalism, and Expert Decision Making

Federal resource management efforts were heavily influenced by the Progressive Era. At the heart of the early conservation movement was a "gospel of efficiency," as termed by Samuel P. Hays.[29] Under this approach, aesthetics were subordinated to the utilitarian, the voice of the people subordinated to that of the expert. Pisani observes: "Foresters decided how much timber to cut each year; agronomists decided how many livestock the public grazing lands could support and hydrologists decided how much water was available and where to build reservoirs. The 'gospel of efficiency' replaced the gospel of political expediency."[30]

Under this resource philosophy, competing claims to resources were to be resolved through the "scientific calculation of material benefits."[31] This spirit of conservation placed an emphasis on large-scale capital organization, technology, central planning, and expert decision making.

However, under this approach, there was little concern for the role of people or for how democracy was to be fostered during this era. Instead, there was an underlying assumption that the net result of scientific planning would be a more democratic society. Gifford Pinchot suggested that resource management was to produce "the greatest good for the greatest number in the long run." Under this philosophy of resource management, the answer to the question of who is qualified to decide what is the greatest good is "professionally trained scientific resource managers."[32]

Paul Hirt calls this reliance on expert opinion and technology the "conspiracy of optimism"—infusions of technology, capital, and labor were seen as the answer to keeping production levels high and forest ecosystems intact.[33] However, this reliance on expert opinion has come to have profound consequences for the role of the public in political matters. According to Yankelovich:

> [Experts] assume that public opinion is of good quality when it agrees with their own views and of poor quality when it does not. The logic is this: they, the experts, are well informed; the public is poorly informed. Give the public more information, and it will agree with them. But what if even after being better informed, the public still does not agree? Rarely do the experts conclude that the public has a different point of view equally worthy of consideration.[34]

Self-governance is undermined by the increasing level of expertise in government.

Moreover, it is instrumental reasoning that drives decisions about resources, not democratic processes. Too often, there is an overwhelming use of rational decision making to the exclusion of other approaches that seek to recognize community values. Rational decision making is characterized by logical decision trees that lead to a single "best" decision.[35] Benefit-cost analysis, as has already been suggested, is often at odds with larger democratic principles.

A Politics of Interests

As the federal structure to manage resources in the West formed, a corollary politics of interests also emerged. This type of politics was in part encouraged by early federal policy, which offered free land, water, minerals, and lands for grazing to settlers. The underlying philosophy was one of unrestricted access and use. Across the West, attitudes developed equating federal property with personal property. Though federal subsidies and eastern money often underlay western resource development, many also viewed federal lands in provincial terms. As Representative Charles Taylor of Colorado once noted about grazing in the West: "We felt that was our . . . unrestricted right, to graze stock upon the free, open public domain."[36]

Much of this attitude was codified in law. Charles Wilkinson refers to the laws and policies that emerged during this period as the "Lords of Yesterday," arguing that laws which seemed sensible in a time when resources were believed to be inexhaustible are now outmoded and offer enclaves of protection and privilege to a few at the cost of devastated rangelands, denuded forested areas, and a loss of habitat.[37] He observes further, "The law is resolutely protective of established interests, and much of that protectionism is profoundly subtle. Too many of the rules lawyers learn by rote and sell as immutable truths to all the rest of the society are doctrines heavily tilted in favor of existing vested interests."[38]

Jeffersonian politics and early federal land policy envisioned a West peopled with yeoman farmers, building new communities in a large and open society.[39] Instead, we have a society where different interests are treated very differently, depending upon their ability to engage in the dominant expert exchange of information, their political and economic power, and the extent to which their interests are established and institutionalized. It is odd that the very groups who owe their present livelihood to past federal policies that provided roads, water, timber, minerals, range, and other resources to extractive industries at subsidized rates are those who often complain the most strongly to big government. What they are really objecting to, of course, is any alteration of the beneficiaries of federal power that would leave them less well-favored.

Further, federal agencies often promote divisiveness and polarization of interests because "in too many cases, they exert authority instead of sharing power."[40] Resource institutions in particular have been described as insular, hierarchical, focused on products, and protective of turf. Information about how resources should be managed rarely, if ever, flows up the hierarchy of the organization, or even from agency to agency. Further, interest groups interact with the agency and are not encouraged to engage in a dialogue among themselves or with members of the public. These distorted power relationships dominate government and are embedded in political institutions.

The dramatic increase in visibility and power of the environmental movement that became clear in the 1970s held out great promise for lessening the environmental damage and democratizing natural resources decision making. In all, over two dozen pieces of federal legislation, including the National Environmental Policy Act of 1969, the Clean Water Act, and the Federal Land Management and Policy Act of 1976, were passed during this period. These laws directly introduced environmental values into decision making about natural resources and opened up additional avenues for citizens to participate in those decisions.

However, managers and citizens alike have found many of the methods developed to meet public participation requirements lacking. Many efforts to include the public are merely formal exercises with little relationship to final outcomes. Ironically, this lack of public involvement serves to increase controversy because it forces interested parties to take extreme stands in order to be heard. Further, planning by agencies such as the U.S. Forest Service often does not encourage deliberation among diverse interests. Administrative review often removes contentious issues, the very issues that are rightly the subject of public deliberation, from the final report.[41]

The great majority of national environmental groups have adjusted to the dominance of expertise and interest-group driven politics by joining rather than attempting to change the political process. They have hired their own bureaucratic managers and scientific experts and carved out areas of special expertise in which they are regarded as legitimate participants in issue networks. Robert Gottlieb argues that while environmental groups have secured a place at the negotiating table and are now powerful organizations, "the interest group identity for mainstream environmentalism seems more entrenched than ever." Through lobbying, lawsuits, and appeals, these groups have strengthened the role of environmental values in federal decision making, but they have done little to build a sense of public deliberation. Gridlock and schisms between the national environmental groups and "alternative environmental groups, grassroots networks and community-based groups, as well as direct-action and more ideologically oriented 'green' organizations" is growing.[42]

Reinventing Democracy

Policies developed to manage the nation's federal lands are a wonderful lens through which to view not only the development of the western landscape, but also the development of American society, particularly long-standing patterns of politics. As this essay shows, the western political landscape has been shaped by a pull between elements of Jeffersonian democracy and Madisonian politics, with a politics based on vested interests predominating throughout much of the West's history. However, in recent years, community-based organizations dedicated to the protection and well-being of particular places are evidence that notions of Jeffersonian democracy are not lost or forgotten.

Many of these efforts share characteristics that reflect the tenets of democracy espoused by Jefferson. First, these efforts are grassroots, bottom-up efforts composed of neighbors, often taking the form of community organizations. Further, these groups are oriented toward action and show an ability to form networks with other groups and governmental entities. Greider notes the growth of pockets of democratic renewal across the nation, from the South Bronx to East Los Angeles. He observes a process that is Jeffersonian in character: "For them, democracy means building their own political organizations, drawing people together in a relationship that leads to a real political power. In a sense, they are reinventing democracy from the group up, starting in their own neighborhoods."[43] In the last five to seven years, there has been an explosion of such groups as the Arizona Riparian Council, the Friends of the Santa Cruz River, the Friends of the Columbia River Gorge, the Upper Rio Grande Consortium, the Sonoran Desert Alliance, and a host of other groups forming around local and regional concerns.

Across the West, neighbors are forming partnerships between themselves and with federal agencies, states, conservation organizations, and others to discuss environmental issues and work on restoration and improvement efforts.[44] In fact, the most successful efforts are those which involve the formation of "unlikely coalitions," grassroots groups that bring together diverse people with very different views about how land should be managed. These efforts to improve the landscape seek to define common interests and to institute programs that balance resource extraction activities with the protection of sensitive riparian areas and forests on both private and public lands. In addition, they build better relationships among a variety of individuals, groups, and agencies, seeking "to build bridges" between agency and nonagency people. Common to these endeavors is an effort to include all people with a concern for the land—from land owners to Indian tribes to governmental agencies and environmental groups—in the planning and management efforts.

While better scientific knowledge about the environment is undoubtedly essential, there is a de-emphasis on the role of the expert and more of an emphasis on public deliberation. Natural resource management, while grounded in ecological and other sciences, is as much of a social endeavor as it is a scientific endeavor. It is very much a political process, because the public itself must decide what value to place on issues surrounding natural resource management. It is a type of politics that starts with the people, and it is the relationships people build between themselves and with other mediating institutions and citizen groups that is the source of political power. Citizen groups and individual citizens become increasingly empowered by participating in decisions about resources when they realize their suggestions carry clout. Most significantly, though, public deliberation, rather than public participation, is slowly emerging in some communities. Spurred in part by necessity (as in the case of the Northwest logging communities) and in part because of love of remaining places in other areas, people are meeting on a community level to discuss what the future of the community should be. These efforts foster a sense of public deliberation much richer than opportunities offered through traditional public participation methods.

One of Jefferson's most enduring contributions to American political thought is his faith in the people to govern. He based American democracy on an informed public citizenry that could think, show sound ethics, use good judgment, and discern facts. Corollary to this faith came a deep understanding that each generation has the right to form its own political future. The unfinished revolution is left for each generation to determine their future. Caldwell observes that it was Jefferson's insistence upon "the need for the adaptability of law and institutions to the changing circumstances of society that is the clearest and most pertinent contribution of this thought to the present debate over land use policy and law."[45]

Another contribution of Jefferson is his belief in a sense of place, of the importance of the landscape in developing the young Republic of America. Jefferson and others who followed him believed that the hope of the American dream lay in the American landscape.[46] He looked to the West with hope and saw it as a place where American democracy could grow and place that could enhance and build the American republic. History, however, has shown that while law and politics have served well the aim of providing natural resources for economic development in the West, issues concerning democracy have been ignored or considered only in symbolic terms. Questions of fairness and the welfare of indigenous minorities have been disregarded. The loss of control over resources as much as loss of land has damaged democratic politics as well as rural cultures and the rich diversity so important to western society.

Jeffersonian qualities have been sadly lacking in modern political discourse. Expert decision making, politics of interests, and a lack of public deliberation over decisions about resources characterize western land management. However, the rise of community groups and the increase in citizen participation across the West is evidence of a new community-based politics. The partnerships that are being built across the West are fostering a growing sense of place, a sense of community. There is an awakening in the West coupled with a decline in Washington, an awakening that stems from communities and groups "who wish to protect a region they love from slipping from nature into McWorld."[47] Rejuvenating the tenets of Jeffersonian democracy so central to the founding of this country will require quite different patterns of politics than the politics of interest and the dominance of bureaucratic decision making; a growing emphasis on citizen participation and public deliberation must be encouraged.

NOTES

1. Henry Nash Smith, *Virgin Land: The American West as Symbol and Myth* (New York: Vintage Books, 1950), 15.

2. Richard K. Matthews *The Radical Politics of Thomas Jefferson: A Revisionist View* (Kansas: University Press of Kansas, 1984), 127. Not surprisingly, given the sheer volume of his writings and the contradictions sometimes contained in them, Jefferson has been subject to a number of sometimes competing interpretations. For example, Matthews argues that many scholars have erred in their characterization of Jefferson. He contends, for example, that Jefferson did not fear modernity and the future as J. G. A. Pocock claims, and that he was not heavily influenced by Locke as Drew R. McCoy claims. Matthews, as well as others, argues that Jeffersonian politics is a much more radical democratic politics than previously believed. See Pocock, *The Machiavellian Moment: Florentine Political Thought and the Atlantic Republican Tradition* (Princeton: Princeton University Press, 1975), 119, and McCoy, *The Elusive Republic: Political Economy in Jeffersonian America* (Chapel Hill: University of North Carolina Press, 1980), 11.

3. Quoted in Ralph Ketcham, *Individualism and Public Life* (New York: Basil Blackwell Inc., 1987).

4. Jefferson's embrace of revolution in politics was not shared by his contemporaries. He once noted: "I hold it that a little rebellion now and then is a good thing, and as necessary in the political world as storms in the physical" (quoted in Matthews, *Radical Politics of Thomas Jefferson*, 85).

5. Lynton K. Caldwell, *The Administrative Theories of Hamilton and Jefferson*, 2d ed. (New York: Holmes and Meier, 1988), 106.

6. Matthews, *Radical Politics of Thomas Jefferson*, 82–83.

7. Quoted in Caldwell, *Administrative Theories of Hamilton and Jefferson*, 120.

8. Quoted in Matthews, *Radical Politics of Thomas Jefferson*, 82–83.

9. Quoted in David Mathews, *Politics for People: Finding a Responsible Public Voice* (Chicago: University of Illinois Press, 1994), 106.

10. Quoted in Kemmis, *Community and the Politics of Place*, 11.

11. Thomas Jefferson, "Observations on Meusnier's Article," January 22, 1786, in Andrew

A. Lipscomb and Albert Ellery Bergh, eds., *The Writings of Thomas Jefferson* (Washington, D.C.: Thomas Jefferson Memorial Association of the United States, 1903–4), 4:158–87.

12. James Madison, *Federalist Paper* No. 10, in Alexander Hamilton, James Madison, and John Jay, *The Federalist Papers* (1788; rprt., New York: Anchor Books, 1961), 30.

13. Lovejoy, *Reflections on Human Nature*, 49, 54. According to Lovejoy, Madison regarded economic self-interest as the driving force of men's actions and he "had *no* 'faith in the people' as *individuals* acting in their political capacity" (51, Lovejoy's emphasis). This view of human nature was shared by many of Madison's contemporaries, including Hamilton and Adams.

14. *Federalist Papers* No. 10, 33. Kemmis, *Community and the Politics of Place*, notes that Hegel offered another perspective by arguing that he believed that it was not until the American frontier closed, and America had no more room to expand, that a republic would begin to form in America. Hegel regarded the availability of large open space as making it possible for America to postpone developing a strong sense of politics.

15. Paul Rahe, *Republics: Ancient and Modern* (Chapel Hill: University of North Carolina Press, 1993), 734.

16. Kemmis, *Community and the Politics of Place*, 12.

17. It was commonly held during this time that republics, which require a great deal of interaction among the citizenry, must be small. Jefferson, however, argued "that, contrary to the principle of Montesquieu, it will be seen that the larger the extent of country, the more firm its republican structure" (quoted in Rahe, *Republics*, 743).

18. Caldwell, *Administrative Theories of Hamilton and Jefferson*, xix.

19. Richard White, *It's Your Misfortune and None of My Own: A New History of the American West* (Norman: University of Oklahoma Press, 1993), 57.

20. William E. Smythe, *The Conquest of Arid America* (London: The McMillan and Co., Ltd., 1907), xviii.

21. Quoted in Donald J. Pisani, *To Reclaim a Divided West: Water, Law, and Public Policy, 1848–1902* (Albuquerque: University of New Mexico Press, 1992), 73.

22. Ibid., 293.

23. Smythe, *The Conquest of Arid America*, viii.

24. Quoted in Pisani, *To Reclaim a Divided West*, 293.

25. Wallace Stegner, *The American West as Living Space* (Ann Arbor: University of Michigan Press, 1987), 36–37.

26. Helen Ingram, *Water Politics: Continuity and Change* (Albuquerque: University of New Mexico Press, 1990); updated version of *The Patterns of Politics on Water Resources: The Case of New Mexico's Role in The Colorado River Basin Bill* (Albuquerque: Institute of Government Resources, University of New Mexico Press, 1969).

27. Donald Worster, *Under Western Skies: Nature and History in the American West* (New York: Oxford University Press, 1992), 15.

28. Ingram, *Water Politics*.

29. Samuel Hays, *Conservation and the Gospel of Efficiency: The Progressive Conservation Movement* (Cambridge: Harvard University Press, 1959).

30. Pisani, *To Reclaim a Divided West*, 330.

31. Hays, *Conservation and the Gospel of Efficiency*, 249.

32. Philip Foss, "Introduction: Public Land Policy," in *Federal Lands Policy* (Wesport, Conn.: Greenwood Press, 1987), xiii.

33. Paul Hirt, *A Conspiracy of Optimism: Management of the National Forests since World War Two* (Lincoln: University of Nebraska Press, 1994), 293.

34. Yankelovich, *Coming to Public Judgement*, 17.

35. Mary Kweit and Robert Kweit, "The Politics of Policy Analysis: The Role of Citizen Participation in Analytic Decision-making," in Jack Desario and Stuart Langton, eds., *Citizen Participation in Public Decision-Making* (Wesport, Conn.: Greenwood Press, 1987), 19–37.

36. Quoted in W. Voigt, *Public Grazing Lands: Use and Misuse by Industry and Government* (New Brunswick: Rutgers University Press, 1976), 249.

37. Charles Wilkinson, *Crossing the Next Meridian: Land, Water, and the Future of the West* (Washington, D.C.: Island Press, 1992).

38. Charles Wilkinson, *The Eagle Bird: Mapping a New West* (New York: Vintage, 1993), 14.

39. Jefferson warned against the power of financial interests as well. In a letter to President Washington in 1792, he described the political divisions that were forming in the country and urged Washington to form a political party "to rally against the corrupt ambitions of monied interests" (quoted in William Greider, *Who Will Tell the People: The Betrayal of American Democracy* [New York: Simon and Schuster, 1993], 246). He argued further that Federalist financial interests were corrupting Congress and that the people's right to govern themselves was compromised (ibid., 434, n. 1).

40. J. Sirmon., W. E. Shands, and C. Liggett, "Communities of Interests and Open Decision-Making," *Journal of Forestry* 91, no. 7 (1993): 17.

41. Dale J. Blahna and Susan Yonts-Shepard, "Public Involvement in Resource Planning: Toward Bridging the Gap between Policy and Implementation," *Society and Natural Resources* 2, no. 3 (1988): 209–27.

42. Robert Gottlieb, *Forcing the Spring: The Transformation of the American Environmental Movement* (Washington, D.C.: Island Press, 1993), 317.

43. Greider, *Who Will Tell the People*, 222.

44. For examples, see: Doc Hatfield and Connie Hatfield, "Solutions for the Land and People," in *Riparian Management Strategies: Common Threads and Shared Interests*, General Technical Report RM-226, USFS Publication, 147-53; J. Caffrey and J. Rivers, "The Bluewater Creek Story: Rebuilding a Land Ethic," in ibid.; Julia M. Wondolleck and Steven L. Yaffe, *Building Bridges across Agency Boundaries: In Search of Excellence in the United States Forest Service*, research report submitted to the USDA-Forest Service, Pacific Northwest Research Station, in fulfillment of USDA Agreement #PNW 92-0215, 1994.

45. Lynton K. Caldwell, "Rights of Ownership or Rights of Use—The Need for a New Conceptual Basis for Land Use Policy," *William and Mary Law Review* 15, no. 4 (summer 1974): 759–75.

46. D. Cosgrove, *Social Formation and Symbolic Landscape* (London: Croom Helm, 1984), 175–80.

47. Mark Sagoff, "Settling America or the Concept of Place in Environmental Ethics," *Journal of Energy, Natural Resources and Environmental Law* 12 (1992), 374.

MAP 3. "A MAP OF LEWIS AND CLARK'S TRACK ACROSS THE WESTERN PORTION OF NORTH AMERICA FROM THE MISSISSIPPIE TO THE PACIFIC OCEAN BY ORDER OF THE EXECUTIVE OF THE UNITED STATES IN 1804, 5, & 6." BY SAMUEL LEWIS, 1814, FROM AN ORIGINAL DRAWING BY WILLIAM CLARK, 1810. REPRODUCED IN CARL I. WHEAT, *Mapping the Transmississippi West: 1540–1861*, VOL. 2, *From Lewis and Clark to Fremont: 1804–1845* (SAN FRANCISCO: THE INSTITUTE OF HISTORICAL CARTOGRAPHY, 1958). MISSOURI HISTORICAL SOCIETY LIBRARY.

The Lewis and Clark Track Map amounts to a visual encyclopedia of the American West. The map's imperial message is plain: the West should be part of the United States, no matter what other contenders say. Native nations find their place on this map, but what counts is the lay of the land, not its original inhabitants. This map offers a vision of expansive, unitary geography equal to Jefferson's own territorial reach.

CHAPTER SIX

THOMAS JEFFERSON, MISSOURI, AND THE "EMPIRE FOR LIBERTY"

PETER S. ONUF

JEFFERSON'S MISSOURI CRISIS

In his retirement years, Thomas Jefferson sought to extricate himself from the political controversies of the day. Pleading ill health, he told James Donaldson in February 1820 that he was "obliged to withdraw my attention from every thing beyond the walls of my chamber, and particularly from politics."[1] The impulse to retreat from public affairs may have reflected growing discomfort with the causes advocated by Donaldson, a protectionist, and other latter-day "Jeffersonians." Jefferson had always found conflict distasteful, even when leading—or inspiring—the crusade against the "monocrats" and "aristocrats" who had held sway during the Federalist ascendancy in the 1790s. Surely the great battle had been won, and the enemies of republican government had been routed. Jefferson did not want to hear that his political heirs were deeply divided on fundamental questions, such as the tariff, banks, internal improvements, foreign policy; much less would he be willing to take a part in their unseemly squabbling.

Yet one issue did draw Jefferson out, even as he proclaimed his withdrawal from politics. In February 1819, during the waning days of the second session of the 15th Congress, Representative James Tallmadge, Jr., of New York proposed an amendment to a bill providing for Missouri's admission to the union that would have banned slavery in the new state.[2] Though Jefferson could have followed the unfolding controversy in the *Richmond Enquirer*—the only newspaper he subscribed to at this time—he remained silent on the slavery restriction question until December. By then its ominous implications had become all too clear. "I am so completely withdrawn from all attention to public matters," he wrote his old friend Hugh Nelson in March, "that nothing less could [have] arouse[d] me than the definition of a geographical line, which on an abstract principle is to become the line of separation of these States, and to render desperate the hope that man can ever enjoy the two blessings of peace and self-government."[3] Jefferson characterized the controversy as "a fire-bell in the night" that had forced him out of his domestic repose, thus confessing to his own failure to grasp its significance—as he slept through its early phases—and his belated recognition that everything he had struggled to achieve in his political career was suddenly at risk.[4]

Jefferson's aversion to conflict is apparent in the conciliatory and concessive tone that characterizes most of his correspondence.[5] But his letters on Missouri betray no equivocation, no willingness to palliate differences, no concession that the restrictionists might be acting in good faith, no awareness that northern friends might share their scruples. Jefferson first broached the Missouri issue with John Adams in a letter of December 10, 1819, responding to Adams' of November 23. Adams had predicted that the coming session of Congress would produce "thunder and Lightning" on various fronts—including the Spanish treaty ceding Florida (but affirming Spanish dominion over Texas), the manufacturers' campaign for protection, "the plague of Banks," and the question of slavery in Missouri, all complicated by "the bustle of Caucuses for the approaching" presidential election.[6] Barely pausing to salute his old friend, Jefferson impatiently discounted the importance of every issue Adams had raised *except* for Missouri. "These are occurences which like waves in a storm will pass under the ship," he wrote. "But the Missouri question is a breaker on which we lose the Missouri country by revolt, and what more, God only knows."

For Jefferson, who characteristically invoked nautical imagery in times of acute stress, "breakers" conjured fundamental threats to the ship of state, a more profound crisis than the American Revolution itself.[7] "From the battle of Bunker's hill," *before* Jefferson had written the Declaration of Independence, "to the treaty of Paris we never had so ominous a question."[8] In effect, Jefferson suggested, the restrictionists had reversed the course of American history, making a mockery and jest of his own life's work, and returning the United States to that critical period when independence and union remained visionary projections. The "sons" had betrayed the Revolutionary "fathers," Jefferson explained to John Holmes, a former representative from the Maine District of Massachusetts who had supported Missouri's admission in order to promote the district's statehood ambitions—and in defiance of his constituents' pronounced anti-slavery sentiments. "I regret that I am now to die in the belief, that the useless sacrifice of themselves by the generation of 1776, to acquire self-government and happiness to their country, is to be thrown away by the unwise and unworthy passions of their sons."9

Complicated negotiations in Congress culminated in the famous compromise measures of March 1820, authorizing free Maine as well as slaveholding Missouri to draft state constitutions and banning slavery in the remainder of the Louisiana Purchase Territory north of 36°30′ (an extension of Missouri's southern boundary). Congressional controversy flared again in November, however, after Missouri submitted a constitution that prohibited the immigration of free blacks and mulattos into the new state. The tenuous compromise was saved only when Henry Clay devised a new formula, adopted by Congress on March 3, 1821, requiring Missourians to agree that the offensive provision would not be construed in a way that violated the claims of any U.S. citizen to "Privileges and Immunities" in the new state under Article IV, Section 2 of the federal Constitution.

On January 22, 1821, while restrictionists still struggled to block Missouri's admission, Jefferson wrote again to Adams. For conspiracy-minded observers like Jefferson, this second phase of the Missouri controversy was in some ways more ominous than the first: restrictionists would stop at nothing in their campaign to obliterate states' rights and destroy the union. "Our anxieties in this quarter," he reported, "are all concentrated in the question[,] What does the *Holy alliance,* in and out of Congress, mean to do with us on the Missouri question?"10 The identification of anti-Missouri forces with the "Holy alliance," the league of reactionary sovereigns who sought to enforce an antirepublican, counterrevolutionary settlement in Europe, was no mere rhetorical flourish. For Jefferson, the restrictionists' pretended solicitude for the welfare of the slaves was as transparently fraudulent as the cause of "legitimacy" in Europe: the Missouri controversy "is not a moral question," he had written Lafayette in December, "but one merely of power."11

Jefferson shared the prevailing view in his "quarter" that "the Missouri question is a mere party trick," a desperate ploy by Federalists to foster and exploit sectional divisions over slavery to resurrect their moribund and disgraced party.12 But Jefferson moved quickly beyond politics to what he considered the heart of the issue. "The real question, as seen in the states afflicted with this unfortunate population, is[,] Are our slaves to be presented with freedom and a dagger?" The same power that Congress assumed to dictate statehood terms to Missourians would be invoked to free the slaves. Because southerners would never submit to this degradation, the union would be dissolved—perhaps, in every essential sense, it already was—and a struggle for power ("another Peloponnesian war to settle the ascendancy among them") inevitably would ensue. "Or," Jefferson asked his old friend, "is this the tocsin of merely a servile war?" Jefferson again imagined his own death, hoping that he and Adams would not live to witness the carnage: "Surely they will parley awhile, and give us time to get out of the way."[13]

Jefferson's stand on Missouri has proven an embarrassment for modern admirers, an occasion for righteous moralizing by his critics, and a confusing combination of the two for everyone else. John Chester Miller strikes a characteristic note, concluding that "the Missouri dispute seemed to mark the strange death of Jeffersonian liberalism."[14] In no respect was this fall from grace more conspicuous than on the issue of slavery restriction. For it was Jefferson himself, in his draft of the Territorial Government Ordinance of 1784, who proposed to ban slavery from the new western states.[15]

My goal in this essay is neither to exonerate Jefferson nor to explain away his stand on Missouri. Instead, I want to offer a broader interpretation of Jefferson's political philosophy, and of his ideas about western political development, that will show that the agonies Jefferson suffered over efforts to block the admission of the new state of Missouri reflected fundamental tensions in American liberalism during its formative years. They resulted from his understanding of, and commitment to, the principle of equality, the foundational principle of his "Empire of Liberty." Jefferson did not retreat from a commitment to civil liberties, or embrace a notion of states' rights in order to defend the interests of southern slaveholders. From the very beginning of his political life, Jefferson recognized the central importance of the autonomy, integrity, and *equality* of republics as corporate entities—as well as of the republican institutions that alone could guarantee the equal rights of self-governing individuals within the new states. The 1784 ordinance was a bill of rights for new western states, and its lasting significance was to establish new state equality—incorporated in the Northwest Ordinance of July 13, 1787—as the fundamental principle of an expanding federal republic.

Beginning with the Missouri controversy and moving backward, I shall explain how Jefferson's conception of a powerful and perpetual union was a casualty of its own logic, as well as of the more familiar sectional division over slavery extension. As with so many other aspects of Jefferson's thought, the story begins—or should I say, ends?—with a paradox. The survival and prosperity of Jefferson's "Empire of Liberty" depended on disentangling and distinguishing America from Europe, freedom-loving Republicans from vicious and corrupt sovereigns and subjects. Before 1819, Jefferson had every reason to think that the great federal republican experiment would be a success, and that the frontier against Europe and European influences would become progressively more secure. The events of 1819–21 challenged this complacency in fundamental ways. Jefferson was increasingly hard-pressed to define the difference between foreigners and fellow Americans—and increasingly conscious of the "geographical line" that separated Americans from each other.

"The idea of a geographical line once suggested will brood in the minds of all those who prefer the gratification of their ungovernable passions to the peace and union of their country," Jefferson wrote Massachusetts congressman Mark Langdon Hill in April 1820.[16] This "idea" was that fundamental differences of interest—and principle—divided Americans, making them foreigners to each other. No longer restrained by bonds of union, the disunited states would find themselves in a state of war, governed only by their "passions." Jefferson, the prophet of intractable sectional divisions, thus anticipated the American Civil War. What he saw was an image of Europe, the negation of everything the new nation stood for, and "treason against the hopes of the world."

Jefferson's dilemma was that he was not simply a witness to these terrifying developments, but a participant in them. No one had a more portentous sense of what was at risk: nothing less than the survival and success of the great experiment in republican government that Jefferson's Declaration had helped launch in 1776. Yet no one felt more keenly the sense of sectional grievance, the "renewing irritations" that "kindle[d] such mutual and mortal hatred" and unleashed such "angry passions." Jefferson could plumb the depth of such feelings because he shared them; he knew that the union he cherished was in jeopardy because he could not stop himself from imagining its destruction. It is hardly surprising that Jefferson, torn between the need to preserve the Revolutionary fathers' great achievement and the irresistible impulse to demolish it, should speak of "suicide"—or that he should displace this death wish, or murderous impulse, onto others: the rising generation, with its "unwise and unworthy passions," or the dangerous demagogues beyond the "geographical line," who "have ever had in view [the union's] . . . separation."[17]

For Jefferson, liberty and union were inextricable: the destruction of one necessarily entailed the destruction of the other. It was only by sustaining the federal republic that the essential distinction between Europe and America could be sustained. This was the fundamental "geographical line" the American Revolutionaries had established between Old World and New World: the line Jefferson had extended to the west through the Louisiana Purchase and that Madison had recently vindicated in the War of 1812, the second war for American independence; in the wake of the Spanish Empire's collapse, this was the "meridian of partition through the ocean which separates the two hemispheres."[18] But as the line between North and South appeared so suddenly, and in such heightened contrast, that other line dimmed to the point of disappearing.

The connection between the Missouri crisis and Jefferson's conception of the global significance of the American Revolution became clear during the interval between the two phases of the crisis, in the summer and fall of 1820. Jefferson could then confidently reaffirm that "the principles of society" in Europe and America "are radically different."[19] The escalating pattern of sectional grievance might be irreversible, but Jefferson now imagined that destructive passions would be spent in the process of its demolition: the "traitors" would then come to their senses, recognizing that their real interests, rightly understood, depended on founding a new and more durable union.

Northern leaders might think that they had established "a line of separation" between slavery and freedom in the West, Jefferson wrote South Carolina congressman Charles Pinckney in September, but they would discover a "very different" line if they did not abandon their campaign against southern institutions and the union disintegrated: "as manufacturing and navigating States, they will have quarrelled with their bread and butter." Yet if the northerners' rational calculations of interest provoked sober second thoughts, the impulse to reunion would reflect their better natures. "After a little trial they will think better" of separation, Jefferson confidently predicted, "and return to the embraces of their natural and best friends."[20]

Jefferson imagined this happy reconciliation of the sectional crisis—the counterpoint to the themes of death and destruction that dominate earlier and subsequent correspondence on Missouri—in more extravagant, and revealing, language when in October he wrote to Richard Rush, the American minister at the Court of St. James' in London and son of Jefferson's old, now deceased friend, Benjamin Rush. Should the "schism be pushed to separation, it will be for a short term only," he told Rush: "two or three years' trial will bring them back, like quarrelling lovers to renewed embraces, and increased affections." The emphasis on affective and affectionate ties, on a sentimentalized conception of bonds of union—joined by God, and which no man (or foreign power) dare put asunder—spoke to the fundamental premise of Jeffersonian social and political theory. Liberty and equality of the contracting parties, whether individuals or states (in this case, the new state of Missouri), were the essential preconditions of true and lasting union. Only by securing this equality—defined as the absence of any external coercion or control—could lasting commitments and obligations be voluntarily undertaken, and the passions that fostered social harmony be given full scope.

Yet Jefferson could not sustain this optimistic gloss on the Missouri question in the face of renewed congressional controversy (over the new state's constitution), his irrepressible animus against his Yankee tormentors, and his anxieties about emancipation and servile insurrection. Jefferson's misgivings were already apparent in the letter to Rush, as he speculated on what the controversy might look like from the European perspective. Even if "the experiment of separation" should result in a stronger union, the immediate effect would be to reinforce the contempt of the European powers for republican government:

> Were we to break to pieces, it would damp the hopes and the efforts of the good, and give triumph to those of the bad through the whole enslaved world. As members, therefore, of the universal society of mankind, and standing in high and responsible relation with them, it is our sacred duty to suppress passion among ourselves, and not to blast the confidence we have inspired of proof that a government of reason is better than one of force.[21]

Jefferson could not pretend that the "passions" of his countrymen were any different from the passions that moved the despots and destroyers of Europe. He could only hope that Americans would return to their senses, and to first principles, once the damage had been done. In the meantime, the new nation's example would no longer inspire the "whole enslaved world." The crucial line of distinction between New World and Old—the premise of Jefferson's statecraft and the practical test of his political philosophy—had ceased to exist.

Jefferson's cosmopolitan perspective reinforced his sense of the significance of union, and the agony he experienced in imagining its demise. From this perspective, the union was an integral whole, just as the Americans constituted a single people. To acknowledge fundamental differences among Americans—differences that would make a durable union impossible—was to acknowledge that Americans were no different than Europeans. This was another way of saying that republican governments, and the republican "character" they presumably fostered in the people at large, could not preserve peace and harmony in America: the states could guarantee neither their own existence as republics, nor the integrity of the American people as an all-embracing union of liberty-loving Republicans.

Jefferson was convinced that securing the sovereignty and equality of the respective states—for him, the central issue of the Missouri controversy—was the essential condition for guaranteeing republican government and promoting a durable union. Disunion could only be attributed to the restrictionists' contemptuous disregard for that essential condition, and to the political ambitions that lurked beneath their self-righteous "Jeremiads on the miseries of slavery."[22] Thus far, Jefferson's formulation of the problem echoed arguments of anti-restrictionists in Congress and the press who projected the entire responsibility for the crisis onto their partisan opponents, beyond the "geographical line." Yet if Jefferson had convinced himself of his and his region's blamelessness, he had—from the cosmopolitan perspective that made the American Revolution meaningful for him as an epochal event in world history—proven far too much. For if the restrictionists were such obdurate opponents of state equality, and if this were the fundamental premise of the federal system, then it was hard to envision any future circumstances in which union with them would be possible.

When the restrictionists cynically exploited "the virtuous feelings" of northerners who opposed slavery, they linked "a marked principle, moral and political, with a geographical line," and that line, "once conceived, I feared would never more be obliterated from the mind."[23] The projection of a line that threatened to reduce the southern states to a subordinate, minority status under a "consolidated" federal regime unleashed Jefferson's boundless hatred for his northern enemies. Such hatred, he knew, had embroiled Europe in a neverending sequence of bloody wars, and the very existence of such feelings constituted a definitive refutation of his gospel of love in affectionate union. In imagining northerners as foreigners, he obliterated the line between Europe and America, and so became complicit in the very "treason against the hopes of the world" with which he charged the rising generation.[24]

UNION AND DISUNION

Jefferson's idealized conception of the American union prepared the way for his radical disillusionment during the Missouri crisis. Jefferson was convinced that the axioms of European political science did not apply in America. From the European perspective, the size of the American republic was its greatest liability. As the new nation projected its authority across the continent, republican institutions would have to be jettisoned in favor of the despotic forms that enabled the great European kingdoms to rule far-flung subject populations; otherwise, the proliferation of new states would strain the bonds of union to an early breaking point, and an American system of disunited sovereignties would soon be indistinguishable from its European prototype. But Jefferson turned this familiar logic inside out, insisting that the states' republican constitutions and their equal standing under the federal compact would secure perpetual peace. "Contrary to the principle of Montesquieu," he told an old European friend in 1817, "it will be seen that the larger the extent of country, the more firm its republican structure, if founded, not on conquest, but in principles of compact and equality."[25] State "equality," the formal capacity to engage in the compact, was the essential condition for creating a true union; as long as the federal government upheld that fundamental principle, the union would endure.[26]

Jefferson's thinking about the nature of the federal union could be as confusing to his contemporaries as it has been to subsequent commentators. "Union," the affectionate embrace of like-minded individuals or states, was in his more extravagant formulations indistinguishable from "disunion," the protean condition of equals who, in their uncoerced and independent condition, were alone capable of such affectionate engagements. This conflation of union and disunion, whole and parts, was most conspicuous in Jefferson's most confident and optimistic moments, as, for instance, when he looked toward the emergence of "a great, free and independent empire" on the Pacific coast. Let republican institutions be planted there, he wrote John Jacob Astor in 1813, and it hardly mattered that—at this point—there would be no formal, constitutional connection with the Atlantic states, for it would inevitably follow that "liberty and self-government" would spread "from that as well as this side" until "their complete establishment over the whole." The crucial thing was to keep the English, with their "habitual hostility to every degree of freedom," from interfering with Astor's settlement on the Columbia River.[27]

Jefferson's casual attitude toward union among American Republicans was thus counterpointed by his anxieties about European interference. Europeans—English in the Northwest, or French in the Mississippi valley—could alone Europeanize American politics, exporting their balance of power (or, rather, terror) to their imperial outposts on the American continent and enlisting credulous Americans in their unholy alliances. An extraordinary letter to John Breckinridge in August 1803—written after the successful negotiation of terms with Napoleon for the purchase of Louisiana, but before Senate ratification of the purchase treaty—best illuminates Jefferson's paradoxical thinking. Responding to Federalist predictions that the overextended union would collapse, with disastrous consequences, Jefferson insisted that there was no reason for the "Atlantic States" to "dread" the separation of the "nations" on the "western waters":

The future inhabitants of the Atlantic and Mississippi States will be our sons. We leave them in distinct but bordering establishments. We think we see their happiness in their union, and we wish it. Events may prove it otherwise; and if they see their interest in separation, why should we take side with our Atlantic rather than our Mississippi descendants.[28]

Jefferson could be sanguine about the prospects of disunion because it would *not* bring into existence new nations that would be "hostile" to each other, as were England and France. Indeed, it was only because "the French nation" had been so suddenly, even miraculously, dislodged from New Orleans, that Jefferson could assume this disinterested, benevolent posture about the political future of the West.[29] Whether or not they chose to remain in the union, westerners would not be foreigners: they would be our "descendants," bound to us—and to each other—by "relations of blood [and] affection." Their "happiness" was in a profound, almost genealogical, sense *our* happiness: recognizing this, their eastern fathers and brethren would never attempt to preserve a political connection by force of arms.[30]

Jefferson's theory of union rested on the same premises and was in a fundamental sense indistinguishable from his notions of intergenerational equity.[31] The development of Jefferson's political philosophy and his plans for educating Virginia's youth were closely linked. Spending on education constituted the grand and significant exception to Jefferson's minimal state, for this was precisely the kind of public investment that would foster the welfare of the rising generation without wasting its future prospects.[32] Jefferson's most elaborate discussion of the character of the federal union emerged out of his proposals for a three-tiered school system in Virginia, and the implications he drew from these proposals for reforming the state's constitution. His projected "ward republics," as he explained to Joseph Cabell and Samuel Kercheval in 1816, would simultaneously provide for the schooling of young people and the political education of their fathers through active participation. Not surprisingly, these letters are the canonical texts for theorists who celebrate Jefferson as a "strong democrat." Yet they also, and not coincidentally, constitute his most systematic effort to divide and subdivide authority, and they did so in ways that called into question the very possibility of government itself.

For Jefferson, the necessary condition of an active citizenry was equality, defined as noninterference and the absence of coercion by other citizens situated at the same level in the ascending hierarchy of authorities, or by any "higher" authority that should seek to exceed its strictly delegated powers.[33] Jefferson's most schematic elaboration of his "gradation of authorities" can found in his letter to Kercheval of July 12, 1816:

> We should thus marshal our government into, 1, the general federal republic, for all concerns foreign and federal; 2, that of the State, for what relates to our own citizens exclusively; 3, the county republics, for the duties and concerns of the county; and 4, the ward republics, for the small, and yet numerous and interesting concerns of the neighborhood;

and in government, as well as in every other business in life, it is by division and subdivision of duties alone, that all matters, great and small, can
be managed to perfection. And the whole is cemented by giving to every
citizen, personally, a part in the administration of the public affairs.[34]

He might have added, as he did in his earlier letter to Cabell, that his system
finally "ends in the administration of every man's farm by himself," thus
constituting a comprehensive theory linking individual rights to a federal
constitutional design.[35]

The notion of layered authorities was hardly original with Jefferson; it can
be traced through Madisonian federal theory to classical antecedents.[36] What is
most notable about Jefferson's formulation, however, is the way the entire
scheme is infused with, and transformed by, liberal premises.[37] Every successive level of association is called a "republic," suggesting that, according to
its respective purposes, each government at every level is complete and self-
sufficient. *Equality* is the operative term, and for Jefferson that term was naturally equated with *sovereignty*. Thus, just as Jefferson's conception of ascending
layers made possible the conflation or confusion of individual rights (the
familiar liberal notion of "equality") with the rights of corporate associations
(the equality of states, the foundational premise of liberal internationalism, or
the equality of counties or wards), so too conventional notions of sovereignty
could move down through these layers.

Jefferson's confusion about Federalism—was it a scheme of government,
securing a complex division of authority along a vertical axis? or was it the
elective affinity or affectionate union of state sovereignties, distributed spatially
along a horizontal axis and acknowledging no authoritative superior?—is of
much more than theoretical interest. It was his persistent tendency to distinguish true "union" from the design and structure of the federal government
itself and so to conceptualize relations among states and regions in the liberal
language of sovereignty that led him, during the dark days of the Missouri
crisis, to project a "geographical line" across his beloved union—and so imagine its destruction, and wish his own death.

In the course of discussing and defending the three-fifths clause in one of his
letters to Kercheval—four years before the "knell of the Union" aroused him
from his slumbers—Jefferson showed how easy it would be to take that imaginative leap into the abyss. In Connecticut only "freemen" who met a property
qualification and were "admitted by a vote of the freemen of the town" could
exercise the full rights of citizenship. Nonetheless, Connecticut's representation in the House of Representatives was computed according to its entire
population. "So, slaves with us [in Virginia] have no powers as citizens,"

Jefferson explained; "yet, in representation in the General Government, they count in the proportion of three to five." Others might well complain about this manifest inequity, but the agreement on representation was a sacred compact, a pillar of the existing union, and Jefferson would not tamper with it. Nor would he question the wisdom of Connecticut's suffrage exclusions. "In truth," he concluded, "the condition of different descriptions of inhabitants in any country is a matter of municipal arrangement, of which no foreign country has a right to take notice."[38]

Here was the hallowed principle of noninterference, the hallmark of liberal internationalism, and the only effectual guarantee of peaceful relations among independent states. Here too, casually and reflexively, Jefferson could speak of his "country" (Virginia) and of the "foreign" countries that together constituted the "General Government." It was no accident that when Jefferson identified a specific "foreign country" it should be Connecticut, one of the last bastions of Federalist strength and a place where English influence was still palpable, if—he then thought—no longer to be feared.

DESTROYING NEW ENGLAND

The identification of slavery restrictionists with the "Holy alliance" came easily to Jefferson. As the Republicans strengthened their hold on the national government after the "Revolution of 1800," Jefferson saw his Federalist opponents as sectionalists who sought to destroy the union and forge an alliance with their secret British sponsors. During the last days of the War of 1812, New England Federalists gathered at Hartford to consider the possibility of separation or a separate peace with Britain. Though they finally backed away from these extreme measures, the Hartford Federalists stood condemned as traitors when the administration's diplomatic efforts brought the war to a sudden and welcome conclusion.[39] Jefferson exulted in his opponents' disgrace, but worried about their future moves. In the event of another war, desperate Federalists would not hesitate to seek foreign support, and the defeat of Napoleon meant that a Holy Alliance of European legitimists could now direct its united energies against republican America. During the Missouri debates, antirestrictionist Republicans repeatedly invoked the Hartford Convention in order to link restriction with Federalism, and both with traitorous designs against the union. Given continuing anxieties about the new nation's security and misgivings about European intentions, the equations of the Congress of Vienna and the "Congress" at Hartford or of the Holy Alliance in Europe and the campaign against slavery in Missouri did not seem as far-fetched then as they do now. For Jefferson, it was not simply a question of plausible, rhetorically effective parallels, but rather of a dangerous new alignment of antirepublican forces.[40] The "geographical line" that the restrictionists imposed on the new nation inevitably would dissolve the union and so enable the "Hartford nation" to enter into alliance with like-minded Europeans.

Jefferson conducted his war against the Federalists on two fronts. The vindication of American independence and recognition of its equal standing in the family of nations meant that foreign powers would no longer presume to interfere in its domestic politics. (For Jefferson, this principle was equally crucial in his indictments of restrictionists in the Missouri crisis and of the interference of the Holy Alliance in the domestic affairs of other European states.[41]) Meanwhile, the triumph of Republicans at the polls would complete the Federalists' isolation, demonstrating conclusively the futility of further foreign efforts to "anarchise us."[42] One-party rule was the sine qua non of union and the best guarantee against foreign interference.

Jefferson's attitudes toward New England revolved around calculations of the relative strength of the Federalists there and of the prospects for recruiting moderates into the republican ranks. At moments of political crisis—when New Englanders resisted the ill-fated embargo, or failed to rally enthusiastically to the American cause during the War of 1812, or presumed to interfere in the domestic affairs of Missouri in the controversy over slavery restriction—Jefferson was hard-pressed to sustain the conventional and comforting distinction between malignant leaders and their deluded followers. Jefferson had emphasized this distinction between leaders and followers in his inaugural address, when he urged that those "among us who would wish to dissolve this Union or to change its republican form" be left to "stand undisturbed as monuments of the safety with which error of opinion may be tolerated where reason is left free to combat it."[43] Following Jefferson's script, the Republicans routed "error of opinion" in every quarter of the union and demolished the Federalists as a viable national party. But the destruction of the "Essex Federalists" was not yet complete when the outbreak of war with Britain gave them a new lease on life.[44] As a result, Jefferson began to imagine a more sanguinary, less principled sort of "combat" against his old Federalist foes.

Jefferson's ruminations about the fate of New England during the War of 1812 prefigured his response to the Missouri crisis. In both cases, advocates of dangerously unrepublican principles held sway within a specific geographical region; having lost their national base of support, these unreconstructed "monarchists" exploited sectionalist grievances in order to prepare the way for disunion and foreign alliances. Yet, despite these apparent parallels, Jefferson's response to the earlier crisis was profoundly different. In 1813 and 1814 Jefferson welcomed a war with the New England Federalists that he knew the loyal republican states would easily win. The subsequent restoration of the union, purified of the last vestiges of monarchical corruption, would redeem the promise of the American Revolution.

In September 1813, Jefferson outlined the steps that could lead to a war between the states and then to a predictably happy outcome. War undoubtedly could be averted, and Federalists be driven from power by less violent means, if the people of Massachusetts were given the opportunity to "declare themselves members of the Union, and obedient to its determinations:" "put this question solemnly to their people, and their answer cannot be doubtful." The "people"—by whom Jefferson meant that half of the electorate generally inclined to support republican candidates—would be decisively augmented by the "dispassionate part" of "the federal moiety": moderate Federalists would recognize that the state's "vital interests" depended on preserving the union. Because Massachusetts could not even feed itself without imported foodstuffs, exclusion from American ports would make them "look to Europe for the deficiency."[45] Yet, remarkably, after exhaustively rehearsing all the sound reasons that would deter the large majority in Massachusetts from defecting, Jefferson concluded that the High Federalist leadership would nonetheless "brave all these obstacles" and break from the union.

Federalist leaders were "monarchists in principle, bearing deadly hatred to their republican fellow-citizens, impatient under the ascendancy of republican principles, devoted in their attachment to England, and preferring to be placed under her despotism, if they cannot hold the helm of government here." Such men deserved to be destroyed, and Jefferson reveled in the prospect: a temporary Europeanization of American politics would lead to the union's ultimate purification—the elimination of all European influences. "Much of the population" would abandon Massachusetts in the event of war, and the inevitable result would "be an early and humiliating return to the Union."[46]

Jefferson's imaginative scenario enabled him to remove the good Republicans of Massachusetts out of harm's way and so enact a ritual humiliation on the remaining "army of officers." (Jefferson had envisaged a similar, if less violent humiliation in his inaugural address, when he cast his foes as "monuments," or objects of popular mockery and contempt.) The practical effect of this exercise was to draw a "geographical line" between the traitors who stayed and the good Republicans who moved on to friendlier climes. Jefferson was eager to draw such a line at this time both because its extent was so limited (he persisted in the belief that the "Essex Federalists" would succeed only in Mas-

sachusetts and that the other New England states would remain loyal) and because it justified the projection of his own "deadly hatred" against his "fellow-
citizens." Jefferson made Federalists foreigners, and gave them a country of
their own (Massachusetts), so that he could imagine making war on them—
and so persuade himself that *he* was not violating the republican gospel of
peace and affectionate union.[47]

When Jefferson visualized the possible sequence of events in his imaginary
war against Massachusetts, as he did in a letter to William Short in late
November 1814, he recalled the good Republicans of the state from their exile
and accorded them a key role in the hostilities. One possibility was civil war: "if
their administration determines to join the enemy, their force will be annihi-
lated by equality of division among themselves"; "their own people will put
down these factionists as soon as they see the real object of the opposition."
Should desperate Federalists finally "call in the English army, the republicans
[would call in] ours." Here was the opportunity Jefferson—and as he saw it, his
countrymen generally—had been so long awaiting. For the result of Massachusetts' defection and an open alliance with Britain "will only be a transfer
of the scene of war from Canada to Massachusetts; and we can get ten men to
go to Massachusetts for one who will go to Canada."[48] In other words, the
"defection of Massachusetts" would *strengthen* the American war effort: the
rupture of the union would bring its real enemies out into the open, enabling
good Republicans in Massachusetts and her sister states to rally to the cause.

That Jefferson could so confidently assert that the secession of Massachusetts would be a boon to the American war effort is a good measure of his
hatred for his Federalist enemies. Jefferson had always insisted that a strong
union was the crucial barrier to foreign interference and counterrevolution.
But now, in the midst of war, he could contemplate a rupture of the union that
would give the British a significant strategic advantage. Jefferson thought that
the "danger" here was more apparent than real, however, for the differences
that had led to war with Britain were ultimately negotiable.[49] When the British
recognized the futility of attempting to enforce their will on an aroused and
united people, now purged of its former secret enemies, they would withdraw
beyond the line that distinguished "the American hemisphere," with "its separate system of interests," from the European balance of power.[50] But the "Essex
Federalists" would not respond to such rational calculations: they could only
"return" to Europe as individuals in another diaspora of Tory exiles. As long as
they held sway in Massachusetts, the Federalists represented a cancerous and
potentially fatal growth on the American body politic. The ultimate design of
these monarchists, Jefferson explained to John Melish in January 1813, was to

establish their "favorite government [in Massachusetts], from whence the other States may gangrene by degrees."[51] The frustrating history of the Republicans' efforts to extend their influence in the region—and thereby strengthen the union—demonstrated conclusively that further negotiations with such enemies were pointless. Radical surgery was the only solution.

Jefferson's response to the prospect of Massachusetts' secession reflected his overriding concern with preserving the distinction between Europe and America. "The meridian of the mid-Atlantic should be the line of demarkation between war and peace," Jefferson wrote early in 1812, shortly before the beginning of hostilities with Britain that were supposed to vindicate that line.[52] The presence of a monarchist fragment in Massachusetts was a dangerous anomaly in the American system that demanded a preemptive response. But Jefferson could still confidently assume—as he could not in the Missouri crisis—that the threat could be localized and therefore easily removed. In striking contrast to his contemporaneous bromides about harmonious, voluntary, and affectionate union *among Republicans,* Jefferson's prescriptions for dealing with the separatist threat in New England relied on mobilizing the "extended republic's" coercive capabilities. As he wrote in March 1814, "I see our safety in the extent of our confederacy, and in the probability that in the proportion of that the sound parts will always be sufficient to crush local poisons."[53]

Jefferson's hatred of New England was the deep-seated source of the "geographical line" that shattered the tranquillity of his old age. For Jefferson, New England had always been the "anti-republican portion of our country."[54] Before the Missouri controversy, however, he remained confident that the cancer would eventually, and without much "difficulty," be localized and destroyed. It was this very confidence that allowed him to link unrepublican principles with a particular state or region, and so draw a line between "sound" and "unsound" parts of the federal union. The line would be obliterated as soon as the Republican party achieved its long-delayed triumph in these last bastions of Federalist strength—or when the "overwhelming force" of the union destroyed its "anti-republican" enemies on the battlefield.

The unexpected success of American negotiators at Ghent made military measures against Massachusetts unnecessary. But in Jefferson's mind, the devastation of his old foes was nonetheless complete: it was as if they actually *had* broken from the union, and then been reduced to submission. In March 1815 he sketched out the terms of reunion to Henry Dearborn, the Massachusetts Republican who had been his Secretary of War. "Oh, Massachusetts!," he declaimed, "how have I lamented the degradation of your apostasy! Massachusetts, with whom I went with pride in 1776, whose vote was my vote on every public question, and whose principles were then the standard of whatever was free or fearless." Yet it was not too late to "return to the bosom and to the principles of her brethren," for "should the State once more buckle on her republican harness, we shall receive her again as a sister." The triumph of Republicans at the polls would constitute an "act of repentance," making it once again possible to distinguish the state from its corrupt leaders. The state's "wanderings," culminating in the abortive Hartford Convention, could then be reckoned "among the crimes only of the parricide party, which would have basely sold what their fathers so bravely won from the same enemy."[55]

The "crimes" of the Federalists were now cast in the same generational terms Jefferson would invoke during the Missouri controversy. The "venal traitors" who had led Massachusetts to the brink of disunion were parricides intent on destroying the Revolutionary fathers and squandering their legacy of liberty. Jefferson's conception of union thus reached back to 1776, when the fathers had marched forth under the same "standard," while looking forward to a time when the sons would renounce and suppress their unnatural, parricidal impulses by purging the last vestiges of Federalism. As Jefferson's insistently familial language reveals, this union was based as much on affection as on principle: a renewed committment "to the principles of her brethren" would draw this wayward "sister," naturally and irresistibly, back to the "bosom" of her republican family.[56]

Having thus imagined the demise of the Federalists and Massachusetts' restoration to the union, Jefferson could view the political landscape over the next few years in increasingly confident, even complacent terms. This complacency, the sleepfulness so suddenly and traumatically disrupted by the "fire-bell in the night," was a key ingredient in Jefferson's response to the Missouri crisis. And when Jefferson awoke from his slumbers, the magnitude of the threat to liberty and union was immediately apparent. For Jefferson had already drawn a "geographical line" around New England (or Massachusetts) that "coincide[d] with a marked principle."[57]

New England's Federalist leaders, he was certain, had made no secret of their hostility to republican principles—and to the union—during the protracted political and diplomatic crisis that culminated in the War of 1812. That such men should ever return to popular favor, as they did under the pretext of promoting slavery restriction, was either a measure of the people's extreme credulity or of their own "anti-republican" tendencies—it hardly mattered which. What Jefferson most feared was precisely this link between party leaders and followers, "officers" and "soldiers": this was the relationship that made

Massachusetts a "foreign" country during the war, and that would make the self-professed "free" states such a formidable danger to republican liberty during the Missouri controversy.

Dedicated as he was to preserving the fundamental distinction between New World and Old, Jefferson *externalized* all threats to the union: Federalists who challenged administration policy were either dupes of the English or worse, homegrown "foreigners" unresponsive to the claims of prudence, principle, or fellow feeling. Again, it hardly mattered which. Either temporarily, in the case of the war crisis, or permanently, in the case of Missouri, the geographical lines Jefferson projected distinguished "Europe-in-America" from the healthy, still republican, and authentically "American" portions of the union. If the line could be obliterated, as Jefferson so confidently predicted in his meditations on the fate of Massachusetts, the Revolution would be secure against "the unwise and unworthy passions" of parricidal sons. But the line between slavery and freedom, "once conceived," could "never be obliterated from the mind." When this happened Americans would become foreigners to each other, America would become Europe.

Jefferson's rehearsal of the main themes of the Missouri controversy in his earlier responses to antiwar and separatist sentiment in New England strongly suggests that his profound hostility to slavery restriction was *not* prompted by reactionary hysteria, or by an exaggerated solicitude for class or regional interests. To the contrary, Jefferson was stunned by congressional controversy over Missouri statehood because it seemed to fulfill so completely and disastrously the nightmarish script for disunion and counterrevolution that he had glimpsed—and dismissed—in earlier dark moments. That the future of the institution of slavery was at issue is what makes the Missouri debates so compelling to historians. But for Jefferson the legacy of the American Revolution, and of his whole political career, was at stake.

Before their recent humiliation, the Federalists of Massachusetts had conspired to destroy the union, thus drawing the new nation into the vortex of European politics and making America over in Europe's image. Now, incredibly, the new state of Missouri—anxious to *join* and strengthen the union, not to withdraw from or demolish it—was rebuffed at the threshold. Missouri's rejection would mark the death knell of Jefferson's empire of liberty, the expanding union of self-governing republican states that guaranteed peace and prosperity to the New World. The patriotic Republicans—and republican loyalists—who settled the vast frontiers of the Louisiana Purchase would be cast beyond the restrictionists' pale. Here, at a time when his old Federalist foes were supposed to be suffering in "silent but unresisting anguish" as the Republicans established their "decided ascendency" across the union, Jefferson could only look on in horror as neo-Federalist restrictionists seized control of Congress and threatened to destroy his cherished union.[58]

WINNING THE WEST

If the Hartford Convention revealed the disloyalty and antirepublican principles of New England separatists during the War of 1812, the great American victory at New Orleans in January 1815 demonstrated the patriotic fervor of western citizens. "The people of Louisiana are sincerely attached to the Union," Jefferson exclaimed, as he contrasted their patriotism with Massachusetts' "apostasy."[59] Unlike their Yankee counterparts, the Louisianans could not claim republican liberty as their birthright: they had only begun to enjoy the full benefits of self-government with their admission to the union in 1811. Yet, with the timely assistance of the other western states, they had successfully defended New Orleans—and the entire Mississippi valley—from British invasion. The Battle of New Orleans "proved the fidelity of the Orleanese"; it also proved that the city "can be defended both by land and water," and "that the western country will fly to its relief."[60] The British would have received a much warmer welcome, and enjoyed far greater success, had they landed in Boston.

For Jefferson, Andrew Jackson's victory at New Orleans, though it had no effect on the already concluded negotiations at Ghent, was a particularly gratifying vindication of the union's durability in a time of great crisis. Separatist sentiment in Massachusetts showed how foreign powers, or native-born "foreigners" like the Essex Federalists, could jeopardize the union by extending their gangrenous influence throughout the federal body. The timely reaction of the healthy parts of the union, those furthest removed from the source of corruption, constituted the only effective antidote. Jefferson would be inclined to think in such schematic terms after a political lifetime of combating Federalist heresies in New England and of recruiting allies to the republican cause in the new western states. As he looked west, the prospects for an expanding, progressively more populous, prosperous, and powerful union seemed virtually unlimited; meanwhile, eastern apostates and parricides appeared all too eager to squander their fathers' priceless legacy by demolishing the union and so returning to the dark ages of despotic government and neverending war.

Yet, however accurately such comparisons and juxtapositions hinted at underlying tendencies and ultimate prospects, Jefferson understood that they represented at best only an imperfect sketch of the federal republic's present circumstances. After all, the great majority of New Englanders (once they came to their senses) were good Republicans, dedicated to the preservation of the union. Nor was Jefferson under any illusions about the motives and character of the adventurers and speculators who flocked west, where unsettled conditions and the settlers' ignorance and credulity gave such scope to their selfish ambitions. Jefferson's exultant response to the American triumph at New Orleans reflected his consciousness of these ambiguities, and his sense of relief is palpable. The British invasion was only the latest—and, Jefferson imagined, the last—of a series of crises that had tested western loyalties to the union. Having demonstrated such extraordinary "fidelity," westerners could claim as a matter of right, once their numbers were sufficient, the full benefits of self-governing statehood and admission to the union.

That Missourians should be drawn toward the union, by voluntary "attraction" instead of coercive "impulse," was not a foregone conclusion when American settlers first flowed into the region.[61] It was instead, Jefferson could argue as he reviewed the history of the region over two decades, the result of his own diplomatic triumph in securing Louisiana to the union (1803), of the responsiveness of his and subsequent administrations to settlers' legitimate grievances and demands, of timely action against Aaron Burr and his co-conspirators (1806–7), and, above all, of the remarkable success of the Republican party in inculcating "federal and republican principles" in a widely dispersed and rapidly growing electorate.

Jefferson emphasized the importance of party mobilization for the security of the union in a remarkable letter to Republican editor William Duane in March 1811. "During the *bellum omnium in omnia* of Europe," the "union of all [this country's] friends" was absolutely essential in order

> to resist its enemies within and without. If we schismatize on either men or measures, if we do not act in phalanx, as when we rescued it from the satellites of monarchism [in the election of 1800], I will not say our *party,* [for] the term is false and degrading, but our *nation* will be undone. For the republicans are the *nation.*[62]

Beginning in Jefferson's second term, the deepening diplomatic crisis with Britain over neutral rights, the ultimately successful resistance to a commercial embargo (particularly in New England) that was supposed to offer a peaceful alternative to war, and ominous portents of divisions in republican ranks all served to exacerbate anxieties about the future of the union, and therefore to reinforce the identification of "nation" and "party." But if the union was once again at risk, as it had been in the crisis of 1798–1800, Jefferson and his followers could take comfort from the collapse of Burr's Conspiracy, one of the few successes of the President's second term. The union had proved strongest where, by all conventional accounts, it should have been most vulnerable.

The conflation of "union," "nation," and Republican party was reflexive for Jefferson, and characteristically self-serving. Yet it was as much the result of what Jefferson heard from constituents as it was a projection of personal and party ambitions. In late 1806 and early 1807, Jefferson was inundated with adulatory addresses from every part of the union urging him to stand for a third term. Loyal Republicans extolled Jefferson's "pacific system of policy, so congenial with our hearts, and with the great principles of our representative government."[63] "Your solicitude to preserve the enjoyments of peace to our country, amidst the storms which agitate the world," as a committee of New Yorkers told Jefferson, "demands the approbation of every virtuous patriot."[64] Many feared that if Jefferson retired, a succession crisis would unleash the "hydra of *apostasy*," as "the enemies of our principles . . . sow[ed] the seeds of disunion amongst us."[65] "Foreign enemies and *domestic Traitors*" like Burr— who was not yet in custody—were naturally linked;[66] it was imperative that Jefferson remain in office so that, in the words of the Maryland legislature,

the same wisdom which has guided and protected us thus far may be able to annihilate the demon of conspiracy[,] the offspring of desperate and abandoned men who backed by foreign aid expect to benefit and aggrandize themselves from the destruction of that Constitution which has exalted us to our now elevated station."[67]

It was Aaron Burr's preparations for his descent down the Mississippi, with the intention of launching an unauthorized private war against Spanish Mexico, and perhaps of seizing New Orleans in order to seduce the western states from the union, that gave these addresses such an urgent quality.[68] Burr's offers of cheap land, Spanish treasure, and the end of the federal government's territorial regime in Orleans (Louisiana) and adjacent territories constituted the first great test of the loyalties of western territories and states since the Louisiana Purchase. Westerners rushed to reassure Jefferson that "no real or visionary prospect of advantage will ever induce us to sever that bond of union which is our only security against domestic violence and foreign invasion."[69]

Westerners could demonstrate their loyalty in 1806–1807 simply by *not* responding to Burr's seductive appeals: there was as yet no need to take up arms. Indeed, the genius of the American system, "where every citizen is a soldier, and every soldier a citizen," was to preserve peace until the time when "life, liberty and independence" were truly threatened; the resources of the union would be correspondingly enhanced, as would the patriotic determination of a grateful and growing population to repel all "those who may unjustly asail us."[70] The federal republic would become powerful, even unconquerable, if its leaders recognized and honored the distinction between war and peace. Of course, this was a distinction never recognized by despotic regimes, with their standing armies, their predatory policies toward their own subjects, and their aggressive designs against one another.[71] Jefferson's pacific system insulated the new nation from the "throes & convulsions which afflict the European world:" "behold[ing] the effusion of human blood, which flows from the wounds of slaves, to satiate the unbounded thirst for power & ambition, obliges us still more to approbate those measures of policy which have averted from us similar horrors & calamities."[72]

Jefferson recognized that the preservation of the union depended on common principles and common interests—the themes repeatedly struck in the public addresses he received during the Burr crisis—and not on the exercise of force, even against those who were temporarily led astray. On November 27, 1806, Jefferson issued a proclamation warning against any unauthorized "military expedition or enterprise against the dominions of Spain" and "enjoining all faithful citizens who have been led without due knowledge or consideration to participate in the said unlawful enterprises to withdraw from the same without delay."[73] Jefferson conducted his campaign against Burr by mobilizing public opinion, not a military force, and by urging local and federal authorities along the conspirator's route to initiate appropriate legal measures.[74] Then he could only wait, "looking with anxiety to see what exertions the Western country will make."[75]

For Jefferson, this test of western loyalties was a great plebiscite, a massive election campaign in which westerners determined their own political future. The collapse of the Burr Conspiracy was one of Jefferson's most gratifying moments, even if—thanks to Chief Justice John Marshall—its leaders did not receive the punishment they so richly deserved.[76] Burr's failure offered the "most remarkable . . . proof" of the "innate strength of our government." "Apprised . . . that there were traitors among them," an aroused citizenry "crushed by their own strength what would have produced the march of armies and civil war in any other country."[77] "On the whole," Jefferson told William C. C. Claiborne, the territorial governor at New Orleans, "this squall, by showing with what ease our government suppresses movements which in other countries requires armies, has greatly increased its strength by increasing the public confidence in it."[78] The American system's great "strength," its exceptional character, was grounded in the people's confidence in a "mild and efficient Government" that would *not* send armies into the field at the slightest provocation and, equally importantly, in the government's confidence in the people.[79]

The survival and strength of the federal republic depended on reciprocal trust and the recognition of an identity of interests between republican citizens and their elected leaders. But Jefferson never assumed such trust, or imagined that all Americans would always recognize their own best interests. Burr's imperial ambitions thus constituted a critical test of Jefferson's "pacific system," of whether the government was capable of pursuing measures that would build trust and confidence. Far from remaining inert, as some critics supposed, the administration actively sought to shape public opinion, encouraging and exploiting expressions of support from all quarters of the union. Appeals to Jefferson to stand for a third term reinforced and reflected his own sense of the perilous conjunction of European war, "insurrectionary enterprize" on the western frontiers, and schism in the Republican party. To conceive of the crisis in these terms—to recognize these connections—was the necessary precondition for its resolution. Conceived as yet another crisis of the union, the Burr Conspiracy provoked the sentiments of loyalty and national identity that constituted the union's only durable foundation. "The fidelity of the western country was not to be shaken," Jefferson exulted, and the union emerged from its crisis with renewed vigor.[80]

Though some leading Burrites may have been Republicans—including Senator John Smith of Ohio and an embarrassingly large contingent from Kentucky, where Federalists took the lead in exposing and resisting Burr's plans—Jefferson could only interpret the conspiracy's collapse as a triumph for the administration party.[81] He was convinced that Federalists expected the union to fall apart, sooner or later, whether or not they actively supported Burr; they "chuckle" at the notion "that the people of the US are qualified for self government."[82] And after Burr was apprehended, Jefferson complained to his congressional lieutenant, William Branch Giles, the Federalists happily made

> Burr's cause their own, mortified only that he did not separate the Union or overturn the government, and proving, that had he had a little dawn of success, they would have joined him to introduce his object, their favorite monarchy, as they would any other enemy, foreign or domestic, who could rid them of this hateful republic for any other government.[83]

For Jefferson, Burr was a sort of honorary Federalist (as he had most certainly been an opportunistic Republican) who shared and acted on their notorious contempt for the "federal and republican principles." Burr "has meant to place himself on the throne of Montezuma," Jefferson shuddered, "and extend his empire to the Alleghany," thus destroying the federal union, the only effective barrier to the Europeanization of American politics.[84]

Jefferson's conception of union depended on the common principles and harmonious interests of republican citizens across the continent. Westerners' loyalty during the Burr crisis vindicated this conception; Jefferson was also gratified by the swift action of local authorities. "The promptitude and energy displayed by your State," Jefferson wrote Governor Edward Tiffin of Ohio, "has been as honorable to itself as salutary to its sister States." Though conventional wisdom called for a powerful federal presence along the frontier, the collapse of the conspiracy confirmed Jefferson's faith in a radically decentralized federal regime. Here was "a happy illustration," he told Tiffin, "of the importance of preserving to the State authorities all that vigor which the Constitution foresaw would be necessary, not only for their own safety, but for that of the whole."[85]

In Jefferson's scheme the "energy and enterprize" that guaranteed national security came from below, from the determination of patriotic citizens to defend their own liberties and those of their countrymen.[86] Instead, the (apparently paradoxical) effect of eschewing a strong central government and respecting the autonomy and agency of the state governments was to *increase* the total amount of force that could be raised when the union was truly threatened. The genius of the American system, as Jefferson envisioned it, was that the firm foundation of popular patriotism made the federal constitutional superstructure of limited, checked, and balanced powers a potentially great, ultimately irresistible force in a war-torn world. Respect for constitutional limitations was the best guarantee that the nation's "resources"—and the confidence of the people—would not be squandered "on dangers which have never happened."[87] When war finally did come, and the people were persuaded of the justice of their cause, American victory was assured.

From the beginning of his administration in 1801, Jefferson celebrated the new nation's increasing population, prosperity, and power. "We contemplate this rapid growth," he assured Congress in his first annual message,

> not with a view to the injuries it may enable us to do others in some future day, but to the settlement of the extensive country still remaining vacant within our limits [and] to the multiplication of men susceptible of happiness, educated in the love of order, habituated to self-government, and valuing its blessings above all price.[88]

Of course, these were just the sort of liberty-loving Republicans to resent and resist "injuries" inflicted by others, and the implicit warning to the new nation's imperial neighbors—including the Spanish in Louisiana—was clear. "We feel ourselves strong, and daily growing stronger," Jefferson wrote William Short in October 1801: "the day is within my time as well as yours, when we may say by what laws other nations [in this case, the British particularly] shall treat us on the sea. And we will say it."[89]

Jefferson's prospectus for America's future power betrayed misgivings about the character of westerners—what if they were *not* properly "educated" and "habituated" to the virtues of "self-government?—and the vulnerability of the union before it came into the fullness of its latent powers.[90] Burr and his fellow conspirators hoped to exploit this vulnerability, seducing westerners before their republican principles and loyalty to the union were irrevocably fixed. But Burr miscalculated, and Jefferson was gratified by the proof this failure offered that his "pacific system" already operated effectively across the western frontiers, even among the "Orleanese Creoles."[91] Combined with the timely interposition of local constitutional authorities, the political mobilization of republican loyalists against Burr demonstrated—at least to Jefferson's satisfaction—that westerners were prepared to meet any military challenge. Predictions of future strength thus gave way to the conviction that the union was already strong enough.

Jefferson's confidence was reflected in the aggressive posture his administration assumed in the deepening conflict with the European belligerents over violations of American neutral rights. In a remarkable letter to Kentuckian James Brown in late 1808, Jefferson suggested that Burr's failure had not only demonstrated the futility of separatist assaults on the union, but that there was as little to "fear [from] foreign invasion." Educated in federal and republican principles, Jefferson's countrymen transformed what the followers of Montesquieu considered the new nation's greatest liability—its size—into its greatest asset. As long as Americans resisted the seductive appeals of "foreign adventurers, and native malcontents," as long as they upheld and perfected a federal union that expressed and cultivated their better political natures, the line of separation between Europe and America would remain impregnable. "For myself," Jefferson told Brown, even in the "most flattering periods" of Burr's Conspiracy, "I never entertained one moment's fear. My long and intimate knowledge of my countrymen, satisfied and satisfies me, that let there ever be occasion to display the banners of the law, and the world will see how few and pitiful are those who shall array themselves in opposition."[92] The United States was, after all, as Jefferson had proclaimed in his first inaugural address, "the strongest Government on earth."[93]

"Who can limit the extent to which the federative principle may operate effectively?" Jefferson asked in his second inaugural address.[94] When Jefferson looked westward, he foresaw no limits. But such limits would become painfully clear as the unreconstructed "monarchists" of New England sought to subvert Jefferson's commercial diplomacy and then "Mr. Madison's War." If expansion to the west vindicated Jefferson's conception of union, the treason of eastern "parricides" threatened to destroy it. A union that would not embrace Missouri was not the same union that Jefferson and the Revolutionary fathers had established with the Declaration of Independence in 1776.

FIRST PRINCIPLES, LAST RITES

The Declaration of Independence is the classic statement of Jeffersonian liberalism. The "self-evident" "truths" set forth in the second paragraph justified the colonists in severing all links with a British sovereign who had "evince[d] a design to reduce them under absolute despotism." "All men are created equal," wrote Jefferson, and "they are endowed by their creator with inherent and inalienable rights; that among these are life, liberty, & the pursuit of happiness." Instituted in order "to secure these rights," governments derived "their just powers from the consent of the governed." Equality was the ultimate rationale for independence, dissolving all connections with the old imperial regime. For Jefferson, it was also the fundamental premise of a new federal republican system. George III's manifest design was to establish "an absolute tyranny *over these states*"; by destroying the colonies as political communities, he would deprive the colonists of their liberty and property. To vindicate their rights as individuals, Americans would have to rally to the defense of their states, and those states in turn would have to forge an effective federal union. At each stage in this process, the consent of equals—individuals or states—was predicated on the absence of coercion or prior connection: disunion was the necessary precondition of union.[95]

Jefferson's federal design in the Declaration is most fully elaborated in passages (deleted by his congressional colleagues) that set forth his idealized version of the imperial relationship. "We might have been a free and a great people together," Jefferson wrote, "but a communication of grandeur & of freedom it seems is below [the] dignity" of "these unfeeling [British] brethren." In Jefferson's imaginative account of colonial history, the first settlers in America had *already* established their independence through exercising the fundamental right of expatriation: "these [settlements] were effected at the expense of our own blood & treasure, unassisted by the wealth or the strength of Great Britain."[96] This original independence should have been the foundation for lasting union (a formulation many of Jefferson's colleagues probably found bafflingly paradoxical). "In constituting indeed our several forms of government," he explained, "we had adopted one common king, thereby laying a foundation for perpetual league & amity with them." In other words, a federal (treaty) relationship securing the equal rights of every member of the great imperial family would have been the constitutional foundation for "a free and a great" Anglo-American nation. But instead of offering peace, as family feelings naturally enjoined, the British chose to make war against the colonies, so giving "the last stab to agonizing affection."[97]

Nearly fifty years later, in 1821, when—in the midst of the Missouri crisis— Jefferson drafted his "Autobiography," he was still disgusted with his "pusillanimous" colleagues for excising these passages, as well as the clause "reprobating the enslaving the inhabitants of Africa." Determined to set the record straight, Jefferson now offered his own version of the Declaration alongside the version adopted by Congress. Far from agreeing with most subsequent commentators that the excisions *improved* the text, eliminating potentially embarrassing and certainly confusing passages that would have alienated readers and listeners at home and abroad, Jefferson remained convinced that his message had been mutilated.[98] It was the motivations of the excisers, not his own, that demanded a closer look, for "the sentiments of men are known not only by what they receive, but what they reject also."[99] Jefferson, for his part, would stand by the "sentiments" his colleagues had denounced in 1776: they, not he, were the ones concerned with rhetorical effects. And the principles he had articulated in 1776 were of much more than historical interest in 1821: fidelity to those principles alone could preserve the union and vindicate American independence.

Jefferson's colleagues had revised his text for the same reason so many of them had dragged their feet on the question of independence itself. "The pusillanimous idea that we had friends in England worth keeping, still haunted the minds of many," Jefferson recalled. "For this reason, those passages which conveyed censures on the people of England were struck out, lest they give them offence." Jefferson presumably risked "offence" by postulating a familial relationship, even an identity, between the British and American people: the violation of these natural ties was the most hideous possible crime. Unwilling to recognize the hideousness of this crime, Jefferson's cautious colleagues revealed the limits of their own commitment to independence, a lingering sense of connection that would ultimately give rise to a monarchical party that was determined to reestablish British authority in the new nation on the most humiliatingly unequal terms. In retrospect, Jefferson may have imagined that his draft of the Declaration had drawn a "line of demarcation" between patriotic advocates of American principles and the reactionary avatars of the European old regime. But the blurring of that line by the mutilation of his text had left the door ajar for lukewarm friends and secret enemies to call themselves Revolutionaries—and then to subvert independence from within.

Jefferson's account of Congress' deliberations in 1776 thus constituted a kind of preface to the "history of the parties" he hoped some good Republican would undertake (in refutation of the Federalist version offered by John Marshall's *Life of Washington*) and that was told in the *Anas*, the three volumes of documents and commentaries on Jefferson's term as Secretary of State that he collected in 1818.[100] But more was at stake in the "Autobiography" than getting the history of the Declaration right—or setting the stage for a proper understanding of the 1790s—and this was most conspicuously apparent in Jefferson's comments on the excision of his blistering attack on George III for "wag[ing] cruel war against human nature itself" by enslaving Africans and then resisting all colonial efforts to stop the slave trade. The question remained compelling in 1821: why had Jefferson's colleagues forfeited the opportunity to stake out the moral high ground? Why would they hesitate to dissociate themselves from this nefarious traffic in human beings, or to lay responsibility for this "piratical warfare" at the feet of the supposedly "CHRISTIAN king of Great Britain?"[101]

Jefferson offered two related explanations for the failure of fellow congressmen to follow his lead on slavery, beyond the "pusillanimous" unwillingness of moderates who secretly hoped for reconciliation with the British. One was economic interest: "the clause . . . reprobating the enslaving of the inhabitants of Africa, was struck out in complaisance to South Carolina and Georgia, who had never attempted to restrain the importation of slaves, and who on the contrary still wished to continue it." The other explanation was more complex and problematic, but much more relevant to the situation of American politics in 1821, and this was the bad conscience of congressmen from the northern states. "Our northern brethren also I believe felt a little tender under those censures," wrote Jefferson, "for tho' their people have very few slaves themselves yet they had been pretty considerable carriers of them to others."[102] Northerners had an interest in the slave trade that they—unlike the Carolinians and Georgians—were unwilling to disclose; by 1821 this dissembling had evolved into self-righteous, hypocritical denial. (It was an article of faith for Jefferson and like-minded Old Republicans that northern prosperity continued to depend on slave-based plantation agriculture after the abolition of the slave trade in 1808.) Astonishingly (to Jefferson), northern restrictionists now had the gall to turn his moral indictment of George III back on Jefferson and his fellow planters—the long-suffering victims of a "piratical warfare" that had enriched no one more than the northerners themselves.

Jefferson's tortuous logic—either in 1776 or in 1821—hardly seems compelling to us today. Yet Jefferson did establish, to his own satisfaction at least, that he had taken the most advanced possible position on slavery in 1776: he was prepared to identify the cause of American freedom with the "most sacred rights of life and liberty" of enslaved Africans.[103] But cautious congressional colleagues held back because they were not fully committed to a final break with Britain. Now, in the Missouri crisis, restrictionists feigned a solicitude for the slaves that could only be attributed to their determination to reverse the outcome of the American Revolution. Heedless of the "blessings of peace and self-government" that union alone could preserve, restrictionists raised the slavery extension issue as a "party trick" in order to gain power.[104] Yet, as any sincere opponent of slavery should know, emancipation was "more likely to be effected by union than by scission."[105] Restrictionist rhetoric notwithstanding, the real enemies of freedom in 1821, as in 1776, were those who resisted American independence and subverted the affectionate, harmonious union of citizens and states that was its only guarantee.

The passionate, blood-soaked language of rage and betrayal that Jefferson's colleagues excised from the Declaration—and that he restored in his "Autobiography" in 1821—was the same language that spilled out, seemingly beyond authorial control, in his despairing response to the Missouri crisis. Just as George III had administered "the last stab to agonizing affection" by waging war on the colonies, the American people—driven to distraction by the restrictionists—were now committing a hideous act of "suicide on themselves, and of treason against the hopes of the world."[106] In both cases family bonds were violated by "unfeeling brethren." Jefferson repeatedly recognized this perfect, awful symmetry: as he wrote William Short in April 1820, for the present generation "this treason against human hope, will signalize their epoch in future history, *as the counterpart of the medal of their predecessors,*" the Revolutionary fathers.[107]

The powerful feelings manifest at these two crucial epochs may provide important clues to Jefferson's psychology. But we should respect Jefferson's sense of the principles involved in both crises. Jefferson certainly did not believe that his resort to such highly charged language was prompted by propagandistic impulses to arouse and manipulate the anger of others (in the Declaration) or by a therapeutic impulse to give vent to the morbid sentiments of a disappointed and deluded old man (in his letters on the Missouri crisis). To invoke his own language against such reductive psychologizing, Jefferson might insist that reason and sentiment, the "Head and the Heart," were always in dialogue with one another, and nowhere more momentously than in the construction and preservation of the American union.

Jefferson was both a constitutionalist, a man of reason ever vigilant against abuses of power, and a sentimental nationalist who believed in the natural harmony and affectionate union of all freedom-loving people. It was the duty of the head, with its "science," to guarantee the equality and integrity—the self-possession and self-preservation—of every free man and every free state. But "morals were too essential to the happiness of man to be risked on the incertain combinations of the head. She laid their foundations therefore in sentiment, not in science." Reason could devise a constitutional order that was the essential precondition of a union that it was itself impotent to achieve. The American Revolution was the greatest testimonial to the power of the heart, Jefferson explained to Maria Cosway in his famous letter of October 1786: "If our country, when pressed with wrongs at the point of the bayonet, had been governed by it's heads instead of it's hearts, where should we have been now?" The answer was: dead, "hanging on a gallows as high as Haman's."[108]

Union was meaningless without equality—an equality that made consent possible, and gave rise to fellow feeling and affectionate attachment. But by the same logic, equality was meaningless without union. It was an apparently paradoxical formulation that Jefferson himself could no longer sustain in the wake of the Missouri crisis.

Jefferson was sorry to be in Philadelphia in the summer of 1776, for the real work of nation making was being done back in Virginia and its sister states, where new republican governments were being constituted. On his return to Virginia, Jefferson would more than compensate for having missed the chance of drafting the new state constitution (which he soon came to see as radically defective) by his herculean efforts as a republican lawmaker, law reformer, and executive.[109] And in 1784, during another brief tenure as a Virginia delegate to Congress before leaving for Paris, Jefferson took the leading role in drafting the first ordinance for the government of the union's western territory.

The rhetorical contrast between the 1784 Ordinance and the emotionally charged Declaration could not be greater. Yet, for Jefferson, they were clearly complementary expressions of his conception of the American union—first from the heart, and then from the head. For it was crucial in 1784, as massive settlement of the West was already beginning, to lay down the fundamental principles that would govern relations between new states and old. The challenge was to create the conditions for union that the British had so conspicuously failed to secure for their erstwhile countrymen in America. The expansion and perfection of the union—and of American nationhood—depended on fostering republican government on the western frontier, on not recapitulating the tragic errors of the British by establishing a despotic, colonial regime.[110]

Jefferson's anticolonial vision rested on two integrally related premises. First, once a new western state (defined according to boundaries prescribed by the ordinance) crossed a minimal population threshhold (twenty thousand free inhabitants), it should proceed to draft its own constitution, subject only to the proviso "that their respective governments shall be in republican forms, and shall admit no person to be a citizen, who holds any hereditary title." Then "whensoever any of the said states shall have, of free inhabitants, as many as shall then be in any one the least numerous of the thirteen original states, such state shall be admitted by it's delegates into the Congress of the United States, *on an equal footing with the said original states,*" given the assent of the requisite number of existing states under the Articles of Confederation.[111] Significantly, in Jefferson's scheme, a "state" existed as a self-constituted political community *before* it claimed admission. There would be no confusion then—as there was in the case of Missouri—about Congress' role in state constitution writing, or in determining a state's "republican" character. For as Jefferson clearly intended in 1784, a state could only be a republic if it constituted itself, without outside interference, and if it were received into the union "on an equal footing."[112]

When Jefferson was in Paris, his ordinance was subjected to successive revisions and was ultimately superseded altogether by the Northwest Ordinance of July 13, 1787. Jefferson was troubled by these changes—most notably the redefinition of new state boundaries and provisions for a more elaborate scheme of "temporary" territorial government under congressional authority—but could take comfort in the fact that his successors had reaffirmed his fundamental principle, that new states be admitted "on an equal footing with the original States."[113] New state equality was essential to an expanding, harmonious union, just as the equality of the original states was the fundamental premise of the union Jefferson and his fellow Revolutionaries had established in 1776. This was the principle the restrictionists attacked in the Missouri crisis. In doing so, they rendered the federal Constitution a dead letter; they also revealed—and provoked—the hostile feelings that made affectionate union impossible and so betrayed the promise of Jefferson's Declaration of Independence.

The controversy over the admission of Missouri as a slave state constituted a crisis for the federal union. Few contemporaries personalized this crisis as much as Jefferson; most hoped that a spirit of compromise would preserve and sustain the union. Where Jefferson harked back to 1776, and so identified union with independence, the compromisers of 1820–21 invoked the inspiring example of the federal convention of 1787 and the "bundle of compromises" that had then enabled James Madison and his fellow founders to form a more perfect union.[114] In retrospect, with the devastation of the Civil War in view, we are inclined to honor Madison's union (inadequate as it may have been in the final crisis) and to lay the blame for its destruction at the feet of Jeffersonian states' rights advocates whose "union" proved to be no union at all.

The uncompromising, self-righteous, and dangerously doctrinaire Jefferson forms a striking contrast to the moderate, conciliatory, and statesmanlike Madison, who devoted so much energy in his waning days to the preservation of his union.[115] Thus, even as Madison disowned the states' rights doctrines that he and his fellow Republicans had flirted with in 1798, Thomas Ritchie and the nullifiers of Virginia and South Carolina claimed Jefferson as their patron saint. After all, as Jefferson had written in his original version of the Kentucky Resolutions in October 1798, "where powers are assumed which have not been delegated [by the federal Constitution], a nullification of the act is the rightful remedy."[116] The genealogy of secession—from 1861 back to 1798, and then to 1776—seems straightforward enough; it was a genealogy that Jefferson's words and deeds authorized, and that Madison, defending the legacy of 1787, resisted to his dying day.[117]

Much can be said for this juxtaposition of Madison and Jefferson. But the story of Jefferson's Missouri crisis—not to mention the lifelong collaboration of these devoted friends—suggests that the juxtaposition obscures as much as it illuminates. Most revealing is the contrast between Jefferson's despairing, self-dramatizing, and ultimately tragic perspective on Missouri, and the (characteristically American) note of optimistic self-righteousness struck by the southern states' rightsers and proto-nationalists who invoked the authority of his principles.[118] Jefferson and Madison shared a common sense of foreboding about the future of the union, even as their legacies were deployed by opposing camps in the ideological crossfire that led to the Civil War. Or, it may be more accurately said that Jefferson, more deeply pessimistic than his friend, believed that the union had *already* been rent by the restrictionists' "geographical line," probably irrevocably. It was not an outcome he could view with equanimity. For Jefferson, the Missouri crisis marked the fundamental failure of the Revolution itself; far from welcoming the opportunity to put the states' rights "principles of 1798" into practice, Jefferson considered the fatal necessity of doing so a kind of death. To return to the first principles of 1776 was not to start afresh, an opportunity to invent the world anew; in sounding the "knell of the Union," in committing this "treason against the hopes of the world," the protagonists in the Missouri crisis had enacted the last rites for the great American experiment in Federalism and Republicanism. The obverse of the "medal" that had been struck to honor Jefferson and his fellow Revolutionaries was now being inscribed to the everlasting dishonor of their parricide sons.

A suddenly disillusioned old man, Jefferson may have indulged himself in a solipsistic fantasy of death and destruction. Yet in glimpsing the horrors of civil war, Jefferson was much more than a prophet of doom. Jefferson's despair in 1820 and 1821 illuminates the promise of 1776, the vision of a new world order founded on enlightened principles that inspired many Americans with patriotic fervor. It also raised to the fore fundamental dilemmas of American liberalism that his countrymen would not face and could not resolve. The Missouri crisis juxtaposed the claims of state equality, self-constitution, and noninterference, the foundational premises of Jeffersonian Federalism—and liberal internationalism—against restrictionist assertions that regimes founded on slavery could not be "republican" because they were not based on the free consent of their peoples.[119] In effect, the natural rights language of Jefferson's Declaration was turned against the equally "natural" rights of states to assert their equality and independence and so join in affectionate union.

These were—and are—America's dilemmas, not just Jefferson's. How can we reconcile the claims of individuals with the claims of states? How can guarantees of liberty and equality be made to serve, as Jefferson believed they must, as the threshhold of harmonious union and true nationhood? How can we promote the sense of community, the dedication to common principles, the national identity, that would make rights claims liberating and empowering? I offer these questions with trepidation, and a not quite hopeful spirit, for they were questions that drove a despairing Jefferson to imagine his own death and the destruction of his cherished union, thus "rendering desperate the experiment which was to decide ultimately whether man is capable of self-government."[120]

NOTES

The author is grateful for the criticism and advice of Andrew Burstein, Joseph J. Ellis, Joanne B. Freeman, Kevin Gutzman, Michael F. Holt, Stephen Innes, Melvyn Leffler, James E. Lewis, and Herbert Sloan.

1. Jefferson to James Donaldson, February 7, 1820, in Jefferson Papers, Library of Congress (microfilm edition).

2. For Tallmadge's amendment, February 13 and 15, 1819, see *Annals of the Congress of the United States, 1789–1824,* 42 vols. (Washington, 1834–56), 15th Cong., 2d sess. (House), 1166, 1170. The standard work is Glover Moore, *The Missouri Controversy, 1819–1821* (Lexington: University Press of Kentucky, 1953). On Jefferson's response, I am indebted to Dumas Malone, *The Sage of Monticello,* vol. 6 of *Jefferson and His Time* (Boston: Little, Brown, 1981), 328–61. For a more critical discussion of Jefferson and the Missouri crisis, see John Chester Miller, *The Wolf by the Ears: Thomas Jefferson and Slavery* (New York: Free Press, 1977), 221–52.

3. Jefferson to Hugh Nelson, March 12, 1820, in Andrew A. Lipscomb and Albert Ellery

Bergh, eds., *The Writings of Thomas Jefferson,* 20 vols. (Washington, D.C.: Jefferson Memorial Association of the United States, 1903–4), 15:238.

4. Jefferson to former congressman John Holmes (of Massachusetts), April 22, 1820, in ibid., 249.

5. For excellent discussions of Jefferson's "voice"—and the tension, if not contradiction, between an accommodating, concessive tone and the imperatives of partisanship—see Robert Dawidoff, "Man of Letters," in Merrill D. Peterson, ed., *Thomas Jefferson: A Reference Biography* (New York: Scribner, 1986), 181–98, and Douglas Wilson, "Jefferson and the Republic of Letters," in Peter S. Onuf, ed., *Jeffersonian Legacies* (Charlottesville: University of Virginia Press, 1993), 50–76. For a brief review of this issue, and further citations, see Onuf, "The Scholars' Jefferson," *William and Mary Quarterly,* 3d ser., 50 (1993): 690–92. The most comprehensive study of Jefferson's letter writing is Andrew Burstein, *The Inner Jefferson: Portrait of a Grieving Optimist* (Charlottesville: University of Virginia Press, 1995).

6. John Adams to Jefferson, November 23, 1819, in Lester J. Cappon, ed., *The Adams-Jefferson Letters: The Complete Correspondence between Thomas Jefferson and Abigail and John Adams,* 2 vols. (Chapel Hill: University of North Carolina Press, 1959), 2:548.

7. For Jefferson's nautical imagery, I am indebted to Burstein, *Inner Jefferson,* chap. 3.

8. Jefferson to John Adams, December 10, 1819, in Cappon, ed., *Adams-Jefferson Letters,* 2:548–49. For a sympathetic brief account of this correspondence, see Joseph J. Ellis, *The Passionate Sage: The Character and Legacy of John Adams* (New York: Norton, 1993), 113–42; for commentary on Missouri, see 138–42. Not surpisingly, Adams was "utterly averse to the admission of Slavery into the Missouri Territory" (John Adams to William Tudor, November 20, 1819, quoted in Ellis, *Passionate Sage,* 140). But Adams tactfully avoided such assertions in his correspondence with Jefferson, hopefully suggesting that the controversy might "follow the other Waves under the Ship and do no harm." (John Adams to Jefferson, December 21, 1819, in Cappon, ed., *Adams-Jefferson Letters,* 551). It is apparent, however, that Adams could not understand why Jefferson was so upset by the Missouri affair. Taking a longer view of the nation's prospects, Adams assumed the role of a "Cassandra," predicting that "this mighty Fabric [would be rent] in twain, or perhaps into a leash" by the disunionist schemes of "another Hamilton" or "another Burr"; in the end, there might be "as many Nations in North America as there are in Europe" (Cappon, ed., *Adams-Jefferson Letters,* 551). But Jefferson did not believe that rogue spirits such as Burr or Hamilton could ever endanger the union again; the whole point of his analysis was that union was threatened from within, *not* by separatists, but rather by neo-Federalist consolidationists who sought to destroy states' rights. The Missouri crisis resulted from rejection of the settlers' efforts to *join* the union, and not from any original intention of theirs to break away from it. Finally, Adams could broach the possibility of the Europeanization of North America with philosophical equanimity; such a prospect was abhorrent to Jefferson, as we will see below. Jefferson did not respond to this letter; perhaps Adams' rather whimsical, humorously pompous language ("mighty Fabric" and "leash" of independent nations, suggesting a pack of dogs and evoking a conventional view of the state of nature where the "dogs of war" were unleashed) was sufficient to tell Jefferson that Adams was not taking him seriously.

9. Jefferson to John Holmes, April 22, 1820, in Cappon, ed., *Adams-Jefferson Letters*, 15:250. For a brief discussion of this letter, see Paul Finkelman, "Jefferson and Slavery: 'Treason against the Hopes of the World,'" in Onuf, ed., *Jeffersonian Legacies*, 211–12.

10. Jefferson to John Adams, January 22, 1821, in Cappon, ed., *Adams-Jefferson Letters*, 2:569, my emphasis. For another reference to "our Holy Alliance of restrictionists," see Jefferson to Joseph Cabell, January 31, 1821, in Lipscomb and Bergh, eds., *Writings of Thomas Jefferson*, 15:311. Jefferson was urging expeditious action on his cherished plans for the University of Virginia—a place where Virginia boys would not be seduced by restrictionist principles, as he supposed was happening at Princeton, where "more than half [the students] were Virginians."

11. Jefferson to the Marquis de La Fayette, December 26, 1820, in Lipscomb and Bergh, eds., *Writings of Thomas Jefferson*, 15:301. At this point, he had concluded that the controversy was a "wave," not a "breaker": "the boisterous sea of liberty indeed is never without a wave, and that from Missouri is now rolling towards us, but we shall ride over it as we have over all others" (ibid., 300–301).

12. Jefferson to Charles Pinckney, September 30, 1820, in ibid., 280. For a discussion of partisan motives that offers substantiation for this perception, see Moore, *Missouri Controversy*, 66–83.

13. Jefferson to Adams, January 22, 1821, in Cappon, ed., *Adams-Jefferson Letters*, 2:570. For a slightly earlier, more circumspect formulation of these concerns, see Jefferson to Albert Gallatin, December 26, 1820, in Merrill D. Peterson, ed., *Thomas Jefferson: Writings* (New York: Library of America, 1984), 1447–50.

14. Miller, *Wolf by the Ears*, 231–32. Merrill Peterson writes that the controversy "threw Jefferson into the deepest political malaise of his entire life." Peterson, *Thomas Jefferson and the New Nation: A Biography* (New York: Oxford University Press, 1970), 997–98. Peterson, Dumas Malone, John Chester Miller, and Garrett Ward Sheldon all suggest that Jefferson's "malaise" was at least in part attributable to his concerns about the consolidationist tendencies of the Marshall Court (exacerbated by *McCulloch v. Maryland* [1819], but dating back to the early days of his presidency), banks, the protective tariff, and a variety of other issues that seemed ominously interrelated. See Peterson, *Thomas Jefferson and the New Nation*, 988–1004 (noting Jefferson's own disastrous financial affairs in these years); Miller, *Wolf by the Ears*, 226–31 (emphasizing Jefferson's concern that the South-West axis that had dominated American politics was in jeopardy); and Sheldon, *The Political Philosophy of Thomas Jefferson* (Baltimore: Johns Hopkins University Press, 1991), 135–40 (arguing that "the emancipation of slaves occupied a lower position than either his personal lifestyle or the ideal [agrarian] republic for which he had risked his life and fortune," 139.) Jefferson's zeal for state's rights "bordered on fanaticism," concedes Malone—the friendliest of biographers (Malone, *Sage of Monticello*, 356).

15. See the discussion of the antebellum response to Jefferson's ambiguous legacy on slavery restriction in Merrill D. Peterson, *The Jefferson Image in the American Mind* (New York: Oxford University Press, 1960), 189–226, esp. 189–94.

16. Jefferson to Hon. Mark Langdon Hill, April 5, 1820, in Lipscomb and Bergh, eds., *Writings of Thomas Jefferson*, 15:243.

17. Jefferson to William Short, April 13, 1820; to John Holmes, April 22, 1820; to Charles Pinckney, September 30, 1820, in ibid., 247, 249–50, 280–81.

18. Jefferson to William Short, August 4, 1820, in ibid, 263. For an illuminating analysis of the relation of Latin American developments to the politics—and theoretical premises—of American federalism, see James E. Lewis, Jr., "'We Shall Have Good Neighbours': The American Union and the Collapse of the Spanish Empire, 1783–1829" (Ph.D. diss., University of Virginia, 1994).

19. Jefferson to William Short, August 4, 1820, in Lipscomb and Bergh, eds., *Writings of Thomas Jefferson,* 15:263.

20. Jefferson to Charles Pinckney, September 30, 1820, in ibid., 15:281.

21. Jefferson to Benjamin Rush, October 20, 1820, in ibid., 284. See also Jefferson to Albert Gallatin, December 26, 1820, in Peterson, ed., *Jefferson: Writings,* 1450: "should this scission take place, one of it's most deplorable consequences would be it's discouragement of the efforts of the European nations in the regeneration of their oppressive and Cannibal governments."

22. Jefferson to Charles Pinckney, September 30, 1820, in Lipscomb and Bergh, eds., *Writings of Thomas Jefferson,* 15:280.

23. Jefferson to Charles Pinckney, September 30, 1820; Jefferson to William Short, April 13, 1820, both in ibid., 280, 247.

24. Jefferson to John Holmes, April 22, 1820, in ibid., 250.

25. Jefferson to M. Barbe de Marbois, June 14, 1817, in ibid., 130–31.

26. For a fuller discussion of these themes, see Peter S. Onuf and Nicholas G. Onuf, *Federal Union, Modern World: The Law of Nations in an Age of Revolutions, 1776–1814* (Madison: Madison House, 1993).

27. Jefferson to John Jacob Astor, November 9, 1813, in Lipscomb and Bergh, eds., *Writings of Thomas Jefferson,* 13:433; see also Jefferson to John Jacob Astor, May 24, 1812, in ibid., 150–51.

28. Jefferson to Sen. John Breckinridge (Ky.), August 12, 1803, in ibid., 10:409–10.

29. Jefferson rehearsed the alternative scenario in an anxious letter to Robert R. Livingston, written before the crisis was resolved, April 18, 1802: "the day that France takes possession of N. Orleans fixes the sentence which is to restrain her forever within her low water mark. It seals the union of two nations who in conjunction can maintain exclusive possession of the ocean. From that moment we must marry ourselves to the British fleet and nation" (Peterson, ed., *Jefferson: Writings,* 1105). It is curious that Jefferson, the notorious Anglophobe, should here imagine not just an ad hoc alliance (thus responding to diplomatic exigencies in a way that "realists" so admire), but should talk of a lasting "union" between the two nations that could be described as a "marriage." The ghost of this marriage is apparent in the letter to Breckinridge discussed above, where Jefferson imagines "an Englishman . . . procuring future blessings for the French nation." It is the French, not the English, who are the "foreigners" in this transaction.

30. For an earlier expression of this theme, see Jefferson to James Madison, January 30, 1787, in William T. Hutchinson et al., eds., *The Papers of James Madison,* 17 vols. (Chicago: University of Chicago Press, and Charlottesville: University of Virginia Press, 1962–91),

9:247–52: Americans could never be brought to "cut the throats of their brothers and sons." Here was the most powerful argument against enforcing restriction, "Wilberforce" wrote in the *Richmond Enquirer*, January 6, 1820: "With what face could we march to the slaughter of our brothers and children, resisting by armed force the invasion of unlicensed power?"

31. Scholars have lavished considerable attention on the "radical" implications of Jefferson's making each rising generation "sovereign" with respect to its predecessors. In the famous letter to Madison (September 6, 1789, in *Jefferson: Writings*, ed. Peterson, 962), Jefferson wrote that "between society and society, generation and generation there is no municipal obligation, no umpire but the law of nature." This was, Jefferson explained, precisely the condition of independent states under international law: "by the law of nature, one generation is to another as one independant nation to another." The passing on, from generation to generation, of an enormous public debt constituted a de facto "state of war" (disguised by the forms of municipal law) between the dead (who squandered the common wealth with which they had been entrusted) and the living. But Jefferson's manifesto should not be construed as a "declaration of war" between the generations: to the contrary, the constitutional protection against the accumulation of such debts that he urged on Madison and his congressional colleagues would preempt all grounds of future contention along generational lines. Generational equity was thus analogous to state equality: it would facilitate the "union" of fathers and sons by eliminating all artificial obstructions to their natural harmony and affection. The antitype of Jefferson's affectionate, familial regime was *aristocracy,* the institutional embodiment of intergenerational inequity and the corrupt foundation of the European old regime. Jefferson was thus extending and elaborating what he took to be the fundamental principle of the American Revolution, the principle that defined the difference between Europe and America; he was *not* advocating redistributionist policies, nor was he seeking to provide a theoretical rationale for evading his own debts to (largely foreign) creditors. My understanding of this dimension of Jefferson's thought is indebted to Herbert Sloan, "'The Earth Belongs in Usufruct to the Living,'" in Onuf, ed., *Jeffersonian Legacies,* 281–315, and to the fuller treatment in Sloan's *Principle and Interest: Thomas Jefferson and the Problem of Debt* (New York: Oxford University Press, 1995). For a suggestive discussion of the kind of intergenerational relations Jefferson hoped would emerge in Virginia and in the new nation generally, see Harold Hellenbrand, *The Unfinished Revolution: Education and Politics in the Thought of Thomas Jefferson* (Newark: University of Delaware Press, 1990). The natural relationship of father and son—recapitulated in the classroom in the relationship between mentor and student—constituted Jefferson's paradigm for affectionate union.

32. This incoherence in Jefferson's conception of the minimal state was suggested to me by Robert A. Gross of the College of William and Mary.

33. Jefferson to Joseph Cabell, February 2, 1816; to Samuel Kercheval, July 12, 1816; to Kercheval, September 5, 1816, in Lipscomb and Bergh, eds., *Writings of Thomas Jefferson,* 14:417–23; 15:32–44; and 15:70–73. See the stimulating discussion in Matthews, *Radical Politics of Thomas Jefferson,* 77–95.

34. Jefferson to Samuel Kercheval, July 12, 1816, in Lipscomb and Bergh, eds., *Writings of Thomas Jefferson,* 15:38.

35. Jefferson to Joseph Cabell, February 2, 1816, in ibid., 14:421.

36. Onuf and Onuf, *Federal Union, Modern World,* 74–91.

37. My analysis in the following paragraphs has been strongly influenced by William John Antholis, "Liberal Democratic Theory and the Transformation of Sovereignty" (Ph.D. diss., Yale University, 1993), esp. chap. 4, "Thomas Jefferson and the American Dissolution of Sovereignty." Jefferson did not "dissolve" sovereignty by transmuting it into the "fiction" of popular sovereignty, but rather by discovering it—and seeking to give it efficacy—*everywhere,* in the claims of distinct generations, or in the various levels of self-government. On popular sovereignty, see Edmund S. Morgan, *Inventing the People: The Rise of Popular Sovereignty in England and America* (New York: Norton, 1988).

38. Jefferson to Samuel Kercheval, September 5, 1816, in Lipscomb and Bergh, eds., *Writings of Thomas Jefferson,* 15:72. The "sacred compact" argument was subsequently elaborated by "An American" in *Missouri Question,* no. 5, *Richmond Enquirer,* January 13, 1820.

39. The best history of New England separatism in this period is James M. Banner, Jr., *To the Hartford Convention: The Federalists and the Origins of Party Politics in Massachusetts, 1789–1815* (New York: Knopf, 1970). For a good brief discussion of Jefferson's animus toward New England, see Robert E. Shalhope, "Thomas Jefferson's Republicanism and Antebellum Southern Thought," *Journal of Southern History* 42 (1976): 539–42.

40. The negotiators at Ghent were awaiting the "result, not of the Congress of Vienna, but of Hartford," Jefferson wrote his old friend M. Correa de Serra, December 27, 1814, in Lipscomb and Bergh, eds., *Writings of Thomas Jefferson,* 14:225.

41. See Jefferson to Pres. James Monroe, June 11, 1823, in ibid., 15:435: "the matter which now embroils Europe, *the presumption of dictating to an independent nation [in this case, Naples] the form of its government,* is so arrogant, so atrocious, that indignation, as well as moral sentiment, enlists all our partialities and prayers in favor of one, and our equal execrations against the other." My emphasis.

42. Jefferson to Lafayette, February 14, 1815, in ibid., 14:251.

43. Jefferson's First Inuagural Address, March 4, 1801, in *Jefferson: Writings,* ed. Peterson, 493.

44. Before the outbreak of war, Jefferson discussed the possibility of "a separate treaty between [Britain] and your Essex men" (Jefferson to Gen. Henry Dearborn, August 14, 1811, in Lipscomb and Bergh, eds., *Writings of Thomas Jefferson,* 13:73).

45. This unnatural dependency would put Massachusetts in the anomalous and untenable position of Britain's remaining American colonies. On the Jeffersonian reliance on America's agricultural productivity as a key to an effective foreign policy, see Drew R. McCoy, *The Elusive Republic: Political Economy in Jeffersonian America* (Chapel Hill: University of North Carolina Press, 1980) and J. C. A. Stagg, *Mr. Madison's War: Politics, Diplomacy and Warfare in the Early American Republic, 1783–1830* (Princeton: Princeton University Press, 1983).

46. The quotations in the previous two paragraphs are all from Jefferson to James Martin, September 20, 1813, in Lipscomb and Bergh, eds., *Writings of Thomas Jefferson,* 13:382–83.

47. If war should break out between Massachusetts and the union, "it would be a contest

of one against fifteen," Jefferson wrote James Martin, September 20, 1813, in ibid., 383. For further comments on the "defection of Massachusetts" and the "factionists of Boston," see Jefferson to William Short, November 28, 1814, and Jefferson to John Melish, December 10, 1814, in ibid., 14:217–18 and 221.

48. Jefferson to William Short, November 28, 1814, in ibid., 217–18.

49. Jefferson discounts the "danger from the defection of Massachusetts" in his letter to William Short, November 28, 1814, in ibid., 217.

50. Jefferson to Baron Alexander von Humboldt, December 6, 1813, in ibid., 22.

51. Jefferson to John Melish, January 13, 1813, in ibid., 13:209.

52. Jefferson to Dr. John Crawford, January 2, 1812, in ibid., 119.

53. Jefferson to Horatio G. Spafford, March 17, 1814, in ibid., 14:120. Jefferson's brief for the extended republic was, of course, a recapitulation of James Madison's *Federalist* No. 10: "the influence of factious leaders may kindle a flame within their particular States, but will be unable to spread a general conflagration through the other States" (Jacob E. Cooke, ed., *The Federalist* [Middletown, Conn.: Wesleyan University Press, 1961]), 64.

54. Jefferson to Dr. Elijah Griffith, May 28, 1809, in Lipscomb and Bergh, eds., *Writings of Thomas Jefferson,* 12:285.

55. Jefferson to Henry Dearborn, March 17, 1815, in ibid., 14:288–89.

56. Ibid., 289.

57. Jefferson to John Holmes, April 22, 1820, in ibid., 15:249.

58. Jefferson to Albert Gallatin, June 16, 1817, in ibid., 135.

59. Jefferson to Henry Dearborn, March 17, 1815, in ibid., 14:287–88.

60. Jefferson to William H. Crawford, February 11, 1812, p.s. of February 26, in ibid., 244.

61. For the analogy of the union to "the planetary system," see Jefferson to John Melish, December 10, 1814, in ibid., 221.

62. Jefferson to Col. William Duane, March 28, 1811, in ibid., 13:28–29. For an excellent discussion of this theme, see Roger H. Brown, *The Republic in Peril: 1812* (New York: Columbia University Press, 1964).

63. Kent Co., Del., Democratic-Republicans to Jefferson, January 13, 1807, Jefferson Papers, DLC.

64. New York General Republican Committee to Jefferson, received December 16, 1806, in ibid.

65. Chenango Co., N.Y., Republicans to Jefferson, January 19, 1807, in ibid.

66. Young Men of Democratic Principles, Philadelphia, to Jefferson, December 1, 1806, in ibid.

67. Maryland Legislature to Jefferson, January 3, 1807, in ibid.

68. The standard account is Thomas Abernethy, *The Burr Conspiracy* (New York: Oxford University Press, 1954). See also Dumas Malone, *Jefferson the President: Second Term, 1805–1809* (Boston: Little, Brown, 1974), vol. 5 of *Jefferson and His Time,* esp. 215–88.

69. Ohio General Assembly Address in support of Jefferson administration, December 6, 1806, in Jefferson Papers, DLC.

70. Chenango Co., N.Y., Republicans to Jefferson, January 19, 1807, in ibid. See also

Orange Co., N.Y., Republicans to Jefferson, December 27, 1806, in ibid: "the finances of our nation are in so flourishing a state . . . (because) they have not been lavished upon '*every speck of War,*' but are still in reserve for real and not imaginary dangers."

71. "Wars of ambition are the offspring of Monarchy; they are incompatible with the genius and the spirit of our excellent constitution. When freemen are summoned to the field of battle it should be to defend and not to sacrifice their happiness and liberties" (New York General Committee to Jefferson, received December 16, 1806, in ibid.).

72. Kent Co., Del., Democratic-Republicans to Jefferson, January 13, 1807, in ibid. Many of the addresses emphasized the "difference between [the Europeans'] Situation and our own." See the Young Men of Democratic Principles, Philadelphia, to Jefferson, December 1, 1806, in ibid.

73. Proclamation of November 27, 1806, in James D. Richardson, ed., *A Compilation of the Messages and Papers of the Presidents, 1789–1902,* 12 vols. (Washington, D.C.: Bureau of National Literature, 1903–9), 1:404.

74. See Jefferson's Notes (on procedure to be followed against conspirators), November 25, 1806, including a list of letters to be written to officials at Pittsburgh, Marietta, Louisville, New Orleans, and other locations, Jefferson Papers, DLC.

75. Jefferson to Gov. William C. C. Claiborne at New Orleans, December 20, 1806, in ibid.

76. Malone, *Jefferson the President: Second Term,* 291–370.

77. Jefferson to Isaac Weaver, Jr., June 7, 1807, in Lipscomb and Bergh, eds., *Writings of Thomas Jefferson,* 11:220–21. For similar sentiments, see Jefferson to M. Dupont de Nemours and Jefferson to Marquis de la Fayette, both July 14, 1807, in ibid., 275–76, 277–79.

78. Jefferson to Gov. William C. C. Claiborne, February 3, 1807, in ibid., 151.

79. Young Men of Democratic Principles, Philadelphia, to Jefferson, December 1, 1806, in Jefferson Papers, DLC.

80. Jefferson to James Bowdoin, April 2, 1807, in Lipscomb and Bergh, eds., *Writings of Thomas Jefferson,* 11:185.

81. Malone, *Jefferson the President: Second Term,* 237–38, 360–62.

82. Jefferson to Gov. John Langdon (N.H.), December 22, 1806, in Jefferson Papers, DLC. For such a prediction, see a pamphlet by Joseph Hamilton Daveiss (the Federalist U.S. Attorney in Kentucky, and a leading opponent of the Burr conspiracy in that state), *An Essay on Federalism* (Frankfort?, 1810?), 46: "The farther a state government is removed from the national centre, the less it hears, and sees, and feels, of that government, and the less interest it takes in its concerns. You must, therefore, expect the federative cord to weaken as it is stretched and extended. . . ."

83. Jefferson to William B. Giles, April 20, 1807, in Lipscomb and Bergh, eds., *Writings of Thomas Jefferson,* 11:187.

84. Jefferson to Charles Clay, January 11, 1807, in ibid., 133.

85. Jefferson to Gov. Edward Tiffin, February 2, 1807, in ibid., 147. On Ohio's "patriotism and public spirit," see also Jefferson to Sec. of War (Henry Dearborn), October 27, 1807, in ibid., 385–86.

86. See Jefferson to Gen. John Shee (Philadlephia Republican Militia) and Jefferson to Capt. Charles Christian (Saratoga Rangers), both January 14, 1807, declining offers to mobilize: "I am ever unwilling that [peace] should be disturbed, until greater and more important interests call for an appeal to force." In ibid., 140–41, 141–142, quotations at 140.

87. Jefferson's Sixth Annual Message, December 2, 1806, in Richardson, ed., *Messages and Papers,* 1:410.

88. Jefferson's First Annual Message, December 8, 1801, in ibid., 327.

89. Jefferson to William Short, October 3, 1801, in Lipscomb and Bergh, eds., *Writings of Thomas Jefferson,* 10:287.

90. For further discussion of this point, see Onuf and Onuf, *Federal Union, Modern World,* 179–82.

91. Jefferson to Dr. James Brown, October 27, 1808, in Lipscomb and Bergh, eds., *Writings of Thomas Jefferson,* 12:185.

92. Jefferson to Dr. James Brown, October 27, 1808, in ibid., 183–85.

93. Jefferson's first inaugural address, March 4, 1801, in *Jefferson: Writings,* ed. Peterson, 493.

94. Jefferson's second inaugural address, March 4, 1805, in Richardson, ed., *Messages and Papers,* 1:379.

95. For Jefferson's original draft of the Declaration, with Congress's revisions interlineated, see *Jefferson: Writings,* ed. Peterson, 19–24, quotations at 19, my emphasis. The scholarly literature on Jefferson and the Declaration is vast. For a good recent discussion, see Joseph J. Ellis, *American Sphinx: The Character of Thomas Jefferson* (forthcoming), chap. 2. The definitive work on the political history of independence is Jack N. Rakove, *The Beginnings of National Politics: An Interpretive History of the Continental Congress* (New York, 1979), 87–110. My understanding of Jefferson's sentimental conception of union is indebted to Garry Wills, *Inventing America: Jefferson's Declaration of Independence* (Garden City, N.J., 1978), esp. 259–319, and Jay Fliegelman, *Declaring Independence: Jefferson, Natural Language, and the Culture of Performance* (Stanford: Stanford University Press, 1993). See also the suggestive comments in Gordon S. Wood, "Trials and Tribulations of Jefferson," in Onuf, ed., *Jeffersonian Legacies,* 395–417. Jefferson, writes Wood, "always conceived of his 'empire of liberty' as one of like principles, not like boundaries"; his "contempt for the modern state" was predicated on "his extraordinary faith in the natural sociability of people" (408). For an illuminating discussion of Jefferson's *Summary View of the Rights of British America* (1774) that underscores its federalist premises and nationalist intentions, see Stephen A. Conrad, "Putting Rights Talk in Its Place: *The Summary View* Revisited," in Onuf, ed., *Jeffersonian Legacies,* 253–80. Conrad's reading of this crucial text provides important clues to Jefferson's concerns in the Declaration.

96. *Jefferson: Writings,* ed. Peterson, 23, 22–23. On the "Authority of Migration," see John Phillip Reid, *The Authority of Rights,* vol. 1 of his *Constitutional History of the American Revolution* (Madison: University of Wisconsin Press, 1986), 114–23.

97. *Jefferson: Writings,* ed. Peterson, 23. On the importance of treaties for Anglo-American imperial reformers, see Onuf and Onuf, *Federal Union, Modern World,* 108–13. For a discus-

sion of Anglo-American and American nationalism, see Peter S. Onuf, "Federalism, Republicanism, and the Origins of American Sectionalism," in Edward L. Ayers and Peter S. Onuf, eds., *All Over the Map: Rethinking Region and Nation in the United States* (forthcoming).

98. See, for example, Carl L. Becker, The *Declaration of Independence: A Study in the History of Political Ideas* (paperback ed., New York: Knopf, 1958; orig. pub., 1922), 213: "Congress omitted this passage [on the slave trade] altogether. I am glad it did. One does not expect a declaration of independence to represent historical events with the objectivity and exactitude of a scientific treatise; but here the discrepancy between the fact and the representation is too flagrant." Though Wills, in *Inventing America*, 65–75, challenges the conventional understanding (I believe mistakenly) that Jefferson "resented changes in his document only, or even principally, because this clause was omitted," he agrees that the document was much improved by this excision. Quotation at 74.

99. Thomas Jefferson, Autobiography, January 6, 1821, in *Jefferson: Writings*, ed. Peterson, 100–101; quotations above and in subsequent paragraph at 18. Jefferson carried his story as far as his arrival as Secretary of State in New York in 1790, reaching this point on July 29, 1821.

100. Joanne Freeman, " 'Slander, Poisons, Whispers, and Fame:' Jefferson's 'Anas' and Political Gossip in the Early Republic," *Journal of the Early Republic* (forthcoming).

101. Jefferson's draft of the Declaration, in Jefferson: Writings, ed. Peterson, 22.

102. Jefferson, Autobiography, in ibid., 18.

103. Jefferson's draft of the Declaration, in ibid., 22.

104. Jefferson to Hugh Nelson, March 12, 1820, and to Charles Pinckney, September 30, 1820, in Lipscomb and Bergh, eds., *Writings of Thomas Jefferson*, 15:239, 280.

105. Jefferson to John Holmes, April 22, 1820, in ibid., 250.

106. Ibid.

107. Jefferson to William Short, April 13, 1820, in ibid., 248, my emphasis.

108. Jefferson to Maria Cosway, October 12, 1786, in *Jefferson: Writings*, ed. Peterson, 874–75.

109. For an excellent account of these years, see Peterson, *Jefferson and the New Nation*, 97–240.

110. Peter S. Onuf, *Statehood and Union: A History of the Northwest Ordinance* (Bloomington: Indiana University Press, 1987), 44–54. See also the editorial note and documents on the 1784 Ordinance in Julian Boyd, ed., *The Papers of Thomas Jefferson* (Princeton: Princeton University Press, 1950-), 6:581–617.

111. Report of the Committee, March 1, 1784, in *The Papers of Thomas Jefferson*, ed. Boyd, 6:604. The ban on settlers with hereditary titles was omitted in the ordinance adopted by Congress on April 23, ibid., 613–15.

112. For a suggestive discussion of Jefferson's geopolitical concerns in the 1784 Ordinance, see Robert F. Berkhofer, Jr., "Jefferson, the Ordinance of 1784, and the Origins of the American Territorial System," *William and Mary Quarterly* 29 (1972): 231–62.

113. For Jefferson's misgivings about these revisions, see Onuf, *Statehood and Union*, 50–56. The text of the Northwest Ordinance is reprinted in ibid., 60–64. James Monroe, who played a key role in the revision process, reassured Jefferson that the "most important

principles" of his plan were "preserv'd" in Congress' new "colonial" system (Monroe to Jefferson, May 11, 1786, cited in ibid., 54).

114. For a history of this compromise tradition, see Peter B. Knupfer, *The Union as It Is: Constitutional Unionism and Sectional Compromise, 1787–1861* (Chapel Hill: University of North Carolinia Press, 1991).

115. For an engaging portrait of Madison in his retirement years that substantiates this contrast with Jefferson, see Drew R. McCoy, *The Last of the Fathers: James Madison and the Republican Legacy* (New York: Cambridge University Press, 1989). Madison responded "with far greater equanimity" to the settlement of the Missouri controversy "than many other prominent Virginians"—including his friend Jefferson. Quotation at 113.

116. Draft of the Kentucky Resolutions, October 1798, in *Jefferson: Writings,* ed. Peterson, 453.

117. Madison may have been protesting too much in dissociating himself from the legacy of 1798—and, implicitly, from Jefferson. See Kevin Gutzman, "A Troublesome Legacy: James Madison and the 'Principles of '98,' " in *Journal of the Early Republic* (forthcoming).

118. See Jesse T. Carpenter, *The South as a Conscious Minority, 1789-1861: A Study in Political Thought* (Columbia: University of South Carolina Press, 1990; orig. pub., New York: New York University Press, 1930), and John McCardell, *The Idea of a Southern Nation* (New York: Norton, 1979).

119. See the speech by Sen. Richard M. Johnson of Kentucky, February 1, 1820, in *Annals of Congress,* 16th Cong., 1st sess., 350, explaining what Jefferson "meant" by saying "all men are created equal:" "The meaning of this sentence is defined by its application; that all communities stand upon an equality; that Americans are equal with Englishmen, and have the right to organize such government for themselves as they shall choose, whenever it is their pleasure to dissolve the bonds which unite them to another people. The same principle applied to Missouri will defeat the object of gentlemen who advocate this restriction."

120. Jefferson to William Short, April 13, 1820, in Lipscomb and Bergh, eds., *Writings of Thomas Jefferson,* 15:248.

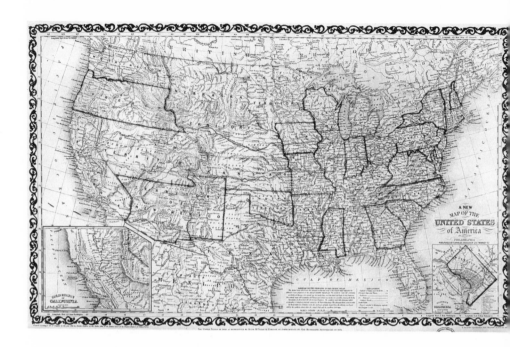

REPRODUCTION FROM *Mitchell's Universal Atlas,* REPRODUCED BY RAND, MCNALLY & CO.,
1956. MISSOURI HISTORICAL SOCIETY LIBRARY MAP COLLECTION.

When the Bent brothers explored the West in the mid-nineteenth century, the old boundaries that marked the territorial ambitions of France, Spain, and Great Britain had vanished or were much changed. Despite those changes, the claims of native people to the land remained. Young's map announces the arrival of a continental power while giving silent testimony to the moral price for Jefferson's "final consolidation" of the American nation.

CHAPTER SEVEN

GREAT DREAMS, GREAT PLAINS
Jefferson, the Bents, and the West

ELLIOTT WEST

My assignment is to shed some new light on the uses of western lands during those years of the nineteenth century that bore the mark of Thomas Jefferson and his ideas about the American West.

That's an impossibly tall order. To trim it down, I will concentrate on a particular part of the West—the Great Plains, specifically the central portion, the 100,000 or so square miles of what is today western Kansas, eastern Colorado, and southern Nebraska. This country is familiar to the reading and viewing public. It is rich in images and heavy with legends about cowboys, cavalry, tenacious sodbusters, and brave mounted warriors. The central plains also have been one of the most vigorously studied parts of the West. The result—a considerable amount of scholarship from historians, anthropologists, archaeologists, and others—can help in asking and answering some basic questions about how the West was used (and misused) in the nineteenth century.

My perspective on that country—my point of reckoning—will be St. Louis, a city that takes proper pride in being the Gateway to the West and the home of a memorial honoring our third president. Specifically, I'll look at the central plains through the lives and lessons of one of St. Louis' most remarkable families—the Bents, a collection of extraordinary men and women who had an enormous influence on western history. By focusing on this one family and on one part of the West, I'll try to turn a hopelessly large task into a more manageable piece of work.

The patriarch of the Bent family, Judge Silas Bent, an eminent civic figure, presided with his wife, Martha, over a sprawling household at Rock Point, today near North Third Street in downtown St. Louis. Their brood of eleven

155

children (eight sons and three daughters) would play prominent and varied roles in the history of their city and the West, as would their descendants. One of Silas and Martha's great-grandsons, for instance, was Montana's Charlie Russell, arguably the West's most famous artist.[1]

The Bents best known to western historians were the first and sixth sons, Charles and William. Their famous careers can be sketched briefly. With a partner, Ceran St. Vrain, and their brother George, William and Charles formed a trading enterprise and established a mercantile outpost, Bent's Fort, along the Arkansas River near present-day La Junta in southeastern Colorado. Through this enterprise, they took in bison robes from several plains tribes— the Cheyennes, Arapahoes, Comanches, Kiowas, and others—and sent them off to St. Louis and New Mexico in exchange for a variety of goods brought in from the those markets. To facilitate that trade, William married Owl Woman, a member of a prominent Southern Cheyenne family.

Charles, in the meantime, settled in northern New Mexico, where he too married into the local elite and quickly emerged as an influential figure in local society, politics, and economic life. Charles became a leading player in the growing trade along the Santa Fe Trail connecting Missouri with New Mexico, some of which passed through Bent's Fort, further adding to the family coffers. With the coming of war with Mexico in 1846, Charles Bent negotiated the bloodless surrender of New Mexico to the U.S., and for that he was named the territory's first governor. Soon after that he was killed in Taos during an uprising against the new regime. William continued the family firm, although his history from that point was not a happy one. He watched the steady decline in the fortunes of his kinsmen, the Cheyennes, and witnessed the gathering conflict between them and the advancing white frontier, conflict which culminated in the infamous butchery at Sand Creek in 1864. He died in May of 1869.

William and Charles Bent had the gift of moving easily among very different realms—the cultural worlds of Anglo, Native, and Hispanic Americans and the geographical settings of the nineteenth century urban frontier, the Southwest, and the Great Plains. That, in turn, offers us the chance to look back from quite different perspectives on what was happening. Through the Bents, we are privy to a multiangled vision of the West and western lands during a time of extraordinary changes.

One angle of vision is that from St. Louis itself. Growing up there early in the century, the Bent brothers would have shared prevailing views and expectations about the country that rolled westward from their city to the Rocky Mountains. The images in their heads were, in a sense, the heritage of Thomas Jefferson. Americans living east of the Missouri River held certain common notions of the plains that had originated during the first years of the century, when President Jefferson had tried to acquire at least some basic facts about the millions of acres he had bought from France in 1803.[2] Jefferson's investigative enterprise resulted in descriptive reports presented to him and to the American public. Out of those reports emerged a series of impressions of the plains that fell roughly into two general categories—a pair of fundamentally contradictory images of the West and how it could be used.

The first image came from the expedition of Zebulon Pike in 1805–7.[3] Based on Pike's reports, the plains appeared as a forbidding desert, desolate and barren and incapable of supporting agriculture, any advanced society, indeed anything but the thinnest and most backward population. That was obviously a discouraging prospect in many ways, but the plains, as desert, also offered a couple of advantages. Restless pioneers, always itchy to move just a little farther west, would finally be stopped short. They would be forced to set down roots in places like Missouri, to take care of their lands, and to cultivate proper and civilized communities. The desert would serve a second purpose. So forbidding and treacherous was this country that it would provide an unbridgeable protective barrier, an impenetrable buffer zone shielding the U.S. from any attack by enemies to the west.

The second image was rooted in the other Jeffersonian expedition, that of Lewis and Clark, who moved up the Missouri and across the northern plains just before Pike left for the South.[4] By this image, the plains appeared far more promising, almost like a garden—a land of potential agrarian abundance. Here was a great land bank that American yeomen could draw upon for generations into the future. In this country fruitful farmlands and modest communities would be bound together in webs of healthy commerce.[5]

These two very different views of the plains were not equally prominent throughout these years. The first forbidding image—the plains as desert— dominated early on, but the second, happier vision was coming on strong by the middle years of the nineteenth century. The impressions carried home by Lewis and Clark, in fact, blossomed into increasingly glowing accounts by 1840s, especially after Kansas and Nebraska were opened to settlement. An 1855 pamphlet described western Kansas and eastern Colorado as a series of fertile valleys deep in rich, black soil, with plenty of building stone, vast deposits of coal, copper, gypsum, and zinc, and thick stands of oak, hickory, and ash. The high plains of the upper Arkansas and Platte, this writer predicted, would "soon be swarming with active, industrious inhabitants," and church spires and courthouse turrets would be "lifting their heads among the hills."[6] The agrarian wealth, some predicted, would soon attract a busy commerce, including a steamship line that would stretch virtually unbroken from the Atlantic, past the Mississippi valley and the prairies beyond, then onto the plains, where ships would chug their way up deep rivers in western Kansas and finally dock at the base of the Rocky Mountains at the site of modern Denver.

The discovery of gold in Colorado inspired even grander visions for the plains. A St. Louis editor wrote that the gold fields would be "the evangel to a new commerce." Hungry miners would soon be fed by grain and cattle from the farmer's paradise that stretched between the Rockies and the Missouri River. Grasslands around Denver could support "millions of cattle," wrote one promoter, and another claimed that streams of the high plains "recall the luxuriance of the tropics, or the magnificence of the ideal world of old navigators." The real money, said yet another, would be found not in gold but in plains farming: "The plow and the scythe will yield a better return . . . than the pan and the pick."[7]

So as the Bent brothers were setting up shop along the Arkansas, and during the thirty years that followed, two dueling visions of the plains and how they might be used were developing among outsiders from the East. These images—the plains as desert and the plains as fruitful gardenland—were the basis of the Jeffersonian legacy for the West. In a larger sense, this Jeffersonian tradition has become part of a deeply entrenched and widely felt vision of what the West is and how it ought to be treated. This perceived West, still much with us today, has pervaded our popular culture, from fiction and art to movies and advertising. All too often, it has influenced public policy toward the country beyond the Missouri. Following the Jeffersonian lead, this popular view sees the West either as the hard country, denying human habitation, or as potentially America's gardenland where society might flower anew. He has been in his grave for 170 years now, but through these images Thomas Jefferson is still with us.

As readers might have guessed, the Jeffersonian images of the West generally and the plains in particular were not necessarily very accurate. This was in fact a tough and dangerous and stingy land, as the first vision suggested, but it was no sterile desert, forbidding human presence and blocking human movement. As for the second image, the plains did indeed offer plenty of opportunities—as well as lots of limits and snares. The truth, in short, was complicated. By taking a closer look at the Bents, and at how they were using their particular western land, we can make a start at grasping the complex world of the plains, and with that we can begin to put those earlier lessons into a larger context.

One way to consider the use of the plains is to stand with the Bent brothers at their famous fort on the Arkansas River in 1833 and look backward in time, not just a few decades earlier to Jefferson and Pike and Lewis and Clark, but centuries backward, into the deep history of the plains. That country had been used for a long, long time. But how? And what might be learned from that old story?

During the past couple of decades, study of the Great Plains has been one of the busiest fields of work among archaeologists and anthropologists. The history of that region before the arrival of Europeans has become much clearer as a result. That history has a lot to teach us.

The human history of the plains is older than that of Jefferson's Virginia. Its story is one of successive waves of occupation, each one adapting to the region's changes in climate and resources, each learning to use what the plains could offer and coping with the region's rigid limits. The earliest arrivals, about twelve thousand years ago, preyed on gargantuan herds of mammoths, horses, bison, and other large animals of the cooler, wetter pleistocene era. During the warmer, drier period that followed, from around 6,000 B.C. to 1,500 B.C., plainsmen developed more diverse economies of foraging, and as one authority puts it, hunted "almost anything . . . that walked, crawled, flew, or swam."[8]

When rainier conditions returned, about 2,500 years ago, natives adapted again, and later, around A.D. 1,000, the earliest plains farmers were planting corn, squash, beans and sunflowers in central Kansas. For nearly three centuries, a remarkable farming culture flourished and spread over the central plains. Along virtually every river and stream of the region today there are the remains of dozens of small villages from this period—many hundreds, perhaps thousands, in all. The population soared. In fact, more Indians were living on the plains eight hundred years ago than at any time before or since.

Then, once more, the climate changed, and with it people's use of the country. The rains slackened and the agrarian culture all but vanished. In its place appeared the pattern of living found by the first Europeans in the sixteenth century. This pattern is particularly important to understanding what followed. Three points are especially pertinent. First, this was a mixed economy. Natives continued to cultivate gardens on a limited scale. They also foraged among a remarkable variety of wild plants and fished and gathered mussels in streams. They hunted all sorts of animals, big and small.

Second, to use the land in those various ways, these Indians had to have free and easy access to the many parts of the plains—its open grasslands, its ponds, springs, and seeps, its rivers and streambeds. Besides their reliance on particular resources, in other words, these plainsmen had to have something else that was just as important—mobility. They devised elaborate strategies that permitted them to move around over large areas. Some recent intriguing evidence suggests that these wanderers may have transplanted and cultivated islands of especially useful plants interspersed at appropriate intervals so that they could more easily make their way around this sprawling region.[9] Early Spanish explorers found some village-dwelling farmers but also many people whom they called *Querechos,* bison-hunting nomads who lived in tents and traveled light with the help of dogs as beasts of burden. The *Querechos* shifted residence with the seasons, roaming and hunting the grassy steppes in summer, then leaving the arid, storm-blown highlands in winter to live on the more hospitable edges of the high plains or finding shelter in protected camps along the streams.

The third point is especially important. Their sophisticated adaptations alone were not enough. Because farming was so limited, the plainsmen fell short in a crucial area. They were in desperate need of carbohydrates and other nutrients that were found most readily in certain cultivated plants, especially corn. Without those vital elements, living on the plains was impossible. Somehow, somewhere, they had to make up that shortage.

They found the answer in another part of their economy: trade. Corn was grown in great quantities both to the west and east, in present-day northern New Mexico and in Missouri and Arkansas. Luckily for the plainsmen, the farmers who lived in those places also had problems. If the plains Indians lacked carbohydrates, these farmers faced a severe shortage of protein, because they could not find enough of the most concentrated form of protein—wild game. But not to worry. As today's new hucksters for buffalo burgers and buffalo chili dogs tell us over and over, plenty of protein could be found grazing and running around in unimaginable quantities not too far away, on the nearby plains.

Here, then, was a natural match. We can think of the plains as a gigantic protein reservoir, while the areas that are now New Mexico, Missouri, and Arkansas were huge carbohydrate storehouses. Not surprisingly, inhabitants of each place turned to each other; the result was a vigorous exchange of products. The central plains became the center of a trading network stretching far to the east and west. Plains hunters exported skins, meat, and fat; their customers sent back corn, other foodstuffs, and probably more.

Archaeologists are just beginning to appreciate the nature and full extent of this trading network. The exchange of goods was especially important when times got tough. Pueblo peoples in the Southwest, for instance, seem to have been badly overhunting the local deer and antelope populations, which made trading for plains bison an even better option than usual. As for the plainsmen, when droughts struck the region, as they inevitably did, the Indians' limited farming became even less dependable. With that, the plainsmen had to rely even more on hunting bison to barter for more southwestern corn.[10]

Plains people were trading just as vigorously toward the east. Once again the bison was the basis of the exchange, this time with the Kadohadacho and other eastern Caddoan groups further down the Red River and over a good part of East Texas. According to a recent speculation, that system reached out much farther. By this argument, several commercial entrepôts in eastern Oklahoma were the pivot of a network reaching from the central plains to the lower Mississippi valley. These Oklahoma trading centers were founded by peoples from downstream on the Arkansas River. Basically, they were middlemen. They pulled goods from the west, processing hides and channeling a variety of bison products eastward, down the river to the great pallisaded urban centers in the densely populated middle and lower Mississippi valley. Those Mississippians, like the Pueblo peoples, were starved for protein and fiber, and so were willing to send back not only garden products but a variety of other items. Especially important were "prestige goods" that show up in considerable numbers in the Oklahoma sites.[11]

This system eventually linked up with the New Mexican trade. Goods from the Pueblos made their way to the trading centers and probably filtered out elsewhere. Pots constructed by southwestern techniques are found in bluff shelters across the Ozarks. The trade entrepôts—the best known was at the Spiro mound in Oklahoma—became storehouses of wondrous wealth. Goods of an astounding range were pulled in and shuttled out over half-a-million square miles. Besides all sorts of bison-related products and tools, there were pots and effigies from Cahokia and other points along the great river, conch shell ornaments from the Gulf coast and Florida peninsula, ear spools and fragments of feathered robes, and a magnificent human effigy pipe probably from the Tennessee and Cumberland valleys. More than goods may have been exchanged. One scholar suggests that the terrible collapse of native population in the lower Mississippi valley, a disaster usually blamed on epidemics introduced by Hernando de Soto in the 1540s, instead was caused by microbial killers, most probably syphilis, carried by traders from other native peoples in New Mexico into the densely populated centers to the east.[12]

Looking back at this system that was flourishing on the eve of white contact, a couple of points are especially worth noting. First, the lessons. People had been using the plains for a very long time. What had they learned? The lessons obviously bore little relation to the Jeffersonian heritage of images of the plains. Was this an impenetrable barrier that would turn back both restless pioneers and ambitious enemies? Hardly. Considering the dynamic movement and spirited trade, the plains look less like no man's land and more like Saturday morning at the mall. As for the vision of an agrarian and commercial empire, there was, it's true, a history of agrarian bloom, but in an earlier time (and very different climate). Looking at the lives of plains natives in the sixteenth and seventeenth centuries, the dream of thriving villages surrounded by green fields bound to the outside world by a bustling commerce was ludicrous.

The experience of the centuries prior to the Bents' arrival instead suggested a few stern lessons. Plains resources were abundant, inadequate, and diffuse. There were enormous amounts of some things, but not nearly enough of others, and essentials that *were* there were scattered among varied habitats. Consequently, people lived by a kind of double dependence. They had to be able to move around and reach the various parts of the plains in order to piece together those scattered necessities. And they had to have reliable access to the world outside so they could acquire what they could not find at home. We might sum it up with a few ground rules: keep moving, learn to use as much as possible close at hand, and reach outside for the rest. And finally: take care not to push too hard or ask too much from the plains, because plenty can go wrong.

A second point can be made, looking back into the deeper history of the plains. This way of life might seem faintly familiar to anyone who has read much western history. That old system of trade, in particular, was strikingly similar to the one we know from the plains of the eighteenth and nineteenth centuries. In the 1750s bison meat and hides were being sent to French entrepôts along the Mississippi and to Spanish outposts in the Southwest; in return, French and Spanish traders carried back to the plains a variety of foodstuffs as well as European goods: firearms and powder, metal points and scrapers, pipes, pots, blankets, and more. Then, in the early 1830s, the Bents and St. Vrain established their post on the Arkansas at a key point chosen to control the bulk of the business flowing onto and out of the southern and central plains.

Seen from this angle, in other words, the Bents, so often described as innovative businessmen, look like something else. Charles and William were simply stepping into an ancient economic arrangement, a well-worn series of commercial grooves linking the plains with areas on either side, taking advantage of their personal connections at both ends. They were not trailblazers; they just moved in and pre-empted some of the continent's oldest trading routes.

From this perspective, the Bents' story reminds us of the antiquity of plains society and the persistence of patterns in the ways that country had been used. It also teaches us how, Jeffersonian images notwithstanding, those very old patterns were cautionary tales about the limitations of the plains, practical reminders about what people could and couldn't do there.

But that is only one angle on the Bent brothers; there is more meaning to squeeze out of their story. If the Bents were in one sense inheritors of old ways of using the land, from another perspective they were promoters of new ones. The Bents show us that in the middle years of the century, the plains were experiencing some of the most profound changes of their long history, changes that held some disturbing messages for anyone drawn to those Jeffersonian visions that were flowering to the east.

Change No. 1: The Bents took a prominent hand in introducing a new and different kind of commerce. Charles was one of several figures—among them Lucien Maxwell, Charles Beaubien, James Webb, and John Kingsbury—whose work in New Mexico helped open the St. Louis-Santa Fe trade. Between 1840 and 1860, this traffic grew from about a hundred wagons a year to nearly two thousand. The products moving over this road ranged from furs and dry goods to raw wool, hardware, whiskey, mining equipment, and bottled beer.[13]

Notice something about this trade: its purpose was not to exchange products from the plains for goods in distant places, but simply to connect markets on either side. Its vigor was limited only by demand at either end of the trail. The Bents, that is, were encouraging an entirely new sort of business—an aggressive, rapidly growing trade in which the plains and Plains Indians took on a very different meaning. The plains became simply country to cross, and its people something to deal with on the way.

This commerce was part of something a good bit larger—a swelling flood of people and animals moving over the plains on their way to other places. The most visible examples were the overland travelers and freighters who moved up the Platte River, heading for California and Oregon and other points west. The overland migration to the Pacific coast was one of the great folk wanderings of the century. Between 1841 and 1865, nearly a third of a million Americans crossed the plains. It was as if half of Missouri in 1850, or all of Wisconsin, or all of Arkansas and Florida combined, packed up, jumped in wagons, and headed up the Platte River. Many other gold seekers and farmers lit out for the Southwest and the Pacific coast along the Santa Fe Trail, many of them stopping for supplies and rest at Bent's Fort.

This traffic, like that of the Santa Fe trade, considered the plains not as a place to live in, or to trade with, but a place to move through. They thought of this country in terms of a phrase used by the Indian agent and the former mountain man Thomas Fitzpatrick: "a disconnecting wilderness" between older settlements to the east and new ones on the Pacific.[14] Travelers avoided most of the plains—the great hordes packed themselves densely onto the trails that ran closely along the rivers—but the part they *did* use, they used very heavily indeed.

The plains, in other words, acquired a new meaning and a new purpose. We might call this an economy of transit. Vital resources—grass, water, wood—

were used temporarily, for several months every year, basically as fuel for migration. What was the function of the plains? Their function was to support travelers and their animals on their way to somewhere else.

Change No. 2: The Bent brothers also played a central role in another new development. The main reason they built their fort and set up business on the Arkansas was to persuade a large and important group of Indians, the Cheyennes, to move into that region and live there permanently. They succeeded. In doing so, the Bents were major players in one of the most momentous developments in the region's history: a great shuffling of populations in the eighteenth and nineteenth centuries and the arrival of several new peoples on the plains: Comanches, Kiowas, Cheyennes, Lakotas, and others. These people were, in part, shoved there by an expanding white frontier, but they were also drawn into that country by opportunities: the herds of bison, vast pasturelands, and the possibility of trade through merchants like William Bent.[15]

One striking result was a spectacular rise in Native American population on the plains. Between the 1820s and about 1860, the number of people living year-round on the central plains more than doubled, from about eight thousand to nearly twenty thousand.[16] That's not so much by modern standards; Kansas or Nebraska today has dozens of modest-sized towns with more people than that. However, compared to what the plains had been supporting up until then, this was a stunning development. And there was more. These fresh arrivals were bringing with them something else the plains had not known until relatively recently: horses, and lots of them. Plains tribes kept anywhere from six to twelve horses per person, so by the 1850s Indian herds totaled somewhere between 100,000 and 200,000 animals.[17] Think of it this way: whatever else it was, this Native American immigration, encouraged in part by the Bent brothers, was also an important zoological event. It represented a massive intrusion of new life forms, human and animal, into the country.

As these new people moved onto the plains, they made a discovery that we have to understand if we are to grasp what was to follow. Like all new peoples who have ever moved onto the plains, the Cheyennes found that as they pursued new opportunities, they also had to commit themselves to new ways of life. The way of life was similar to that of earlier peoples of the plains, the ones described a few pages back, who were first seen by Europeans. Like those earlier nomads, the *Querechos,* the Cheyennes had to follow a distinctive annual pattern. In the summer, the most generous time of the year, these mounted hunters roamed over the highlands in search of bison. Covered with nutritious short grasses in the warmer months, the plains were one of the world's greatest grazing grounds. It was one great pasture, larger than western Europe.

But by October, things were changing. Then, when the nights began to chill, the Cheyennes' new way of life became much more treacherous and demanding. At any point between October and April, frigid storms could sweep out of the north, sucking the life out of anyone caught on exposed ground. As white soldiers would discover a little later, this country could become some of the most dangerous on the continent.

The Cheyennes met this threat by the method used by those earlier inhabitants. In mid-autumn, they moved off the highlands and into protected enclaves along the rivers. These enclaves represented only a tiny portion of this huge region, but it was only in these few places that the Indians could hope to survive. Only there could they find what they had to have—water and wood, grass for their horses, and shelter from the blast.

In a sense, then, the Cheyennes were continuing an old tradition. They adopted a pattern of life essentially like that of those early nomads. But there were two big differences. Now there were a lot *more* people living by that ancient pattern, and this much larger crowd had with them a lot of animals that the land had never before been asked to feed.

So Charles and William Bent were instrumental in encouraging and facilitating two changes of enormous significance. In many ways, these two developments were quite different, but they had a couple of things in common. Both pulled more people and many more animals onto the plains, and those people and animals were concentrated in particular on a small portion of that large region—the river valleys, where travelers crossed on their way west and where Indian herdsmen retired for the winters.

The result can be stated very simply. The valleys of the Arkansas and Platte Rivers, those vital but vulnerable habitats, suddenly were given a burden of use that far surpassed any in the past—and, I would argue, a burden heavier than any since.

It is easy to overlook, for instance, the number of oxen, cattle, horses, mules, and sheep that trudged up the Pacific Trail. During the gold rush, maybe 150,000 head took the trip every year. Even as the human traffic slowed, that of the animals picked up. For every person crossing the plains in the mid-1850s, there were a dozen animals, upwards of 200,000 a year. "It seemed as if Missouri would be totally drained of cattle," a traveler wrote in 1857.[18] The huge freighting outfits using both the Oregon and Santa Fe Trails usually brought ten or more oxen for every wagon. It all added up to two gigantic streams of horses, mules, oxen, sheep, and milch and beef cattle lumbering and bawling and chewing their way up and down the basins of river grasses. Pasture was overgrazed as much as four miles off the trails. The thousands of wagons tore and chewed great corrugations in the land, up to five hundred yards wide, destroying ground cover and triggering erosion that left desiccated gullies as much as seventy feet deep. As for the trees, as late as the 1830s cottonwood groves could be found in much of the valleys, and occasionally thick woodlands, but the men and women who drove all those animals were cutting them fast; by the 1850s, travelers wrote of going up to two hundred miles seeing hardly a tree and boiling their tea water with knots of dry grass. You could travel the whole Platte valley, one wrote, and "not [find] a stick . . . large enough for a switch."[19]

But don't forget those people involved in the second change. In the winter, Native American pastoralists were bearing down on the same places after travelers had passed through. Observers reported villages, in some cases stretching up to eighty miles along the streams, concentrated in the best pastures and woodlands. Herds of up to twenty, thirty, and even fifty thousand horses congregated in spots along the Arkansas. George Bent, William's son, recalled seeing as a boy animals grazing for fifty miles above and below the family fort.[20] And as winter residents, the Indians cut trees even more eagerly than the whites, both for fuel and for green shoots of young cottonwoods to feed their animals in the worst weather.

In short, that double set of changes the Bent brothers were encouraging drew together into a powerful ecological force that was focused with terrible intensity on one part of the plains, the river valleys. The consequences were troublesome for those farmers and freighters headed for the Pacific. For the Plains Indians, the results were calamitous. They, after all, had to get most of what they needed from the land, and what they needed was going fast.

Tough times. And they got worse. From 1849 to 1862, the central plains were struck by some of the worst droughts of the century.[21] This must have seemed like a brutally cruel trick. Recent studies show that the years right before this, from 1825 to 1849, were the wettest during the entire 350-year period from 1600 to 1950. It was during that quarter century, remember, that the new Indians were crowding in. In other words, when the Cheyennes were drawn to the central plains, they were seeing it greener and lusher and deeper in pasture than it had been since before the founding of Jamestown, or would be until the middle of the Truman administration. Then the rains slowed, and with that the Indians had to make it in a very different world. The vast highland grasslands held back most of their best, and hunting there became a much chancier business. The horses, already weak from heat and thirst, had to walk more and more for less and less. The Kiowas' pictorial calendar for 1855, an especially dry year, seems especially strange on the face of it. It shows a man who appears to be seated with his legs straight out in front of him, depicting "the summer of sitting with legs crossed and extended"—so called because the heat and lack of rainfall that season forced Kiowa riders to stop and rest their thirsty, exhausted animals often even on short marches.[22]

The blistering summer droughts, that is, had the same practical effect as the frigid winters: they made the highlands virtually useless to the Indian hunters. Native Americans responded by heading—where else?—to the rivers, which, after all, offered the best options. But those valleys were already battered and overgrazed. Now they had to support the Indians and their herds in summer *and* winter, just as tens of thousands of gold seekers were beginning to pour up the river trails.

So if we can re-imagine our way back to the St. Louis of the 1850s, then look westward from here onto the plains, the view is a strange one indeed. Those were the years when the Jeffersonian vision of the plains was coming to full bloom. Yet even as that was happening, the plains were offering up some of the most dramatic demonstrations of just how wrong that vision was. As boosters were predicting a country of vast pasturelands sprinkled generously with cattle, of steamboats chugging along wide rivers that flowed through verdant fields and past tidy communities bustling with commerce, the current inhabitants of the plains were experiencing an environmental disaster equal in its way to the most infamous ones over the next century—the ranching crisis of the 1880s, the Dust Bowl of the 1930s, the drought and farming collapse of the 1950s. As Jefferson's heirs looked toward a bountiful future of open-ended possibilities, the Cheyennes were learning hard lessons about the land's fragility and the iron constrictions around how people could use it.

Those lessons would soon help build into the Cheyennes' crisis of the 1860s, which culminated in the slaughter at Sand Creek in November of 1864. These events were tragedies as well for William Bent. At Sand Creek were his sons Charles and George, his future son-in-law, Ed Guerrier, and many other Cheyennes, white and mixed-blood kinsmen, and friends.

It is a cliché among western historians to call William and Charles Bent men who lived in two worlds. Unlike most clichés, however, this one is even truer than it is usually meant. The Bents not only straddled the cultural divides between Anglo-, Hispanic-, and Native-Americans, but they also lived between the chronological worlds of older and newer uses of the plains and their resources. As such, they have a lot to teach us about the nineteenth-century West and its deeper past.

In the Bent family are even a few hints of the future. In that regard, I'll introduce, very briefly, one last Bent brother—Silas, eleventh and youngest child and namesake of the household patriarch. Born in 1820, Silas is practically unknown to western historians, but his life was, if anything, as remarkable as those of his two famous siblings.[23]

While Charles and William looked for their fortunes farther into the continent, Silas turned to the sea. After entering the navy, he became one of the century's greatest hydrographers. In the early 1850s, as things were really unraveling for William and the Cheyennes on the plains, he was sailing with Matthew Perry to Japan. There he became the first non-Asian to discover and map the Japanese current (or *Kuro Siwo*), which he called "the Black Tide." He went on to describe generally the movements of the ocean streams around the Pacific. That alone would have assured Silas' reputation, but he was not finished. In a brilliant paper in 1869, the year of his brother William's death, he argued that those ocean currents were intimately connected to the prevailing patterns of climate and weather of North America, especially its western portion.[24]

Even then, Silas was not through. By the 1880s he had left the navy, returned home, and headed, of all places, out west to the Arkansas valley, where he began ranching near Bent's Fort. There he took what he had learned in his earlier odyssey—tracking the tides and currents of the Pacific, fitting together intricate global webs of weather, the interplay of continents and seas, streams in the ocean, and rivers of air—and applied it all to the adopted plains homeland of his older brothers.

In 1885, while visiting back in St. Louis, Silas Bent delivered a lecture before the national cattle growers' convention.[25] The plains, he argued, was no agrarian wonderland, and it never would be. Dominated by climatic patterns spawned on the Pacific, by systems that rolled eastward and over the Rockies, its potential would always be restricted by scant and erratic rainfall that supported only limited amounts of essential resources. What should be done? Accept it, for one thing, and for another: change our land laws to reflect the realities of the plains.

Here, a few years after John Wesley Powell said virtually the same thing about the arid lands farther to the west, and only a year before drought and blizzards would devastate the ranching industry, Silas Bent was arguing for a fundamental rethinking of the ways the plains ought to be used. He was, in a sense, bringing the remarkable Bent family full circle. Using what he learned half a world away, he confirmed what his brothers had discovered in their years along the Arkansas (and what tens of thousands of Native Americans had been learning for centuries)—that the West has limits that are quickly reached, and that it ought to be approached gingerly and with a healthy humility. He was, perhaps, taking a first tentative step, in the words of this book's title, "from conquest to conservation."

For us, the Bent brothers suggest the need to understand the West and its lands, not through the flawed visions that grew from the time of Thomas Jefferson, but through Jefferson's larger legacy, a commitment to intellectual breadth and a practical knowledge of living with the possible. If we are to use its lands wisely, we must learn from the West's basic nature, from its deep history, from its people's many errors, and from its place in a larger world.

NOTES

1. The best single work on the Bents remains a classic of western history, David Lavender, *Bent's Fort* (Garden City, N.Y.: Doubleday and Co., 1954). See also Quantrille D. McClung, *Carson-Bent-Boggs Geneaology* (Denver, Colo.: Denver Public Library, 1962), and its supplement (1973).

2. I am writing here from the perspective of society in the eastern United States. The images described below were new to persons in that region, but similar perceptions had been around for some time, the result of earlier Spanish, French, and English contact with this region. On the older origins of these images, see John L. Allen, "New World Encounters: Exploring the Great Plains of North America," *Great Plains Quarterly* 13, no. 2 (spring 1993): 69–80.

3. The best edition of Pike's journals is Zebulon Montgomery Pike, *Journals,* 2 vols., ed. Donald D. Jackson (Norman: University of Oklahoma Press, 1966). On Pike's expedition, see also W. Eugene Hollon, *The Lost Pathfinder: Zebulon Montgomery Pike* (Norman: University of Oklahoma Press, 1949).

4. The journey of Lewis and Clark has inspired more investigation and writing than any other government-sponsored expedition in our history, including, I suspect, the modern space program. Of the many versions of their journals, the best is also the most recent (and in fact not yet complete), Gary E. Moulton, ed., *The Journals of the Lewis and Clark Expedition* (Lincoln: University of Nebraska Press, 1983–). Scholars have studied many aspects of the expedition, including its medical history, scientific investigations, relations with Native Americans, geographical perceptions, and much more. The best single-volume history is still John Bakeless, *Lewis and Clark: Partners in Discovery* (New York: William Morrow and Co., 1947), although there is room for a much better one.

5. The basic source on the perceptions of the West emerging from the Lewis and Clark expedition is John Logan Allen, *Passage through the Garden: Lewis and Clark and the Image of the American Northwest* (New York: Dover, 1991). Essential to the Jeffersonian vision of the West's promise for the new republic was not just its agrarian potential but also its value for a national commerce. On the importance of this commercial vigor to the Jeffersonian dream, see especially Drew R. McCoy, *The Elusive Republic: Political Economy in Jeffersonian America* (Chapel Hill: University of North Carolina Press, 1980).

6. Walter B Sloan, *History and Map of Kansas and Nebraska: Describing Soil, Climate, Rivers, Prairies, Mounds, Forests, Minerals, Roads, Cities, Villages, Inhabitants, and Such other Subjects as Relates to that Region—Politics Excepted* (Chicago: Robert Fergus, 1855).

7. *St. Louis Daily Missouri Democrat*, November 24, 1858; Parker and Huyett, *The Illustrated Miners' Hand-Book and Guide to Pike's Peak* . . . (St. Louis: Parker and Huyett, 1859), 14–17; LeRoy R. Hafen, ed., *Colorado Gold Rush: Contemporary Letters and Reports, 1858–1859* (Glendale, Calif.: Arthur H. Clark Co., 1941), 207, 225, 231; Leroy R. Hafen, *Pike's Peak Guide Books* (Glendale, Calif.: Arthur H. Clark Co., 1941), 160, 184, 250, 285.

8. The quotation is from Waldo R. Wedel, *Central Plains Prehistory: Holocene Environments and Culture Change in the Republican River Basin* (Lincoln: University of Nebraska Press, 1986), 72. For a selection of other literature on precontact history, see Karl H. Schlesier, ed., *Plains Indians, A.D. 500–1500* (Norman: University of Oklahoma Press, 1994), Waldo R. Wedel, *Prehistoric Man on the Great Plains* (Norman: University of Oklahoma Press, 1961), Wedel, *Central Plains Prehistory*, and two articles by Wedel, "Some Problems and Prospects in Kansas Prehistory," *Kansas Historical Quarterly* 7 (May 1938): 115–32, and "Toward a History of Plains Archeology," *Great Plains Quarterly* 1 (Winter 1981): 16–38. See also George E. Hyde, *Indians of the High Plains: From the Prehistoric Period to the Coming of Europeans* (Norman: University of Oklahoma Press, 1959). A special issue of *Nebraska History* has a series of articles that brings together the latest scholarship on native history before arrival of Europeans.

9. Richard Stoffle, Henry F. Dobyns, Michael J. Evans, and Omer C. Stewart, "Toyavita Piavuhuru Koroin, 'Canyon of Mother Earth': Ethnohistory and Native American Religious Concerns in the Fort Carson-Pinon Canyon Maneuver Area," United States Army/National Park Service Report, 1984.

10. Katherine A. Spielmann, *Interdependence in the Prehistoric Southwest: An Ecological Analysis of Plains-Pueblo Interaction* (New York: Garland Publishing Co., 1991); Katherine A. Spielmann, "Coercion or Cooperation? Plains-Pueblo Interaction in the Protohistoric Period," and Timothy G. Baugh, "Ecology and Exchange: The Dynamics of Plains-Pueblo Interaction," both in Katherine A. Spielmann, ed., *Farmers, Hunters, and Colonists: Interaction between the Southwest and the Southern Plains* (Tucson: University of Arizona Press, 1991), 1–17, 107–27.

11. Frank F. Schambach, "Some New Interpretations of Spiroan Culture History," in James B. Stoltman, ed., *Archaeology of Eastern North America: Papers in Honor of Stephen Williams*, Archaeological Report no. 25 (Jackson, Miss.: Mississippi Department of Archives and History, 1993), and "Spiroan Entrepôts at and beyond the Western Border of the Trans-Mississippi South," *Caddoan Archeology Newsletter* 4, no. 2 (July 1993): 11–26.

12. Schambach, "Spiroan Entrepôts," 16.

13. J. Evarts Greene, *The Santa Fe Trade: Its Route and Character* (Worcester, Mass: Charles Hamilton, 1893); Thomas D. Hall, *Social Change in the Southwest, 1350–1880* (Lawrence: University Press of Kansas, 1989), 150–54; Walker Wyman, "Freighting: A Big Business on the Santa Fe Trail," *Kansas Historical Quarterly* 1, no. 1 (November 1931): 17–27.

14. Thomas Fitzpatrick to A. Cumming, November 19, 1853, in *Report of the Commissioner of Indian Affairs, 1853*, 370.

15. Joseph Jablow, *The Cheyenne in Plains Indian Trade Relations, 1795–1840*, Monographs of the American Ethnological Society 19 (New York: J. J. Augustin, 1951), 58–60; Donald J. Berthrong, *The Southern Cheyennes* (Norman: University of Oklahoma Press, 1963), 17–22.

16. Estimating the populations among seminomadic peoples on the central plains during these years is necessarily speculative. The figure of twenty thousand persons using this country during any given year is, I believe, reasonable, even conservative, based on what evidence there is. For various estimates, see Jacob Fowler, *The Journal of Jacob Fowler,* ed. Elliott Coues (Lincoln: University of Nebraska Press, 1970), 65; *Report of the Commissioner of Indian Affairs, 1845;* Thomas Fitzpatrick to Thomas H. Harvey, September 18, 1847, in *Report of the Commissioner of Indian Affairs,* 1847, 243–49; Thomas S. Twiss to Col. Cumming, November 14, 1855, Office of Indian Affairs, Letters Received, Upper Platte Agency, 1855; J. W. Whitfield to Superintendent of Indian Affairs, January 5, 1856, op cit.; Thomas S. Twiss to Secretary of Interior, *Report of Commissioner of Indian Affairs, 1856,* 96–98; William Bent Annual Report in *Report of Commissioner of Indian Affairs, 1859,* 137–39.

17. For estimates of horses per person based on numerous observations of Cheyennes, see Jurgen Doring, *Kulturwandel Bei Den Nordamerikanischen Plainsindianern: Zur Rolle des Pferdes bei den Comanchen und den Cheyenne* (Berlin: Dietrick Reimer, 1984).

18. Louise Barry, *Beginning of the West: Annals of the Kansas Gateway to the American West, 1540–1854* (Topeka: Kansas State Historical Society, 1972), 1008, 1081–84, 1158; James Ure journal, 1856, Historical Department, Church of Jesus Christ of Latter-Day Saints, Salt Lake City, Utah; Arthur M. Menefee, "Arthur M. Menefee's Travels Across the Plains, 1857," *Nevada Historical Society Quarterly* 9, no. 1 (spring 1966): 11.

19. A more detailed discussion of the impact of white overlanders and freighters on the valleys of the Platte and Arkansas can be found in my essay "Land," in Eliot West, *The Way to the West: Essays on the Central Plains* (Albuquerque: University of New Mexico Press, 1995), pp. 13–50. For a few sources that describe that impact, see, for the Santa Fe Trail: Thomas J. Farnham, *Travels in the Great Western Prairies, the Anahuac and Rocky Mountains, and in the Oregon Territory* (London: Richard Bentley, 1843), 1:54, 91; George Bent correspondence to George Hyde in folders 14, 20, and 22, Bent-Hyde Papers, Western History Collection, University of Colorado Library; J. Nielson Barry, "An Excerpt from the Journal of E. Willard Smith, 1839–1840," *Annals of Wyoming* 15, no. 3 (July 1943): 288; George Rutledge Gibson, *Journal of a Soldier Under Kearny and Doniphan, 1846–47,* ed. Ralph Bieder (Glendale, Calif.: Arthur H. Clark, 1935), 144, 147, 163–65; Lt. E. G. Beckwith, *Report of Exploration for a Route for the Pacific Railroad, by Capt. J. W. Bunison, Topographical Engineers, near the 38th and 39th Parallels of North Latitude, from the Mouth of the Kansas River, MO, to the Sevier Lake, in the Great Basin,* H. Doc. 91, 33d Cong., 2d sess., 1855, 27–28; Ralph Bieber, ed., "Diary of a Journey to the Pike's Peak Gold Mines in 1859," *Mississippi Valley Historical Review* 14, no. 3 (December 1927): 365; Abraham Robinson Johnston journal in Ralph Bieber, ed. *Marching with the Army of the West, 1846–1848* (Glendale, Calif.: Arthur H. Clark, 1936), 87–90; "Diary of Mrs. A. C. Hunt, 1859," *Colorado Magazine* 21, no. 5 (September 1944): 161–70.

For the Platte River valley, see: Osborne Cross diary, June 8, 1849, in Raymond W. Settle, ed., *The March of the Mounted Riflemen: First United States Military Expedition to Travel the Full Length of the Oregon Trail* (Glendale, Calif.: Arthur H. Clark, 1940), 68, 71, 298, 308; Leo M. Kaiser and Priscilla Knuth, eds., "From Ithaca to Clatsop Plains: Miss Ketcham's Journal of Travel," *Oregon Historical Quarterly* 62, no. 3 (September, 1961): 273, 279; Lydia

Milner Waters, "Account of a Trip Across the Plains in 1855," *Quarterly of the Society of California Pioneers* 6, no. 2 (June 1929): 64; Donald Jackson and Mary Lee Spence, *The Expeditions of John Charles Fremont . . . Travels from 1838 to 1844* (Urbana: University of Illinois Press, 1970), 1:194; J. Robert Brown, "Journal of a Trip Across the Plains of the U.S. from Mo. to Cal," entry for June 1, 1856, copy of manuscript journal, Newberry Library.

20. Fowler, *Journal of Jacob Fowler,* ed. Coues, 65; George E. Hyde, *Life of George Bent, Written From His Letters,* ed. Savoie Lottinville (Norman: University of Oklahoma Press, 1968), 37; James Bordeaux to Supterintendent of Indian Affairs, *Report of the Commissioner of Indian Affairs, 1854.*

21. The most extensive study is Merlin Paul Lawson, *The Climate of the Great American Desert: Reconstruction of the Climate of Western Interior United States, 1800–1850* (Lincon: University of Nebraska Press, 1974). See also Harry Weakly, "A Tree Ring Record of Precipitation in Western Nebraska," *Journal of Forestry* 41 (1943): 816–19, Frederick E. Clements, "Drought Periods and Climatic Cycles," *Ecology* 2, no. 3 (July, 1921): 181–88, and Edmund Schulman, *Dendroclimatic Changes in Semiarid America* (Tucson: University of Arizona Press, 1956), especially 85–89.

22. James Mooney, *Calendar History of the Kiowa Indians* (Washington, D.C.: Smithsonian Institution Press, 1979), 300.

23. Allen Johnson, ed., *Dictionary of American Biography,* c.v. "Silas Bent" (New York: Charles Scribner's Sons, 1943).

24. Silas Bent, *An Address Delivered before the St. Louis Historical Society . . . upon the Thermometric Gateways to the Pole; Surface Currents of the Ocean and the Influence of the Latter upon the Climate of the World* (St. Louis: R. B. Studley & Co. Printers, 1869). One reason that Bent's paper did not have a greater influence on the scientific community may have been that he also argued, incorrectly, that Pacific currents flowed into the arctic and were connected eventually to those of the Atlantic.

25. Silas Bent, *Meteorology of the Mountains and Plains of North America as Affecting the Cattle Growing Industries of the United States. An Address Delivered Before the Cattle Growers' Convention* (St. Louis: R. Studley and Company, 1885).

CHAPTER EIGHT

THE EXHAUSTED WEST
A Last Look at Landscape

MARY CLEARMAN BLEW

The local legend, when I was growing up on a small ranch in Fergus County, Montana, was that the county seat, Lewistown, was the exact geographical center of the state. In fact, the story went, the *exact* center of Montana was the drainpipe of the kitchen sink in a certain old brick mansion. High school teachers tried to explain to us that a land surveyor could never be so accurate as to pick out a single town, let alone the drainpipe of a kitchen sink, as the *exact* center of an irregularly shaped state, but we third- and fourth-generation Montana kids knew better.

In 1986 that old brick house with its kitchen sink and its drainpipe was torn down and replaced by a McDonald's, but I can still stand at the top of Main Street Hill and see, through the Golden Arches, what I once thought was permanent and enduring: the green watered lawns and weeping willows around the Fergus County Courthouse, the old Carnegie Library with its slitted windows and moldering stone steps, and, farther down the hill, the tops of cottonwoods shading the cattywampus streets. In the distance lies prairie and the blue shoulders of the Judith Mountains. On a clear day I can even see the outline of the Bear's Paw Mountains, faint as a cloud on the Montana highline, along the Canadian border.

On slow summer days it is almost possible to believe that Lewistown has segued into a perpetual *D.C. al fine*. Its ninety-year-old hotels and banks and store buildings are built from dressed sandstone or locally fired dark red bricks to last another century. The Bon Ton on Main Street still spreads its striped awning, still offers "cards for all occasions, fountain service, books and magazines—your coffee-break headquarters," with heavy glasses upside down on a towel behind the soda fountain, freshly sliced lemons, and ice in a bin. Down the street the white-marble façade of the Montana Building, all six stories of it, gleams in dusty afternoon sunlight. Then the jangle of bars, the neon cowboy hats and cocktail glasses, the Moose Lodge and the Coast to Coast store. Where the historic T. C. Powers Mercantile used to display drygoods and quality footwear in a hush of decorum behind plate-glass doors, an Anthony's store now fills the windows with marked-down western wear and props its doors open to the sidewalk to send odors of linoleum and special-shipment sales goods into slow traffic.

Central Montana is a beautiful place. Fresh spring water, thousands of gallons a minute of the purest water in the world, gushes out of its foothills and flows through Lewistown on its way to the Judith River. Antelope drift through the fabulous grasslands, and white-tailed deer browse among the chokecherries and aspens at the bottoms of coulees. The subtle colors of wildflowers—Indian paintbrush and wild sweetpeas and prairie flax—burnish the sidehills. The coyotes have come back, after years of being systematically poisoned, and at night their insubstantial yammer haunts the ridges. Cougars have been seen in the foothills. There is talk of wolves. And the price of land has recently veered toward the stars as an overflow of wealthy urban fugitives has sought an alternative to Aspen or Sun Valley or Whitefish.

My great-grandfather, a land surveyor, came to Montana with the Northern Pacific Railroad in 1882. He wrote home about the resources of the Judith Basin, its water and timber and deep grass, and he left the railroad and filed on a homestead to raise sheep and eventually survey most of Fergus County for the land rush of 1910–1914. My great-grandfather believed that he was bringing pastures and gardens to fruition in an empty landscape. I listened to the family stories, and eventually I discovered the frontier myth spinners, and learned from novels like A. B. Guthrie's *The Big Sky* still another way to understand the place where I was growing up.

But in spite of my reading—or perhaps because of it—I thought my life as a skim-milk Montana ranch kid was anything but colorful. Somewhere might exist the West I was reading about in the novels of Zane Grey. Texas, I thought, was a likely locale, or Arizona. Or perhaps everything exciting had happened in the past. Nobody I knew in Fergus County was shooting his way out of bars or riding with the Hash Knife Outfit or being pursued through the Purple Sage by hostile Mormons. My family and all our neighbors lived in a perfectly ordinary way, using teams of horses to mow and buck rake and stack their hay, coming back to the house tired at night for a supper cooked on a wood stove, and later telling stories around the kitchen table or reading Zane Grey or Norman O. Fox by the light of kerosene.

I did know a family of Mormons. They had bought a ranch on the bench above us and were trying to make a living raising potatoes. Their children, Dixie and Bradley, went to the one-room district school with my sister and me. The most exciting thing any of those Mormons ever did was get in a fistfight with the big boss of the Deerfield Hutterite colony over irrigation rights. I never saw the fight, of course, but I heard the men telling about it. I suppose they embroidered it—how old Eli Stahl, the Hutterite, was big and fat and bearded and thought he could bluff little Jack Grover, but he hadn't known that Jack was an amateur featherweight boxer—*You should have seen it, by God! Jack hit that fat bastard so hard he fell right into his own irrigation ditch.* It would be years before anything about that episode would strike me as *story,* and western story at that.

I couldn't have known that my ordinary world had for years been shaped and altered by the expectations and desires of the "outside," that for more than a hundred years painters and writers from "civilization" had been venturing west and bringing back word of strange animals, exotic landscapes, and colorful customs. The last thing I could have supposed was that my family and I might be "local color." And I remember being surprised, in about 1975, to get a note from the editor of a literary journal; he rejected a short story I had submitted to him, but added, "God, how I envy you, living out there in that beautiful country."

Nor could I have imagined living in a museum. Just before I left Montana in 1987, I took my aunt to visit a homestead museum in Hill County, on the Montana highline where I had been living. My aunt was born in 1910 and had grown up on a homestead herself. She looked at the replica shack with its washtub and wood stove and lanterns and remarked, "I just hate it when I see things on display that I, personally, have *used.*"

In his essay "On Going Back to Sawtooth Valley," the Idaho writer John Rember reflects on his childhood in the (relatively) pristine Sawtooth and how, just after World War II, he and his family were thrilled by the advent of electrical power service. Returning as an adult to live in the Sawtooth, Rember is struck by the changes in his remote and protected valley, where rivers teem with fish-hatchery salmon and trout, and federal legislation protects the scenery:

> There has been talk of burying the main power lines that run along the highway in order to enhance the pastoral values of the valley yet another degree. The power company doesn't think it's practical. The cold of the

winters here would make it impossible to dig down to a frost-damaged line. But I hope they figure out a way to get around that problem, because along with the Forest Service I think it would look better. The lines are a visible reminder of our intimate connection to the world that lies outside the valley walls, where acidic coal and great silt-ridden dams and plutonium produce the electricity that keeps this house bright at night. I don't like being reminded of that connection. I'd prefer that it be hidden, for the lights to go on as if by magic.[1]

Like John Rember, I know how exciting it was when the Rural Electrification Administration strung its poles down through the Judith River breaks in 1946 and brought us the possibility of instant light from a bare bulb hanging from the kitchen ceiling. I remember the fascination of a flush toilet. What could be more wonderful than a handle that pushed down, followed by a gush of water? What better luxury than not having to trek from a warm bed to an outhouse through rain or snow?

But nostalgia is a bad risk for any writer. I look back at my description, in *All but the Waltz*, of haying season in central Montana in the 1940s. I wrote it knowing that my own children had little idea of the work that once seemed so mundane to me, and I am struck now by my wistfulness:

> Haying season . . . is a water bottle clinking with diminishing ice, coated with bits of leaf and grass and fine pulverized dust in its shady uncut corner of the meadow. A shower of sparks and a shriek from the grinder from the log shed where my father is sharpening sickles. Meals of cold fried chicken and potato salad thrown on the table by my mother, who has dashed in from a day on the buck rake. But haying season belongs to the men. Their dirty slanted Stetsons and grimed faces, white teeth and hand-rolled cigarettes. The texture of their voices, the way their Levi's fit, the way they ride the mowers with their legs braced and their gloved hands full of lines. Their glamor.[2]

Historical reconstruction has for years been the task of many writers in the West. Their purpose has been to restore, according to Jon Tuska, "*man in nature,* not the denatured, mechanical, sterile world that increasingly has come to serve as a backdrop for human activity in other kinds of fiction"; or, according to Greg Morris, "to reinterpret the historical circumstance of the West and, thereby, the nation,"[3] citing as examples Ron Hansen, Molly Gloss, and Ivan Doig.

Ivan Doig and I grew up in Montana on far-apart ranches and—although we knew nothing of each other—graduated from Montana high schools in the same year. Many of Ivan's memories stir mine. Here is his description of haying season, from his novel *English Creek:*

> I believe I am right [says Doig's narrator, the teen-aged Jick McCaskill] in saying Pete was the first rancher in the Two country to use a power buckrake: an old automobile chassis and engine with a fork mounted on it to buck the hay in from the field to the stack . . . Thus the internal combustion engine roared into the Reese hayfields and speeded matters up, but it also left dabs of hay behind it, scatterings which had either blown off the buckrake fork or which it simply missed. The scatter raker was the gatherer of that leftover hay, which otherwise would be wasted. In place on my rake seat, I now clucked to Blanche and Fisheye, reined them toward the part of the meadow Pete had been bucking in loads from, and my second summer of scatter raking was begun.[4]

Doig is a scrupulous researcher. When his narrator describes a scatter rake as "a long axle—mine was a ten-foot type—between a set of iron wheels [which] . . . carries a row of long thin curved teeth, set about a hand's width apart from each other, and it is this regiment of teeth that rakes along the ground and scrapes together any stray hay lying there,"[5] we can be certain that this is just what a scatter rake looked like and how it worked. But Doig's care, his exactitude, and his attention to detail in these descriptions only emphasize that his scene is already so remote that it must be documented.

Nostalgia? Only, I think, in his loving attention to detail. But many of Doig's readers will find here not memories, or historical documentation, or even, in his description of the first power buckrake, an inkling of the coming transformation of labor-intensive family ranch work into full mechanization and the economics of agribusiness. Rather, they are likely to expect, and find, the romance of the past.

"My people sent me to the desert as a child so I would learn how to work," writes William Kittredge, who has anchored his own reinterpretation of western history in the wanton and far-flung ranching and farming kingdoms of his own family, whose past he sees as anything but romantic. "My life since has been colored by what I got from four or five summers with . . . adults who in fundamental and goodhumored ways were willing to spend their time and lives absolutely on the topic at hand, whether gentling horses or braiding rawhide ropes, with even-handed intelligence."[6] Kittredge, who advises students to write about real work in their fiction, who has made work central in his short stories and essays, also has had to look for his kind of work in the past or remote pockets of the country. When he discovers some (how many?) of the old desert cow outfits refitting their horse-drawn chuck wagons for what they say are economic reasons, he is heartened, though his cost-counting seems perfunctory. "What it comes to is rediscovering reasons for doing the work. Call it the recognition that most of us are eager to live in connection with a specific run of territory and its seasons. . . ."[7]

But work without an economic reason becomes something else. Avocation, perhaps, or ritual, or entertainment: the dude ranch without dudes. "Should the [power] lines ever be buried," writes John Rember about Idaho's Sawtooth Valley, "the road now designated Scenic Highway 75 will look very much like it did in 1956. . . . Some of us who live here will be out digging ditch or fixing fence or working with the horses. Perhaps a bit of pageantry can be detected in our motions."[8]

There lives today a rancher in the lush Deer Lodge Valley of Montana who still bucks in his hay with teams of horses and stacks it with a beaver slide within clear view of Interstate 90. Because haying season in the Deer Lodge Valley corresponds with the height of tourist season, it is not uncommon to find several cars pulled off the highway and several cameras clicking away at the spectacle of the two harnessed and sweating horses and the old man on the seat of his buckrake in his grimy working clothes. Is he oblivious of his audience?

Again, John Rember:

There are worse lives than those lived in museums. There are worse shortcomings than a lack of authenticity. Trouble with unreality is much preferable to trouble with reality. So I get up in the morning, open the doors to the sun and tree-cleaned air and a river next door that has never known a discharge of treated effluent, look up at mountains that tear holes in the clouds, watch the eagle that has made this stretch of river his home this winter, and consider myself among the luckiest of men. But that's because the place I live in now reminds me that once I had a home in Sawtooth Valley when the fish were wild in the rivers, when our neighbors had always been cowboys and when a flip of the switch brought wonderful, magical, incredible light.[9]

Rember may be right. There may be worse lives than those lived in museums. But I am a writer, and I am committed to probing my past and my present. What if I am doomed to inauthenticity?

Wallace Stegner once called the remaining western wilderness "the geography of hope," although, he noted near the end of his life, it may represent the "wrong kinds of hope."[10] What Stegner had in mind was the continuing cult of individualism and the myth of the Garden of the West, which, he warned, would destroy what is left of our environment and blind us to the kinds of connections that Kittredge and others have urged that we make with each other and with landscape.[11] In "Variations on a Theme By Crèvecoeur," Stegner nominates as cultural hero some native-born writer—

> some Doig or Hugo or Maclean or Welch or Kittredge or Raymond Carver . . . who transcends his culture without abandoning it, who leaves for a while in search of opportunity and enlargement but never forgets where he left his heart . . . [in] towns and cities still close to the earth, intimate and interdependent in their shared community, shared optimism, and shared memory.[12]

Stegner is far from alone in observing the great shift of recent western fiction away from the old stories of the frontier that most of us grew up reading or hearing about. Elliott West, for one, has pointed out that the new western fiction writers have been working at reinterpretation of the past in parallel with the new western historians, and mentions Douglas Unger, James Welch, Patricia Henley, Craig Lesley, Kent Haruf, William Kittredge, Louise Erdrich, and David Quammen as examples. Along with Unger and Kittredge, Greg Morris singles out Ralph Beer, Elizabeth Cook-Lynn, James Crumley, Ivan Doig, Gretel Ehrlich, Richard Ford, Molly Gloss, Ron Hansen, John Keeble, David Long, Tom McGuane, Amy Tan, and myself as voices that "seek both to demolish myth and create myth anew." Alexander Blackburn, drawing from the tables of contents of several recent anthologies of western writing, comes up with a list too long to quote in support of his argument that an honorific like "renaissance" is not inappropriate for writing in the West.[13] From my own neck of the Northern Rockies, I would add the names of Annick Smith and Deirdre McNamer, as well as Kim Barnes, Judy Blunt, Claire Davis, Mary Golden, and Leslie Ryan as writers we will soon hear from.

What we can celebrate in such a rich list is its diversity: the voices of Blackfeet, Chippewa, Sioux, Chinese-Americans, second-generation Finns, the sons of great ranching empires, the sons and daughters of starved-out homesteaders, young men and women who have grown up on reservations and in logging camps, on poultry farms and on faceless urban streets. The stories we tell are multitude, and we can be glad of the many strands where once we believed we had only one or two.

Still, in many ways we are a rear guard, writing as though we lived a century before cyberspace was ever considered. Greg Morris has noted that what we have in common is a conservative style. Many western writers, he argues,

> *want* to believe in the sacred and meaningful relationship between language and the land, because the Old West writers believed in that relationship—it is their link to that tradition, and their means to the source of that tradition's power; but the radical and profound changes worked upon the Western landscape now make such belief difficult. So the New West writers settle for a style that allows a compromise, one that perhaps provides a new rhythm for an altered, abused landscape.[14]

But while the literary link between living western writers and the recently dead—Edward Abbey, A. B. Guthrie, Jr., Norman Maclean, Wallace Stegner—is profound, it does not completely account for our connections between language and landscape. When creation myth overlays landscape, as it does for many Native American writers, the relationship between language and the land is literally sacred. Landscape may be so emotionally charged with a writer's reflection of self that James Welch, for example, can "see into the life of things" in an almost Wordsworthian sense:

> Many times when he was far away, [Welch's Indian lawyer] had envisioned these plains, the rolling hills, the ravines, the cutbanks and alkali lakes, the reservoirs and scrublands, and he always saw life . . . He saw beauty in these creatures [hawk, antelope, rattlesnake] and he had quit trying to explain why. It was enough to hold these plains in his memory and it was enough to come back to them.[15]

And for many of the rest of us, the western landscape is permeated with private associations contained in memory and family narratives. Language is how we move from private silence to communal story.

Will we soon be doomed to inauthenticity? None of us wants to think about the death of landscape, and nostalgia may suffice some of us for a few more years. But we are not the first writers on earth to experience loss. While we fight for the preservation of the last wilderness areas (and allow ourselves to forget that "preservation," as Keats knew, implies a kind of death), as writers we should remember that in story lies possibility.

Meanwhile, back in the plastic world, much is going badly for the man or woman on the paved street. Sven Birkerts, writing recently for the *Chronicle* of the Associated Writing Programs, deplores the monochrome nature of experience that confronts the postmodernist writer:

> Consider this fantasia of the average day of the average American businessman. He wakens to the sound of the clock radio, pads to the bathroom where he shaves his bristles to the background noise of a television news program, which tells him every minute what time it is and updates him almost as often on the weather. He finishes his coffee while he ties his tie, blasts a croissant in the microwave, which he carries along to the car to enjoy on his way to work. The electric garage door lifts, the machine eases forth. Through tinted window glass he notes the look of the sky. The radio has more talk of the weather, some chatter about last night's game. He thinks about his office day as he hurtles along the expressway, zeroes in on priorities as he guides the car down the ramp into the office garage. An elevator then carries him into the building, and the business day begins. Check e-mail, listen to stored messages. Hours pass as he swivels in front of his computer. The long day unfolds in carpeted and climate-controlled rooms, under the crackle of fluorescents. If he has the energy, he takes an hour for racquetball. A yogurt and a roll. More calls, more moving of data. And as the sun sets over the glass towers of his metropolis, he hurries home to a casserole, some Nintendo with the kids, and a few cold ones in front of *NYPD Blue*. There are days, quite a few in fact, when our man does not set foot in what used to be known as the outdoors.[16]

If you are a fiction writer, what do you do with such unpromising experience? Birkerts says that you might look for language that accurately depicts its depletion. Or you might mock, or ironize, or intrude imaginative havoc. You might, as Robert Stone does, remove your character from his electronic womb and set him afloat on the high seas. But your most likely next move, suggests Birkerts, will be to change the subject. Because literature, he insists, must become dangerous again. Literature must lead us back toward a reconnaissance of selfhood. "You move into the past, into the 1950s or 1960s, say; or you betake yourself to some more rural place where the mediation is not yet so total. . . ."[17]

In other words, you will travel west. Along with other fugitives from the concrete, you will enroll in a graduate course in nonfiction creative writing at one of the western universities, and you will distress your instructor with essays about your backpacking trip into the wilderness wherein you found your soul in solitude. You will recognize, adore, and perhaps fight to save the depleted remnants of old-growth forest and unploughed grassland and the last wild salmon and the last bears. Your heart will be in the right place.

What you may not recognize is that the wilderness where you have come to look for your soul is already a museum. You will have mistaken your nostalgia for authenticity. It may take you years to learn, as it has us, that between Wallace Stegner and Sven Birkerts lies an irreconcilable contradiction. None of us can be romantic individuals, testing the depth of our despair against the frontier, and be responsible men and women of the late twentieth century at the same time.

I cannot reconcile myself to the loss of landscape, which for me often is an analogy for my own body, sometimes even an extension of my body, like an outer membrane. And yet I know that I have never owned the landscape.

Any summer afternoon from the top of Main Street Hill you can see the tree-shaded streets of Lewistown, Montana, forty-five degrees off the true north, like a last legacy from those old Metis, the half-breeds who, years before my great-grandfather came west, had traveled out of the Red River country and down from Canada in the aftermath of the first Riel rebellion to build their cottonwood log cabins on the slope where the drain of a kitchen sink would eventually become the center of the State of Montana, and to plant gardens and orchards along the creek bottom, and, as an afterthought, to lay out cattywampus streets between their fruit trees.

In time, 150 families of Metis had settled along Spring Creek. They were sedate in comparison with the white frontiersmen of the mining and wolving camps who were their neighbors, and they must have had their dreams, perhaps not as ambitious as my great-grandfather's dream of the Garden of the West, perhaps closer to Wallace Stegner's dream of responsible connections with each other and with place. Or perhaps they only did what came next as it seemed best. They opened a school in Lewistown in 1881, began the construction of a Catholic church in 1886, and in 1903 sent for nuns to run the school and the St. Joseph's Hospital.[18] Nuns were still running that hospital in 1939 when I was born there, and in 1959 when my first child was born there.

On their journey down to central Montana, the Metis had encountered the Nez Perces with Chief Joseph, fleeing toward their final stand in the Bear's Paw Mountains.[19] Maybe they saw Blackfeet or Crow hunting parties, or met relatives among the Cree. They were not eager to draw attention to themselves. Some of them may have fought and been betrayed in the first Riel rebellion, in 1870. After they settled on Spring Creek, they may have hosted Louis Riel himself a time or two before Gabriel Dumont rode down from Saskatchewan in 1885 to urge him to lead the half-breeds in their second, and bloodier and more disastrous, revolt against Canada.

As a child I never heard a word of Metis history. The descendants of the Metis themselves were known, in our Protestant world, as Catholic *breeds,* to distinguish them from middle-European Catholic *bohunks.* I went to school with a Metis girl called Donna LaFountain, who was ridiculed by cheerleaders for wearing cowboy boots under her skirts. Who could have supposed that Donna's boots and skirts were to become fashionable?

Who could have supposed that our world might have been otherwise?

North of Lewistown, over the tops of the cottonwoods and beyond the Judith Mountains, the gray hills and hollows of the prairie stretch out of sight. Draws and coulees break the superimposed grid of ripening wheat and summerfallow. Chokecherry brush and groves of aspens along the creeks offer occasional shelter all the way to the breaks of the Missouri River along the old Carroll Trail.

Across this landscape in 1885, in Metis settlements and Indian camps at ten- or twenty-mile intervals along the 450-mile trail between Lewistown, Montana, and Regina, Saskatchewan, Gabriel Dumont set up secret relay stations with fresh horses by which he hoped to spirit Louis Riel down across the border to sanctuary in the Judith Basin after he had broken him out of jail in Regina. Captured after his second rebellion, Riel had been convicted of treason against Canada and was waiting to be hanged.

I might write this story for the glamour of a lost cause: how, somewhere out there, lost in distance, in the next coulee or in the ashes of a woodcutters' camp along the Missouri River, Gabriel Dumont still pursues his futile mission. The fleet horses and provisions wait, the rifles are ready. If he can just get Riel as far as the first of his camps, he can evade capture for a long time—but first, there is the matter of the heavily guarded Regina jail.

Or I might write as a historical reconstruction how Riel was hanged for treason on November 16, 1885, and how that was the end of a dream of a native state called "Assiniboia."

But I continue to believe that in story lies possibility. Soon enough, as Birkerts fears, we may all erase our individual selves as we are hooked into the great circuits of cyberspace. We may (tell me we will not!) lose the last remnants of the geography of hope. But story need not be romantic, or despairing, or simplistic, or single-voiced. It need not even reflect landscape. Story, in its search for common ground, can find the links between Metis history and the great-granddaughter of a land surveyor for the homestead frontier. Story can be collective.

I tell students, find your story. Follow it west, if that's where it leads you—chauvinistic talk about western "carpetbagger" writers has more to do with the territorial imperative than it does with literary merit, and many writers from "outside" see us more clearly than we see ourselves—but if it leads you home, don't be surprised. Recognize pageantry when you see it, but remember that life is motion. Treasure your friends. Protect your place and treat it tenderly.

NOTES

1. John Rember, "On Going Back to Sawtooth Valley," in William Studebaker and Rick Ardinger, eds., *Where the Morning Light's Still Blue: Personal Essays about Idaho* (Moscow: University of Idaho Press, 1994), 87.

2. Mary Clearman Blew, "Auntie," in *All but the Waltz: Essays on a Montana Family* (New York: Viking, 1991), 108.

3. Jon Tuska, *The West in Fiction* (1982; repr., Lincoln: University of Nebraska Press, 1988), 26; Gregory L. Morris, *Talking up a Storm: Voices of the New West* (Lincoln: University of Nebraska Press, 1994), xiii.

4. Ivan Doig, *English Creek* (New York: Atheneum, 1984), 225.

5. Ibid., 224–25.

6. William Kittredge, *Hole in the Sky: A Memoir* (New York: Alfred A. Knopf, 1992), 88.

7. Ibid., 172.

8. Rember, "On Going Back to Sawtooth Valley," 87–88.

9. Ibid.

10. Wallace Stegner, Introduction to *Where the Bluebird Sings to the Lemonade Springs: Living and Writing in the West* (New York: Penguin, 1992), xv.

11. Brett J. Olsen, "Wallace Stegner and the Environmental Ethic: Environmentalism as a Rejection of Western Myth," *Western American Literature* 24, no. 2: 133–34.

12. Wallace Stegner, "Variations on a Theme by Crevecoeur," in *Where the Bluebird Sings*, 115–16.

13. Elliott West, "A Longer, Grimmer, but More Interesting Story," *Montana: The Magazine of Western History*, summer 1990, 76; Morris, *Talking up a Storm*, xi; Alexander Blackburn, "A Western Renaissance," *Western American Literature* 24, no. 1: 59–60.

14. Morris, *Talking up a Storm*, xvi.

15. James Welch, *The Indian Lawyer* (New York: W. W. Norton, 1990), 158.

16. Sven Birkets, "The Narrowing Ledge," AWP *Chronicle* 27, no. 1: 23.

17. Ibid.

18. Joseph Kinsey Howard, *Strange Empire* (New York: William Morrow and Company, 1952), 344–45. See also Clemence Gourneau Berger, "Metis Come to Judith Basin," oral history in William W. Thackeray, Jr., ed., *The Metis Centennial Celebration Publication* (Lewistown, Mont., 1979), 15.

19. Berger, "Metis Come to Judith Basin," 15.

CHAPTER NINE

EXPLAINING OURSELVES:
Jefferson, History, and the Changing West

PATRICIA NELSON LIMERICK

When I was in graduate school, we read a great deal of Jefferson, with *Notes on the State of Virginia* popping up all over the curriculum. We certainly read it more often than we read Franklin's *Autobiography*, and, thank heavens, we read it more often than we read the *Federalist Papers*. Perhaps memory exaggerates just how often it was our assigned text, but there is no question in my mind that nearly every professor I had felt that *Notes on Virginia* was a central, illuminating, precedent-setting, and necessary book.

My telephone, back then, was listed in my name, though having my full, feminine name listed in the New Haven directory proved to be a not-so-great idea. At the time that I was reading *Notes on Virginia* for the second or third time, I got a series of irritating phone calls, in which a man would ask me questions like, "What are you wearing?" or, "What are you doing?" Usually, I would just hang up, but on one occasion I decided that graduate training was giving me skills that might be useful in ways I hadn't yet imagined. This time, when my unpleasant caller asked, "What are you doing?" I said, "I am reading Thomas Jefferson's *Notes on Virginia*, and paying particular attention, this time, to the ambivalent pastoralism that characterizes the text, since, while Jefferson's preferences were clearly on the agrarian side, he was quite aware that prosperous nations also embraced commerce and industry, and I'm not sure that Jefferson was able to really believe that the United States could be both prosperous and separate from Europe's business." And so I went on, and on, in this vein, and after, really no more than two or three minutes, I heard a quiet "click." I knew, at that moment, that my intrusive caller would not be bothering me again, and knew, as well, that graduate training had advantages and benefits that I had only begun to explore.

As I read over the essays for this volume and remembered this story, I began to see that phone call as a tribute to just how ill-informed my caller was. He was a victim, I would say, of the "Mount Rushmore Phenomenon," by which Jefferson becomes a tranquil and remote founding father, a man distant in both time and temperament from the agitations and frictions of daily life. Jefferson seemed distant and bloodless and carved in stone, and thus my caller was willing to hang up on *me* if that was the only way to avoid this ponderous topic. And that, combined with the fact that I was clearly and intentionally using Jefferson with just that expectation of his effect, is a tribute to how little either of us knew about Thomas Jefferson, and a tribute, as well, to how willing both of us were to let Gutzom Borglum, sculptor at Mount Rushmore, set the terms of our Jeffersonian perceptions.

The Thomas Jefferson who emerges in essays like Peter Onuf's and Anthony Wallace's is *not* a man whose name you would bring up if you wanted to bore someone into ending a conversation. Onuf's and Wallace's Jefferson was a man very much subject to strong passion—indeed, as both authors remark, to rage. Jefferson could write, with great tranquillity and even with something that approaches a superhuman, above-the-fray omniscience, about human rights and liberty of expression. And yet, when New England Federalists or antislavery activists undertook to exercise some of that liberty of expression, Jefferson was fit to be tied, ready to drive the opposition out of the union so that— paradoxically enough—the union could endure.

Jeffersonian democracy, one learns from Peter Onuf's essay, was a very complicated matter, full of contention, friction, and even violence. In truth, when I finished reading these essays, I was convinced that the American West has enough of its own troubles today, without having to endure a resurgence of Jeffersonian democracy. My point is the obvious one: that there is a world of difference between the abstractions of self-government, as Jefferson memorably and quotably set them forth, and the *practice* of those abstractions, as the parties and sections played them out in the early republic. There was never a golden age of decentralized, self-governing, participatory, consensual government, and in many ways, we should accept that as very good news. It is an easy matter to feel glum about present-day politics, if one thinks of the present in comparison to some happy, lost age of true and consistent democracy. But an essay like Onuf's does us all a world of good in showing us the contentious reality of that not-very-utopian past. The founders, Onuf helps us to remember, were at least as capable as we are today—maybe more capable—of tearing each other up ideologically. In the place of nostalgia for a calmer past, one begins to feel a certain enthusiasm for—or at least peace with—the particular, contentious state of American society into which one happens to have been born.

"Obviously," Merrill Peterson tells us, "though [Jefferson's] spirit and principles still live, he offers no ready solutions to present-day problems." Peterson's observation is especially clear when it comes to Indian people. As a long-time admirer of Anthony Wallace, I took a particular pleasure in the clarity and directness of his argument, an argument seconded by Robert Williams: even if Jefferson had a scholar's interest in Indians, and even a habit of expressing admiration for their oratory and interest in their languages, when it came down to behavior and practice, Jefferson stood squarely behind the process of white land acquisition. Thus, when you hear Wallace's and Williams' exposition of the stark reality of Jefferson's Indian policy, and then you remember Helen Ingram's call for a restoration of Jeffersonian democracy in the American West today, you feel a momentary obligation to warn the Indians, to tell them to get braced for, at the best, another round of coercive assimilation, or, at the worst, another round of naked, forceful seizures of their resources. If you told western Indian people that they were going to have to take part in a restoration of Jeffersonian democracy in the late twentieth century, I would not expect them to respond with applause; nor would I expect much greater enthusiasm from African American people, or from descendants of the Spanish colonists, a group of people of whom Jefferson was not fond.

My point is that there is no way to write race and ethnicity out of the story of either Jeffersonian principle or Jeffersonian practice. One of the most fundamental facts about Thomas Jefferson—maybe *the* fundamental fact about Thomas Jefferson—is that he was a white man, and a landholding white man at that. Scholars of ethnicity in the last thirty years have spent an enormous amount of time analyzing what it has meant to be Indian, or African American, or Mexican American, or Asian American, but scholars of "mainstream" history have spent almost no time analyzing what it means to be "white"; whiteness, on the contrary, simply remains the norm by which the difference of the nonwhites is gauged. We are just beginning our exploration of whiteness, as a culturally and politically constructed phenomenon.

Even though many of us may yearn for a more congenial and flexible age in the future when these distinctions might matter less, no consideration of the applicability of Jefferson's political philosophy to the issues of the contemporary West can get very far until it has reckoned with his whiteness, and with his central role in the invasion and conquest of what became the United States. Thus, I suspect, many historians sit with some discomfort through a presentation celebrating a return to Jeffersonian democracy in the American West today, wanting to say, "It's really a lot more complicated than that."

With that remark, I reach the central structuring idea of this volume—the notion that historians, and historical understanding of Jefferson, might be of some use in figuring out the dilemmas of the American West today. One of the main things historians do, and certainly what they do best, is to repeat some version of the line I used above: "It's really a lot more complicated than that." Elliott West's essay is a fine example of that: what was once a simple story of whites meeting Indians in straightforward contest for the mastery of the Great Plains becomes a complicated matter of changes in weather, livestock, resources, protein, carbohydrates, and overburdened river valley ecosystems. And that is only one element of the complication, because to all these variables of nature and landscape we have to add complex interactions between whites and Indians for at least a half-century before permanent white *settlers* would arrive on the plains. The Jeffersonian West—the mappable, knowable, chartable, assimilatable, controllable, plannable, manageable West—was simply not going to happen. As Jefferson was writing his remarkable instructions, sending Lewis and Clark out to do that first round of mapping, knowing, charting, assimilating, controlling, planning, and managing, the actual West was already much more complex than the mind of any person, even a mind as capacious as Jefferson's, could possibly imagine.

Historians specialize in pointing out complexity. Whether the topic is the political philosophy of Thomas Jefferson or the state of affairs in the American West in the nineteenth or twentieth century, we are guaranteed to say that things are much more complicated than nonhistorians want them to be. This habit has virtually become our identifying trait. If you meet someone who calls himself a historian, and that person doesn't say, within the first five minutes, "It's really a lot more complicated than that," then you may well have uncovered a fraud, a fellow who calls himself a historian but who doesn't even know the club slogan.

This habit, I suspect, has the potential of exhausting other people's patience, of leading to a revolt in which people trying to find a wise way of living in the present give up on historians. I fear, in other words, the onset of a dialogue in which historians say, for instance, "Thomas Jefferson in reality was very complicated," and public policy people say, "That may be, but in the meantime, we have to do *something*. We've got to get our inspiration somewhere, and many of Jefferson's remarks are very inspirational—and, lord knows, they are a lot more inspirational than anything we've heard from you historians."

My conviction is, more and more, that historians are not going to be much good when it comes to charting public policy; intervening in the present and attempting to shape the future is just not our sport. But people who want to shape the future *can* gain something useful from historians. For people reckoning with present-day western issues, historians are useful navigational devices. When, for instance, they hit the turf where Jeffersonian ideals run up against the issue of race, their proclamations of complexity can say to people working in public policy, "This is where the turf gets very shaky and sticky and treacherous. If you do not step very carefully and thoughtfully here, then you are likely to become the next example of the innocent who blundered into the historical equivalent of the La Brea Tar Pits." Historians thus become a kind of intellectual warning system that beeps and chirps and squawks just as someone else begins to insert a foot into what history has shown to be quicksand.

Speaking of warning signals and quicksand, my impression is that the second most complicated aspect of applying Jeffersonian thought to the contemporary American West, second after the issue of race, is the issue of the gap, and even the hostility, between the rural West and the urban West. Seeing the rural West and the urban West in the same picture is, I think, the most vexing and unsettled challenge facing both historians and westerners of every occupation. Indeed, for a number of scholars the way out of this dilemma has been an easy one: just think of the rural West as the *real* West, and consider the urban West to be a parasitic and alien and dismissible intruder into the wide open spaces. Then you can concentrate your attention on the legitimate, scenic, authentic West, and ignore those congested and contested urban places. The particular benefit of this course of action is that you can ignore Los Angeles.

Thomas Jefferson, as Peterson reminds us, traced the stages of civilization from savagery up through the ladder of progress, through "the gradual shades of improving man," until one reaches man's "as yet most improved state in our seaport towns." Peterson is quite right in pointing out to us that this line "suggests how wrong it is to associate Jefferson with some ideal of the primitive, the pastoral, the simple agrarian, of any other archaic state." And yet, even if Jefferson had made some degree of peace with eighteenth-century coastal urbanity, one can be pretty certain that what he did *not* anticipate, in the way of "seaport towns" capping the rise of mankind, was Los Angeles.

You can see evidence of the gap between the rural West and the urban West in the differences between Mary Clearman Blew's and Robert Gottlieb's essays. There are many sources for this gap—which can sometimes turn into tension, friction, and outright hostility in today's West—but when it comes to looking for them and their points of origin, the mind of Thomas Jefferson is, I think, one of the principal sources. In essence, Jefferson's fervent and quotable agrarianism gave a promise to rural people, and in different phases of American history and especially in the last twenty years, rural people have been infuriated by the gap between the respect and rewards promised by Jeffersonian agrarianism and the tough times they face in reality. "Those who labor in the earth are the chosen people of God": consider that statement as something close to a filled-out and completed check, transferring funds and respect and power and status from the American nation to rural people, signed by Thomas Jefferson. And yet, when rural people today try to deposit that check, they find urban environmentalists, or Secretary of the Interior Bruce Babbitt or any number of other federal bureaucrats, standing in their way, informing them that the check is no longer good for deposit, or for anything else. Their resentment is tremendous, and it is hard not to feel that rural westerners were, in many ways, set up for a fall by Thomas Jefferson and his enthusiasm for agriculture. In the same way, our extraordinary difficulty, as scholars, in trying to think clearly about the West—thinking about it, that is, as both our most urban region and as the region where rural issues are at their most heated—is also, at least in part, a legacy from Jefferson.

And what would Mr. Jefferson make of these rural/urban conflicts today? What, for instance, would Mr. Jefferson make of the spotted owl? In the Pacific Northwest today, two sides of Jefferson's mind collide: his curiosity about nature is one legacy, and a legacy that brings us finally a deeper and (dare I say) more complicated understanding of ecosystems; yet the other side, his enthusiasm for hardworking rural people, is another legacy, and one that brings us the hearty working people who put nature to use in the northwest logging towns, who feel themselves to be the real producers. It also brings us the real environmentalists, the ones who are much more closely in touch with nature than urban environmentalists on weekend holidays could be.[1] Jefferson wanted hardworking people to *make use of* the West, and he wanted scientists to *investigate* the West. In the spotted owl controversy, these two ambitions have run into each other head to head. Mr. Jefferson, one imagines, would be very interested in and enthusiastic about the habits and workings of the spotted owl, and equally interested in, and much less enthusiastic about, the strange and unwieldy bureaucratic and judicial systems that are now responding to this instructive information about owls. But I do not know of anything in his writings that would help us cope with this social and ecological dilemma.

When one plays out this exercise of imagining Mr. Jefferson's response to present dilemmas in the West, one thinks repeatedly of Dr. Frankenstein's dilemma. Dr. Frankenstein was the creator of the monster, and Thomas Jefferson was, in many ways, the creator of the West. Setting aside the difficulties of a fictional person communicating with a dead person, one imagines that the two could have had a hell of a conversation, shared a lot of pain and frustration, maybe even formed a support group. The best way to get Jefferson geared up for his support-group meeting with Dr. Frankenstein would be to give him a copy of Robert Gottlieb's essay, so that he could see how much the "empire" side came to dominate the other half of that phrase, "empire of liberty." Imagine Jefferson's response to the federal government's management of its western nuclear facilities, and especially the treatment of the neighbors of the Nevada test site and the Hanford nuclear reservation. Yes, Jefferson was always a great enthusiast for technological innovation and for putting resources to use, and yet it seems distinctly possible that Jefferson's horror and anger over the story of the federal government's Western Atomic Empire might exceed our own. Can anything in Jefferson's ideals and visions help us cope with the enormous problems of the nuclear West? Beyond deepening the intensity of our regrets over the injuries inflicted by a too-powerful government agency, I don't see how.

Imagining Jefferson's response to current western dilemmas is an exercise at the further reaches of uncertainty, but these essays give wonderful demonstrations of how much uncertainty, and variations in judgment, extend into our reading of the past. Placed together, two of these essays give a textbook example of the pleasures and frustrations of historical interpretation. Both Anthony Wallace and John Logan Allen pay particular attention to youthful influences on Jefferson, influences from his father's experience in land surveying, from his father's friend Dr. Thomas Walker, and from the involvement of both of these people in the Loyal Land Company. Both Wallace and Logan provide us with essentially the same facts, but, from there on, it is an invitation to travel to Interpretation City.

For Wallace, Peter Jefferson's surveying activities, Dr. Thomas Walker's enthusiasm for western lands, and the neighborhood elite's involvement in the Loyal Land Company had a very clear impact on Jefferson: they made him an enthusiast for white expansion; they set his sympathies on the side of whites heading west to acquire land. Yes, Jefferson would be curious about Indians, but these youthful influences had settled the question of which side he would be on in the contests of westward expansion.

But then, turn to Allen's essay, and the influence, while it still pushes westward, is cast in another tone entirely. Now Dr. Walker and the Loyal Land Company function to provoke the young Jefferson's geographical imagination, to bring him to life intellectually, to awaken his sense of curiosity about the spaces, and the spatial relationships, lying to the west.

There is no question that the Jeffersonian curiosity and intellectual energy that entrance Allen are very magnetic and very appealing. I remember vividly the experience of reading the Adams/Jefferson correspondence, and reading it in a sustained state of delight over the intellectual vigor of those two old men, who used their restored friendship to explore just about every open and interesting question in the universe. When I neared the end of that rather lengthy correspondence, when I noticed that there were only fifty or sixty pages left, when I realized that I was coming right up on the Fourth of July in 1826, I astonished myself by starting to cry, thinking to myself, "I cannot bear the fact that these two men are about to die." I became, as far as I know (though I suspect that anyone who has read through that correspondence has had the same experience), one of the first people in a century or so to experience the death of Jefferson as a surprise and shock and a personal blow. His geographical imagination—not to mention his political imagination and his technological imagination and his architectural imagination—remains very attractive and very powerful, and if Dr. Walker and the Loyal Land Company did something to get all that imagining started, then in some peculiar way, everyone who has been charged up by reading Jefferson is in their debt.

But surely Wallace's point stands as well—Dr. Walker and the Loyal Land Company did train Jefferson in the ways of empire and in the ambitions of land acquisition. In fact, in the manner of historians instinctually in pursuit of the complicated, one must observe that what seem like contradictory inter-pretations of the influence of the Loyal Land Company may be something closer to intertwined, interdependent interpretations. Geographical imagina-tion and enthusiasm for white land acquisition were perfectly compatible traits, and they both place Jefferson in the era in which he was a full and hearty participant, an era of invasion and conquest of native lands. The pattern of white folks heading off, imaginatively or literally, to get to know the unknown is a basic pattern of empire; sometimes it is directly followed up by military conquest, and sometimes the connection is less direct. So one can have—one *must* have—it both ways: Jefferson as an enthusiastic participant in the dis-placement of natives, and Jefferson as a person whose curiosity about the territory under conquest can still be surprisingly magnetic and engaging.

Historians might well find the interpretative puzzle, a puzzle presented by Robert Williams' response to Jefferson as storyteller, the most challeng-ing and instructive of all. Jefferson remains our collective paradigm-shaper and paradigm-popularizer, and while his judgments of Indians can never do much for Indian self-esteem, there is no reason, Williams argues, why Indians shouldn't put Jefferson's narrative powers to their own use. The American Revolution was *the* precedent-setting uprising against the powers of empire; as Indian people today engage in their own uprisings against empire, they may as well put this analogy to good use. As the Anglo-Saxons had full justice in their resentment of the Norman Yoke, as the patriots had full justice in their rebellion against the British king, just so would the Indian campaign for decolonization carry the clear backing of the Jeffersonian call to justice and self-determination.

Indian people, Williams tells us persuasively, have survived because they are the great utilitarians, willing to pick up what might be useful, whatever the source. Historians, this analogy tells us, may be an extinct subspecies pretty soon, because they are the poorest of utilitarians, the most bound-up by picky concerns of purity and complexity. *Should* historians voice the objection, the objection that Williams is perfectly aware of, that Jefferson never *meant* for his ideas about liberty and self-government to support the cause of Indian tribalism? If they *do* decide to voice this objection, then Williams will have the comfort of knowing that nobody pays attention to historians anyway. To take one poignant and personal example: for any one point that I may have scored, in the last few years, in changing public perceptions of the American West, Kevin Costner has scored a thousand points more. If Indian people begin citing Jefferson as the champion of Indian sovereignty, and if historians, even though sympathetic with the Indian cause, say that this is *not* what Jefferson had in mind, then all that the public will hear is a thin and high-pitched piping in the distance. If one could get Kevin Costner to play Thomas Jefferson, and have Costner's Jefferson stand at the door of Monticello, look toward the West, and make a ringing statement on behalf of Indian rights of self-government, then, I suspect, historical accuracy would be whipped, and yet, I hope, the cause of Indian rights would be much strengthened.

When Peter Onuf tells us that "Jefferson had always found conflict distasteful" and, in his later years, "sought to extricate himself from the political controversies of the day," then irony seems to be very thick in the air, and one feels instantly like responding, "If that's the case, Mr. Jefferson, you chose the wrong line of work." As far as I can tell, one of the principal lessons of this volume is that Jefferson not only failed to extricate himself from the political controversies of *his* time, but he has also ended up front and center in the political controversies of *our* time, too. The moral of this story is pretty clear: the hope to escape from conflict and controversy, while certainly understandable, did not work for Mr. Jefferson, and it is not going to work for us.

Human and environmental affairs in the American West, Elliott West's essay tells us, were already very complicated, and full of conflict, by the 1840s. Over the following 150 years, things got even more complicated: the dilemmas multiplied, the solutions and resolutions looked ever more distant, the riddles and puzzles became ever more challenging, the interest groups and constituencies and factions proliferated. Conquest may have yielded to conservation, but conservation turned out to be a can of worms in itself, loaded with different interpretations and pulled in many conflicting directions. Thus, I am completely bewildered by Helen Ingram's vision of an impending return to intelligent, fair, and open community-based decision making in the West today.

But, like Ingram, I have to find my inspiration somewhere, and there is one place in Jeffersonian thought where, for me, the inspiration holds firm. That, you can probably guess, is in the Adams/Jefferson correspondence. After years of feuding and a refusal to communicate, Jefferson and Adams started writing to each other. From time to time their old conflicts threatened to heat up again and test the staying power of the restored friendship. On one of those occasions, John Adams wrote these words to Thomas Jefferson, "You and I ought not to die, before We have explained ourselves to each other," a sentiment Jefferson ratified in an answering letter.[2]

This may seem like a fairly diminished ambition for the American West, but it is the one that still holds my faith. Before the 1992 election, I doubted that westerners were on their way to consensus, and after the results from the elections of 1994, I doubt it even more. Consensus seems unlikely, but conversation still seems possible, and, in bedrock terms, conversation is worth a great deal. I hold out the hope that westerners—indeed, everyone—can take some inspiration from Jefferson and Adams. Although we seem guaranteed to live permanently with conflict, we can still find, as Jefferson and Adams knew, an enormous value in explaining ourselves to each other.

NOTES

1. For a particularly telling case study of this conflict, see William Dietrich, *The Final Forest: The Battle for the Last Great Trees of the Pacific Northwest* (New York: Penguin, 1992), 11.

2. Lester J. Cappon, ed., *The Adams-Jefferson Letters: The Complete Correspondence between Thomas Jefferson and Abigail and John Adams* (1959; rprt., New York: Simon and Schuster, 1971), 358, 391.

CONTRIBUTORS

JOHN LOGAN ALLEN, Professor of Geography at the University of Connecticut, is a scholar of the exploration and settlement of the American West. His *Lewis and Clark and the Image of the American West* is a classic in its field, and *North American Exploration,* a multivolume work that he edited, is scheduled to appear shortly.

MARY CLEARMAN BLEW is the author of numerous stories and essays on western life, including *All but the Waltz: Essays on a Montana Family* and *Balsamroot.* In addition to her role as Professor of English at the University of Idaho, Blew is active in directing public humanities programs in Idaho and Montana.

ROBERT GOTTLIEB teaches environmental analysis and policy at UCLA. He has written on resource and environmental issues for a variety of national publications, including the *Wall Street Journal* and the *Nation.* He is also the author of numerous books, including *Empires in the Sun: The Rise of the New American West* (with Peter Wiley) and *Forcing the Spring: The Transformation of the American Environmental Movement.*

HELEN INGRAM is the Warmington Endowed Chair in the school of Social Ecology at the University of California, Irvine. Her published work, such as *Water Politics: Continuity and Change,* explores the delicate relation between policy and natural resource allocation in democratic societies.

PATRICIA NELSON LIMERICK teaches at the University of Colorado, where she is also co-chairman of the Center of the American West. Her scholarship, including *The Legacy of Conquest: The Unbroken Past of the American West,* has helped to articulate an environmental approach to western history that is changing popular and academic perceptions of the field.

PETER S. ONUF is Thomas Jefferson Memorial Foundation Professor of History at the University of Virginia. His writings, such as *Statehood and Union: A History of the*

Northwest Ordinance, focus on the expansion of the United States in the early republican period.

JAMES P. RONDA, H. G. Barnard Professor of Western American History at the University of Tulsa, has written extensively on the history of the western frontier. Two of his recent works, *Lewis and Clark among the Indians* and *Astoria and Empire,* were nominated for the Pulitzer Prize in American History.

ANTHONY F. C. WALLACE's books, including *Rockdale* and *The Death and Rebirth of the Seneca,* have influenced anthropologists and historians, scholars and laypeople alike. Professor of Anthropology at the University of Pennsylvania since 1961, he has also worked extensively in the fields of behavioral science and mental health.

MARY G. WALLACE is a Ph.D. candidate in political science at the University of Arizona.

ELLIOTT WEST is Professor of History at the University of Arkansas. Well known as a social historian of the West, his published works have focused on the history of frontier family life. His books include *The Saloon on the Rocky Mountain Mining Frontier* and *The Way to the West.*

ROBERT A. WILLIAMS, JR., Professor of Law and American Indian Studies at the University of Arizona, is an enrolled member of the Lumbee Indian Tribe of North Carolina. He has written *The American Indian in American Legal Thought: The Discourses of Conquest;* he also is author of the leading casebook in American Indian rights.

INDEX